Search and Clear

Search and Clear:

Critical Responses to Selected Literature and Films of the Vietnam War

Edited by
William J. Searle

Bowling Green State University Popular Press
Bowling Green, Ohio 43403

Copyright © 1988 by the Bowling Green State University Popular Press

Library of Congress Catalogue Card No.: 88-70749

ISBN: 0-87972-428-5 Clothbound
       0-87972-429-3 Paperback

For my parents
and
Susan Lee Morris

Contents

Acknowledgments

I am indebted to Ray B. Browne, Pat Browne, and Peter Rollins for giving me the opportunity to gather this collection. Long before the study of Vietnam War literature became fashionable, they provided a forum, through the Popular Culture Association, for the discussion of issues concerning the Vietnam experience. Indeed, many of the essays that follow were originally presented at meetings of the PCA. I also wish to thank John Mulryan whose encouragement in the 1970s legitimized my interest in Vietnam War literature, James Quivey who not only read the literature and several of my drafts but also marshalled the support of the department behind my efforts, and Linda Highland who typed the manuscript in a cheerful and professional manner. I must give my special thanks to Susan Lee Morris, who, in urging her husband to pursue his interest in an area then outside the mainstream of literary study, gave the gifts of time, self, and love.

Introduction

William J. Searle

In Tim O'Brien's now-lionized *Going After Cacciato,* Captain Fahyi Rhallon voices an enduring truth " 'that after a battle each soldier will have different stories to tell, vastly different stories, and that when a war is ended it is as if there have been a million wars, or as many wars as there are soldiers' " (197-98). The compelling motivation behind such tales is suggested by Michael Herr who says of infantrymen in Vietnam, "All had a story, and in the war they were driven to tell it" (*Dispatches* 29). Ward Just in his criticism of the Russian Roulette metaphor in *The Deer Hunter* is more graphic: "In Vietnam there is no lack of facts or images, emotions or metaphors, to choose from. You don't have to reach for them; if they're right, they reach for you. They are inescapable, fingers around your throat" ("Vietnam: The Camera lies" 65).

Captured by their stories, prisoners of war, so to speak, those who convey the experience most tellingly are frequently those who were most immersed in it, veterans all, even those who did not wear a uniform. Given the passion, the special poignance, the concrete grittiness, and the ethical implications of much of Vietnam War literature, the words of Peter Marin concerning the survivors of that war could apply to many who have written about it: "But the nature of the war, and the fact and the feel of it—the conflicts and private struggles of conscience, the horrors that exist simultaneously outside and inside a man—all of these belong to the *vets,* for who else has it in their power to keep us straight, and who else has the knowledge required to do it?" ("Coming to Terms with Vietnam" 55). Imaginative literature of the Vietnam War—plays, novels, nonfiction narratives, poems, screenplays—can render the maze and lead us through it. "It is," James Chace has recently noted, " 'The most important literature being written right now' " ("*Reading the Wind*" 8).

While a great deal of Vietnam War literature is currently in print, and new novels and memoirs continue to replenish the market, the publishing industry, perhaps reflecting public interest, was not always so receptive. Martin J. Naparsteck, writing in 1979, mentions two "insurmountable obstacles" to the publication of manuscripts about

1

Vietnam: the virtual impossibility "for a first novelist to find his way into print these days" and the unpopularity of the war with publishers ("The Vietnam War Novel" 37). Jervis Jurjevics, who worked in publishing for nearly sixteen years, admitted in 1985:

We sat for years in editorial boards and marketing meetings turning down novel after novel.... For a period of time well into the 1970s, the Vietnam novel was really an obscenity.... Ironically some of the ones turned down went on ten years later to win first novel awards. ("*Reading the Wind*" 44)

Apparently the collective amnesia that gripped the country after the Vietnam War was mirrored in the neglect by the publishing business. Timothy J. Lomperis notes that "Bill Ehrhart had to wait ten years for any of his poetry to be published" and Wallace Terry, author of *Bloods: An Oral History of the Vietnam War by Black Veterans* was rejected by 120 publishers! ("*Reading the Wind*" 43-44). Having survived the war, and the indifference if not outright hostility upon their return, initially many authors of Vietnam War literature had to endure the welcome home provided by publishers as well. By the late 1970s, however, "the success of a few films," states Lomperis, namely *Apocalypse Now*, *The Deer Hunter*, and *Coming Home*, "changed the attitudes of the publishers" (44).

Even a cursory glance at the local bookstores, many of which now boast Vietnam sections, will indicate the current popularity of this body of literature. "What is truly remarkable about this literature," writes Lomperis, "is its diversity and tremendous range of experience" (44). Its diversity includes a range in quality, encompassing everything from pot boilers and thrillers, like the *Saigon Commandos* series, to the finely crafted *Going after Cacciato* by Tim O'Brien, a novel Joseph Tetlow says: "Stands with any war novel written in this century by an American" ("The Vietnam War Novel" 36), and Michael Herr's brilliant book *Dispatches* which "may be," Peter Prescott writes, "the best book any American has written about any war" (*Newsweek*, June 19, 1978, 82). The praise for both writers is high indeed as the names of American war novelists like Stephen Crane, John Dos Passos, Ernest Hemingway, James Jones, Norman Mailer, Joseph Heller, and Kurt Vonnegut come to mind. But, as noted above, the body of literature is a steadily increasing one. Just as the Vietnam War films of the late 1970s stimulated publication, so too will the success of Oliver Stone's *Platoon* and Stanley Kubrick's *Full Metal Jacket* bring about a new generation of imaginative literature about Vietnam. Though much of Vietnam War literature is substantial, at times even distinguished, Peter Marin cautions, "Our great texts, and a period of rich understanding, may yet be ahead of us; new books still working in the minds of silent men—and new films may, a decade from now, confront us with the truth of the past in a way we have not yet learned to manage" ("Coming to Terms with Vietnam" 55). A focus on the literature spawned by that war may be likened to aiming at a moving target, one already possessing many moods and capable of great artistic range, to be sure, but one ever in motion, ever growing, stimulated, in part, by changing cultural attitudes and the multiplicity of perspectives.

While primary sources multiply, so too do secondary, as the plethora of Vietnam War literature and related films has attracted increasing attention from the academy, particularly in the form of book-length studies and special issues of periodicals.[1] The collection of critical essays that follows, then, is intended, in part, to continue the critical dialogue on the imaginative literature and selected films of the Vietnam War. But its essays should also fill in gaps only partially treated in earlier studies, stimulate research in a quickly burgeoning field, and, finally, reveal the craft of literary pieces often overlooked by other critics. The goal of imaginative writers and film makers and, this writer believes, critics of Vietnam literature and film as well, is perhaps suggested by Ward Just: "There is a duty to look this war in the face and to look at it without vanity or ego or pretension or narrow idealogy" ("Vietnam: The Camera Lies" 65). While such a goal is difficult, perhaps impossible, to attain, the five-part structure of this collection was devised and the essays therein selected with that end in view.

I

The essays in Section I, "The Quest," explore the ramifications of Philip Beidler's statement that "the war's horror had been implicit in the American character from the outset, a collective tragedy waiting to happen, a prophetic curse hiding at the heart of a whole mythology of culture" (*American Literature and the Experience of Vietnam* 113). Tobey Herzog analyzes an American icon and a cultural legacy, revealing that the better narratives of the Vietnam War often include "the motif of a John Wayne figure confronting a modern Heart of Darkness." He explores the unintentionally humorous film *The Green Berets* to introduce the inadequacy of the John Wayne myth to explore the complexity of Vietnam. Absent from the film, starring and co-directed by "The Duke," are any implications of moral issues or ambiguities, moments of individual self-awareness, admission of emotional or psychological turmoil, or even an attempt to present the numerous ironies and difficulties that appear when an advanced technological society encounters its opposite. The order, control, and purpose embodied in the John Wayne myth, Herzog contends, is addressed but quickly discarded in many a Vietnam War narrative in favor of issues and motifs found in Conrad's *Heart of Darkness:* the folly of imperialism, the impact of a primitive environment on civilized individuals, the shattering of ethical certainties, the attraction toward and the repulsiveness of evil. In some narratives Americans succumb to darker impulses, in others they resist, and in others they are blithely unaware. The best, Herzog asserts, "become introspective plunges exploring the depths of character."

Complementing Herzog's study is Jacqueline Lawson's focus on the structure of nonfiction narratives. Her essay examines the debilitating education endured by many a nineteen-year-old-soldier, a process whereby a naive youth is soon transformed into a disillusioned, cynical veteran, prematurely, utterly aged, an "old kid." According to Lawson, many of the works share an infrastructure of five stages: a call to arms, often inspired by the multiple impact of John F. Kennedy, John Wayne, commentary in the media, and even Saturday morning cartoons upon impressionable youths; a rite of passage experienced during basic training, where a young man's masculinity is broken down only to be restructured; disorientation upon arrival in country, where reality did not correspond with recruiting posters; awareness of one's own mortality in the face of peril, a time when prospective John Waynes wept; and homecoming, where recovery from disenchantment may be less than complete.

Louis Kern's study agrees in principle with Ward Just's advice, "The myths are gathering out there in the Hollywood hills, and while we can still hear the tom-toms, we had best circle our wagons" ("Vietnam: The Camera Lies" 65). During the post-Vietnam era, Kern suggests, the myths of old soldiers neither die nor fade away in film, but reappear in strange mutations. He argues that the popular "MIA-POW/Avenger-Vigilante subgenre of film" is Hollywood's attempt to reconcile American agony over the war with a national mythology of self-confident ascendency. Kern views the combat soldier in Vietnam as "the latest in a long line of macho heroes who incarnated the nation's archetypal self-image," one which is messianic, heroic, potentially violent, whose purest expression is found in the figure of the "Frontiersman/Indian Fighter." But after the loss of Vietnam, Kern notes, "the national mood was post-apocalyptic," and American films of the period, especially *The Deer Hunter* and *Apocalypse Now*, attempted to address the pervasive sense of lost ideals. As their protagonists confront the dark ambivalence at the core of the traditional American self-image, both films, Kern contends, illustrate the failure of American heroic ideals. The atmosphere of shattered national identity in the late 1960s and early 1970s, coupled with a collective desire to deny consequences and to atone for strategic and political "sins of omission," provided fertile ground, Kern believes, for the growth of the Avenger Vet hero in "Vetsploitation" films of the late 1960s and early 1970s, eventually evolving into the MIA-POW films of the late 1970s and early 1980s, in which the utter transformation of the Indian fighter occurs. In brief, the protagonist acquires traits and attributes of the enemy, frontiersman becomes Indian, history is exchanged for fantasy, defeat replaced by victory.

II

In Section II, "Differences and Debts," Nancy Anisfield, Owen Gilman, and Cornelius Cronin, while noting the debts owed by writers of Vietnam War literature to the literature of earlier wars, stress the differences between Vietnam and other conflicts. Anisfield demonstrates that the linguistic environment of novels structured by surrealistic elements, like Tim O'Brien's *Going After Cacciato* and Stephen Wright's *Meditations in Green*, are particularly suited to render the experience of the Vietnam War. The circumstances of warfare in Southeast Asia, she asserts, often undermined efforts to construct the political or the rite-of-passage novel or even to stress the theme of male bonding. Those novels most effective in portraying combat in Vietnam, she argues, contain "time shifts, tone changes, heightened detail, energetic pacing, transitional modes," and climactic incidents in greater concentration and frequency than do novels of earlier wars. Language, too, is intensified, as words are "mixed, mutated, and piled on each other," a bitter brew of military acronyms and G.I. argot, " '60s slang, rock, and drug lingo," and euphemism, resulting in a jungle inspired concoction helpful to distance combat soldiers from harsh situations. The artful use of words and fragments, Anisfield concludes, helps readers simulate combat reality and lends both emphasis and cohesiveness to the novels of Tim O'Brien and Stephen Wright.

Owen Gilman's essay reverberates with the authority and excitement of an insider well aware of the inner dynamics of the military machine as it explores further the crucial differences in language and ambience between the fiction of Vietnam and that generated by other American wars. He contends that the special feature of Vietnam War fiction is its "paradoxical paradigm of nomenclature," a characteristic which encompasses prose texture, word coinage, and style. Unlike science fiction which constructs peculiarities in language to invent its separate world, the terms of Vietnam War fiction, Gilman notes, "came directly—untranslated—from the miasmal ooze of the war itself." Inspired by the rituals of boot camp, sustained by the special weirdness of combat, and needed by soldiers as a coping mechanism, the language of Vietnam War fiction is charged with particularity, intensity, brutality, and irony. As a final point, Gilman mentions that the paradoxical nomenclature has a bright side, a "subtle anti-war bias," but it also entails a dark, fatal attraction to the cruel origin of its intensity.

Concluding Section II, Cornelius Cronin illustrates that Philip Caputo's *A Rumor of War* is both anchored in and departs from the literary tradition of the First World War. By constructing epigraphs from their poetry, Caputo carries on a dialogue with Wilfred Owen and Siegfried Sassoon, reaffirming a range of emotions a soldier may experience, from a sense of camaraderie within ranks to increasing alienation as the slaughter continues. More important, Cronin argues, is the structure of Caputo's book which echoes two contrasting patterns found in memoirs written by British officers. One paradigm, the comical preparation for combat, the disillusionment of battle, and withdrawal to a secure haven, is found in Part One of *A Rumor of War*. The other paradigm, training and exposure to war, separation from the unit to safety, and finally return to battle, is echoed in the tripartite structure of the entire book. However, when this second pattern is applied to *A Rumor of War*, Cronin notes, the uniqueness of the Vietnam experience is seen. When, for instance, Caputo attempts to return to his old unit for combat, he learns that it is returning stateside to be reorganized. Support that soldiers in earlier wars received from the group is thus denied and further exacerbated for all troops in Vietnam by the institution of an individual rather than unit rotation policy, one which undermined unit efficiency and morale. Furthermore the depiction of individual responsibility and consequent guilt is more emphatic in Vietnam War literature than in literature of earlier wars. Finally, American soldiers in Vietnam literature "see themselves more clearly and self-consciously" than those in other wars as Robert J. Lifton's concept of " 'socialized warriors' "—soldiers who are " 'measured by acts of killing,' " their activities, Cronin states, more "self-involving and self-destroying."

III

In a review-article of early Vietnam War fiction entitled "Vietnam Novels: First Draft," Bernard Bergonzi, implying the skill of often overlooked novelists, writes, "The authors are highly responsive to the nuances of soldiers' speech, but they are also strikingly bookish; the names and quotations that occur in epigraphs and allusions would provide a good foundation for a Great Books course, which is one result of sending a well educated citizen army into a bad and unpopular war" (*Commonweal* 27 October 1972). In Section III, "Craft and Techniques," a similar focus on the literary merits of an early novel seldom analyzed by critics informs the essays of Robert Slabey, who writes on James Park Sloan's *War Games,* and James Quivey, who analyzes Asa Baber's *Land of a Million Elephants*; while a consequence of committing a highly literate army to Vietnam is found in several literary masterpieces of that war: David Rabe's *Streamers,* examined by N. Bradley Christie, and Tim O'Brien's twin consideration of the conflict, *If I Die in a Combat Zone* and *Going After Cacciato,* discussed by Eric James Schroeder.

Reminding us that Vietnam not only changed American attitudes about war but also ways of writing about war, Robert Slabey notes the necessity for "new devices, structures, styles, even a new language." Given the era in which most Vietnam novels were published, some also share postmodernist elements of "reflexivity, collage, moral uncertainty, individual reality, and fictions becoming metafictions." A noteworthy example of metafiction in Vietnam War literature, Slabey asserts, is James Park Sloan's *War Games*. Its self-conscious narrator/protagonist, viewing reality through the filter of literature and the popular arts of film and television, frequently echoes the aphorism, irony, and bookishness of Juan Luis Borges; the isolation, ambivalence, and alienation of Franz Kafka; and the satire and absurd comedy of Joseph Heller. Rather than reporting objectively, he observes himself in the process of writing fiction, drawing attention to his techniques and to his participating in "an invented role in a plot of his own devising." The narrator/protagonist's attempt to write the great Vietnam War novel resembles a collage: a melding of facts, fictions, meditations, literary allusions, memories, dreams, reflections. Despite the novel's limitations *War Games* exemplifies "the perils of fiction and the limits of metafiction in writing about an experience that was itself ambiguous, circular, fragmentary, entropic."

James Quivey evokes both the spirit of affirmation and the considerable craft of Asa Baber's *Land of a Million Elephants*, a novel that was seldom reviewed when it first appeared in 1970 and has been virtually overlooked by most critics ever since. Pointing out that the techniques of narrative distance separate the better Vietnam War fiction from the all too common "close to the action" variety, Quivey also notes the refreshing theme of Baber's novel, one which is "positive....reassuring: Wars are a part of time, of the universal symmetry; and Southeast Asia, and the world will survive." Several primary distancing devices help articulate the theme: a narrative point-of-view, essentially "dramatic-objective with occasional slips into omniscience," that prevents readers from identifying with any "character-narrator" or "single identifiable, authoritative voice"; a structure in which no single narrative strand dwarfs the rest; "character equipollence" whereby no single figure dominates the action and discrimination between major and minor characters is often fuzzy; echoes of children's literature, adventure fiction, travel literature, and even Hemingway and Swift, all of which imply an atmosphere of permanence, separating readers from the war; and finally a muted depiction of death coupled with images of regeneration, underscoring the important life-sex-death continuum. All of the techniques, Quivey contends, distance author and reader, allowing "the story to make perhaps the least judgemental, least forced, and most organic thematic statement to be found among the early novels."

N. Bradley Christie notes that long before novels or films of the Vietnam War became popular, the theater audience was receptive to the thorny issues of that war raised by award-winning playwright David Rabe. In *Streamers,* the last play of his Vietnam trilogy, Rabe explores the looming threat of Vietnam on young, impressionable servicemen, as well as the attempt by their older ironic role model to cope with its impact. In a sharply confined setting, characters foil each other, revealing their fears, compassion, and capacity for violence. Both the youthful soldiers and their older counterpart try to disarm the reality of Vietnam: the young by filtering it through vicarious experience provided by the media, the career soldier dealing with his experiential knowledge by "selective short-circuit memory," studiously avoiding the subject. Though set stateside in 1965, in *Streamers* Rabe is very much aware of the two primary means by which Americans dealt with Vietnam in 1976, when his play first appeared.

Eric James Schroeder argues that *Going After Cacciato* contains a resolution of the moral and aesthetic problems O'Brien presented in *If I Die in a Combat Zone.* Labeling O'Brien's nonfiction narrative a "carefully crafted, yet ultimately unresolved memoir," Schroeder states that O'Brien's authorial intrusions imply lessons to be learned, but the point of the lessons is unclear to both reader and narrator. The substitution of aesthetic experience, resorting to war stories to be interpreted by individuals, for moral certitude suggests a shaping of experience, yet the lack of closure, even an "absence of catharsis," undermine that process of ordering in the memoir. *Going After Cacciato,* however, shifts the focus from the resolution of moral ambivalence to the "process necessary to reach such a resolution." To a question, "Do dreams offer lessons?" posed in *If I Die,* O'Brien answers affirmatively in the novel, for his protagonist Paul Berlin can achieve goals through asserting a quiet interlocking of memory and imagination. Whether real or imagined, events only have meaning when it is imposed on them, a lesson, Schroeder believes, that both Berlin and O'Brien learn.

IV

"The contemplation of the literature on the Vietnam War," Timothy Lomperis writes, "is far from mere academic exercise. People still hurt" (37). Part of the pain of the Vietnam experience, amply illustrated in the literature inspired by that war, was the return home, especially society's reluctant accommodation of what it had spawned. "They were my guns and I let them do it," (67) Michael Herr says of his relationship with combat soldiers in Vietnam, a statement that could apply to, but was forgotten by, many, if not most, Americans who remained stateside during the war. The essays by James Robinson, William Searle, and Vicente Gotera in Section IV, "Return and Partial Recovery," examine, respectively, the assumptions behind, the persistence of stereotypes associated with, and a means of addressing the consequences of the Vietnam War.

Since the allegorical aspects of David Rabe's play *Sticks and Bones* highlight political and generational flareups of the 1960s, brushfires caused and sustained by failures in communication, it is appropriate, James Robinson contends, that virtually all of the crucial images of the play are silent ones. He explores the significance of the noiseless slide projections, the broken television, David's imageless and soundless film, and the ghostlike appearance of David's abandoned fiancee Zung. Furthermore Robinson argues that such images operate on a more important level, as a "diagnosis of a national sickness which predates our involvement in Vietnam." Racism, materialism, and self-delusion come under fire in Rabe's play, but equally significant, our failure to comprehend the alienation of returning veterans and our inability to learn from them are dramatized.

After exploring the stereotypes associated with Vietnam veterans perpetuated by both the media and popular entertainment during the 1970s, William Searle, paraphrasing Charles Moskos, writes of a possible motivation behind the surprising acceptance of those harmful cliches by some of the veterans themselves, "Perhaps guilt-ridden, perhaps seeking in an oblique way, respect and deference, otherwise denied them, many of these anti-war vets substituted stories of atrocities for the usual heroic tales told by veterans of more noble conflicts." A favorite stereotype of the time, that of the psychotic Vietnam veteran, reappears in several novels published in the early 1980s, namely Charles Coleman's *Sergeant Back Again* (1980), Robert Bausch's *On The Way Home* (1982), and Stephen Wright's *Meditations in Green* (1983). The protagonists of all three novels, while enduring the war within, achieve partial victories at home, small triumphs which deflate labels attached to survivors of Vietnam. Coleman, Bausch, and Wright, however, unable to avoid popular conceptions, include in their novels other disturbed veterans, who, far less admirable than the major characters, revitalize the "sick vet" image, a cruel legacy of an unpopular war.

Vicente Gotera explains that by employing the familiar short lyric and a basic vocabulary, rather than experimental modes and trendy jargon, Bruce Weigl in *The Monkey Wars* forces complacent Americans to rethink and realize their inability to ameliorate the experience of the Vietnam era. Weigl's plain style—limited diction, mixed etymologies, and sophisticated sound effects—signifies the poet's obsession with his topic, suggests the necessity for attention, and deflates the euphemisms often applied to American conduct of the war. Though many of the collection's poems are not set in Vietnam, the landscapes of America, Europe, and Southeast Asia are linked by subtle gradations of violence. Imagistic associations, subtle connections, allow Weigl to evoke Vietnam without resorting to extremes, "surrealistic bloodshed or dadaistic nihilism," found in some literature of the Vietnam War. Instead, *The Monkey Wars*— where the struggle with the monkey of Vietnam continues "with no surrender in sight"—is ultimately Weigl's "battle to save the enterprise of poetry as something redemptory...."

V

Lastly, in Section V, "Wider Perspectives," Kathleen Puhr, Susan Jeffords, and Thomas Prasch examine, respectively, three separate areas of the Vietnam experience usually neglected by other critics, namely, the depiction of women in fiction, the role of gender in Vietnam representation, and the false assumption of realism in the movie *Platoon*. Electing to focus on American nurses in Vietnam rather than the portrayal of stereotypical American (fiancees, wives, mothers) or Vietnamese (bar girls, hootchmaids, or NVA/Vietcong loyalists) women, Kathleen Puhr notes that in selected memoirs and oral histories American women admit that they were motivated by John F. Kennedy's call to arms, dehumanized Vietnamese in order to cope with the consequences of combat, were emotionally scarred by their duties, endured rejection upon their arrival stateside, and suffered from post-traumatic stress disorder years later, experiences, in short, similar to those of American males who saw combat. Such realism is not often found in several popular novels (Evelyn Hawkins' *Vietnam Nurse* and Leonard B. Scott's *Charlie Mike*), where the female characters, primarily concerned with bedding the most eligible males, are uninformed about politics, unconcerned about ethical issues, and incapable of any insight into any aspect of the undeclared war. A significant exception, according to Puhr, is Patricia Walsh's *Forever Sad the Hearts*, a novel in which the female protagonist is concerned about the harsh ironies of the war, the love interest is more than one-dimensional, and the refreshing perspective of healer versus injurer is often apparent. Treating the after-effects of the war, Walsh's novel implies, can result in a loss of innocence as devastating as surviving first-hand experience of combat.

Susan Jeffords argues that viewing the movie *Platoon* through a "gendered frame" produces an interpretation that slices through political, social, and ethical ambivalence. A case in point surrounds the conflict between Barnes and Elias for Chris Taylor's soul, "a staging of a battle of gender," according to Jeffords. From this perspective, Barnes is representative of the masculine outer world (competitive, divisive, motivated by "things worth dying for") and Elias of a feminine underworld (utopian, bonded, motivated by "things worth living for"). Chris' admission, after his murder of Barnes, that he is "like a child born of two fathers," possessing qualities of both Elias and Barnes, indicates a tendency within Vietnam representation in both film and prose, whereby the masculine appropriates and incorporates the "qualities, characteristics, values" of the feminine within itself, "as a means of producing its own character." The masculine appropriation of the feminine in *Platoon* not only excludes women from the realm of warfare, but also suggests that resolution of issues and indeed "meaning to this life" are "found only within the frame of men, inside the 'platoon'."

Thomas Prasch contends that despite the claims of realism by both reviewers and writer/director Oliver Stone, *Platoon* is essentially a fiction relying on mythic referencing and genre conventions for both plot and theme. Though the film does contain elements of realism, they are surfacial, incidental, subordinated to the fictions of the film, a framework of the *Bildungsroman* containing an allegorical battle between good and evil. He points out Stone's dependence on Scripture, the myth of the hero, and war film genre conventions to underline the allegorical nature of his plot. Prasch also examines implicit contradictions between content and the conventions employed: especially an anti-war realistic surface versus the creation of a warrior hero. Stone's insistence on the realism of the film, Prasch believes, provides both explanation and absolution. If the film's fictions are viewed as realities, the audience not only is able to condemn warfare and evil individuals (conveniently left dead on the field of battle) without castigating veterans in general, but also is able to believe that the war was winnable, a victory prevented by Americans fighting among themselves.

Finally, citations from Peter Marin, Ward Just, and Tim O'Brien which began this introduction may also be used to conclude it. Since virtually all of the authors discussed in the following collection of essays are, in one way or another, survivors of the war in Southeast Asia, the words of Peter Marin concerning Vietnam veterans may, once again, apply to them: "In a sense, they are still walking point for us, confronting a landscape as alien as anything they faced in Vietnam, still doing for the rest of us the dangerous tasks that we pretend do not exist" ("Coming to terms with Vietnam" 52). In part, some of these perilous tasks involve revealing the assumptions that led us into that war, its harsh singularity, its cruel consequences. Down range, of course, the target continues to move, new books and films appear, a fact implied by Ward Just several years ago. Commenting on the time lapse necessary to acquire aesthetic distance, Just voices what he perceives as a similarity between the Civil War and the conflict in Vietnam, "But in both the myths rise organically from the material, the events and the human beings who lived in them, and there will not be one myth but many; with luck, through art, we will come to understand our memories" ("Vietnam: The Camera Lies"

65). Implicit in the words of Just is the power of the imagination, a concern vital to Tim O'Brien, as any reader of *Going After Cacciato* will affirm. Recently, at the 1985 meeting of the Asia Society, a conference devoted to the discussion of the literature of the Vietnam War, O'Brien stated, "When...writing fiction...we're after a kind of truth or clarity" (Lomperis 54). In his concluding remarks, he spoke of the longevity of the fictions, "Who knows, a thousand years from now the facts will disappear—bit by bit by bit—all that we'll be left with are stories" (54). Ironically, it is very likely that the most important "facts" about the war—American values, conduct, conscience—are preserved in the "stories." The tales that we already possess are frequently informative and the truths therein are not ultimately bitter ones, for self-knowledge, as both literature and "reality" have so often revealed, is usually a significant stage for both recovery and regeneration.

Notes

¹Ten of the most noteworthy include: *Journal of American Culture*, "Focus: The Vietnam War," 4 (Summer 1981); Gilbert Adair, *Vietnam on Film: From the Green Berets to Apocalypse Now* (New York: Proteus, 1981); Philip Beidler, *American Literature and the Experience of Vietnam* (Athens: University of Georgia Press, 1982); James C. Wilson, *Vietnam in Prose and Film* (Jefferson: McFarland, 1982); *Critique: Studies in Modern Fiction* 24 (Winter 1983); *Modern Fiction Studies* 30 (Spring 1984); Robin Wood, *Hollywood From Vietnam to Reagan* (New York: Columbia University Press, 1986); John Hellman, *American Myth and the Legacy of Vietnm* (New York: Columbia University Press, 1986); *Cultural Critique*, "American Representations of Vietnam," 3 (Spring 1986); and Timothy J. Lomperis, *"Reading the Wind": The Literature of the Vietnam War* (Durham: Duke University Press, 1987).

Works Cited

Beidler, Philip. *American Literature and the Experience of Vietnam*. Athens, Georgia: University of Georgia Press, 1982.

Bergonzi, Bernard. "Vietnam Novels: First Draft." *Commonweal*, October 27, 1972. pp. 84-88.

Grant, Zalin. "Vietnam as Fable." *The New Republic*, March 26, 1978, pp. 23-24.

Herr Michael. *Dispatches*. New York: Alfred A. Knopf, 1978.

Just, Ward. "Vietnam: The Camera Lies." *Atlantic*, December 1979, pp. 63-65.

Lifton, Robert J. *Home From the War*. New York: Simon & Schuster, 1973.

Lomperis, Timothy J. *"Reading the Wind": The Literature of the Vietnam War*. Durham, N.C.: Duke University Press, 1987.

Marin, Peter. "Coming to Terms with Vietnam." *Harper's*, December 1980, pp. 41-52.

Moskos, Charles. "Surviving the War in Vietnam," *Strangers At Home: Vietnam Veterans Since the War*. Ed. Charles R. Figley and Seymour Leventman. New York: Praeger, 1980. 71-85.

Naparsteck, Martin J. "Vietnam War Novels." *Humanist*, July 1979, pp. 37-39.

O'Brien, Tim. *Going After Cacciato*. New York: Delacorte Press/Seymour Lawrence, 1978.

Prescott, Peter. "In the Quagmire: Rev. of *Better Times Than These*." *Newsweek*, June 19, 1978, p. 82.

Terry, Wallace. *Bloods: An oral History of the Vietnam War by Black Veterans*. New York: Ballantine, 1984.

Tetlow, Joseph A. "The Vietnam War Novel." *America*, July 1980, pp. 32-36.

Section I:
The Quest

John Wayne
in a Modern Heart of Darkness:
The American Soldier in Vietnam

Tobey C. Herzog

"He bought the farm, but he took a lot of them with him."
        Soldier in
        The Green Berets (film)

"Every war is ironic because every war is worse than expected."
        —Paul Fussell, *The Great War and Modern Memory*

I begin this paper about war, movies, American myths, John Wayne, Vietnam, and metaphysical journeys with my own version of an occurrence from David Halberstam's novel *One Very Hot Day* where American combat troops in Vietnam, sitting in an outdoor theater, watch a World War II movie, *The Guns of Navarrone*. In my version, I am sitting in an outdoor theater in Long Binh, Vietnam, (January 1970) watching *The Green Berets* starring John Wayne. In the middle of this romantic portrait of war, a Viet Cong mortar attack sends us scurrying for nearby bunkers. Safely inside, I realize that even from my perspective as a clerk in a relatively secure area, the Vietnam War is not following the typical Hollywood script of a John Wayne movie, especially *The Green Berets*. The incessant noise of the medevac choppers ferrying the wounded to a nearby hospital; the dope, alcohol, and protest music in the barracks; the absence of apparent purpose and progress in the war; and the constant tensions between lifers-draftees, officers-enlisted men, blacks-whites, Americans-South Vietnamese are turning this war into what Michael Herr would later characterize as a "black looneytune." As I later discovered, a similar John Wayne induced disillusionment would be described in poignant ways by many of the Vietnam veterans writing personal narratives and fiction about a war that instead of a John Wayne movie became for them a "heavy trip" into a modern "Heart of Darkness."[1]

16

This transforming of a soldier's innocence and idealism into experience, disillusionment, and self-revelation on the battlefield is not unique to Vietnam narratives but rather underlies much war literature. For example, *The Red Badge of Courage, All Quiet on the Western Front, A Farewell to Arms*, or Wilfred Owen's poetry effectively illustrate this theme. In fact, in his study of literature from World War I, Paul Fussell notes that the paradigmatic memoir from this war portrays this customary change in three stages: (1) innocent preparation for war including a view of war as sport; (2) descriptions of the "unmanning experiences of battle" leading to "disenchantment and loss of innocence"; and (3) reconstruction and consideration, which can result in repudiation of the experiences, insight about the ironies of war, self-awareness, nostalgia, or social estrangement (130). Such a tripartite pattern of innocence, experience, and consideration has obvious archetypal properties and, in various forms, shapes much of the rite-of-passage literature focusing on the education, spiritual growth, or mythic quest of a central character. Not surprising, then, is the presence of this pattern in several significant Vietnam narratives as authors and characters move from unrealistic expectations about war into a search for order and meaning in an experience often seeming meaningless and chaotic, but also—at times—fascinating.

What may be surprising in many of these books, however, is the starting point for this change—the sources of illusions about war, sacrifice, and heroism affecting many American soldiers entering Vietnam. Commenting on one source, John Hellman in *American Myth and the Legacy of Vietnam* notes that "Americans entered Vietnam with certain expectations that a story, a distinctly American story, would unfold" (x). He proceeds to describe the ingredients for this story emerging from the landscapes, values, adventures, and heroes associated with the mythic frontiers of the American West. Not unexpectedly, he cites President Kennedy's "New Frontier" as an embodiment of these myths and a symbolic call for America to "regenerate its traditional virtues while serving future progress" (36). Such an urge to action figures prominently in Philip Caputo's Vietnam memoir, *A Rumor of War*. For the author describes the pervasive influence of the youthful, energetic President challenging young Americans to serve their country nobly:

> . . . we believed in all the myths created by that most articulate and elegant mythmaker, John Kennedy. If he was the King of Camelot, then we were his knights and Vietnam our crusade. (66)

At the same time Kennedy was restoring America's sense of mission and expanding the role of his "Arthurian" Green Berets in Vietnam, another prominent American and mythmaker was at work. John Wayne was waging his own campaign to revive sagging American patriotism and to provide additional materials for the "distinctly American story" believed to be emerging in Vietnam. In 1960, Wayne produced, directed, and starred in *The Alamo,* a movie affirming the indomitable American spirit and promoting the same principles of nation building and adventure underlying Kennedy's New Frontier. Thus, Julian Smith notes that despite their markedly different political views, "John Wayne and John Kennedy were not so terribly far apart. Both were trying to awaken their countrymen from lethargy, to inspire them with tales of courage, to make them feel more energetic" (92). Of course, Wayne and Hollywood had been at this task much longer than the new President and with greater success. Thanks to movies and television, the first true video generation, many of whom would later be fighting in Vietnam, had already grown up on a steady diet of westerns and World War II movies— several starring John Wayne. Referring to this social phenomenon, a character in Charles Durden's novel about Vietnam, *No Bugles, No Drums*, laments that late night movies "have done more to make romantic bullshit outa bad business than any single industry ever known" (85-86). Consequently, as many authors of Vietnam narratives suggest, to identify the dominant romantic illusions of American combat soldiers entering Vietnam and to understand the subsequent changes that many of these individuals underwent, one must comprehend John Wayne's widespread influence on Americans' perceptions of war.

But why was this John Wayne effect so significant? The answer is quite simple. By the early '60s, the Duke, through his movies and political stands, had already approached his present status as a cultural icon representing traditional American values of patriotism, courage, confidence, leadership, and manliness. Over the years, the man and his screen character had become one and the same—a mythical figure. The name of John Wayne was invoked as a verbal shorthand to describe the character of the American warrior-gentleman and to represent for young American males the elements of manhood. American movie audiences had seen Wayne as a cavalry officer, cowboy, soldier, sailor, pilot, seabee, and in 1960 Davy Crockett—frontier hero. Wayne, along with other Hollywood stars, had even appeared in military training films. Out of these appearances emerged widely accepted stereotypes of masculinity, the hero, conflict, and America's foreign policy: an individual/country, while engaged in a simple and ordered conflict, firmly controlling his/its fate and the destiny of those around him/it. But it is against this John Wayne influence and these very stereotypes many of the authors of Vietnam narratives are writing.

In this book *Home from the War*, psychiatrist Robert Lifton examines the impact of John Wayne on American soldiers in Vietnam. He comments that in rap groups, veterans talked of their struggle to free themselves from the "John Wayne thing." He describes its characteristics as follows:

We have seen the John Wayne thing to be many things, including quiet courage, unquestioning loyalty, the idea of noble contest, and a certain kind of male mystique.... But its combat version, as far as the men in the rap group were concerned, meant military pride, lust for battle, fearless exposure to danger, and prowess in killing. (219)

As further evidence of this phenomenon, William D. Ehrhart—a Vietnam veteran, author, and poet—writes in a short memoir about his early combat experience that "I had also at the time a rather unrealistic perception of what it meant to be in the service and fight a war.... I'd grown up on John Wayne, Audie Murphy, and William Holden" (26).

In light of Lifton's and Ehrhart's observations, it is not surprising, then, that direct and indirect references to the John Wayne-Hollywood syndrome appear in many Vietnam narratives. Thus, Ron Kovic in *Born on the Fourth of July* writes about his admiration for sports heroes, war, and John Wayne: "Like Mickey Mantle and the fabulous New York Yankees, John Wayne in the *Sands of Iwo Jima* became one of my heroes" (43). Caputo also mentions Wayne's influence on his unrealistic notions of war: "Already I saw myself charging up some distant beachhead like John Wayne in the *Sands of Iwo Jima,* and then coming home a suntanned warrior with medals on my chest" (6). Black soldiers also refer to this pattern in Wallace Terry's oral history, *Bloods:* "I was brought up on the Robin Hood ethic, and John Wayne came to save people: (4); or "We were so in the spirit that we hurt ourself. Guys would want to look like John Wayne. The dudes would just get in country and say, 'I want a .45. I want eight grenades. I want a bandoleer....' " (35). Finally, journalist Michael Herr in *Dispatches* uses a John Wayne reference to describe the attraction of war: "But somewhere all the mythic tracks intersected, from the lowest John Wayne wetdream to the most aggravated soldier-poet fantasy, and every one of us there a true volunteer" (20).

So, if indeed many American soldiers went to Vietnam bolstered by these John Wayne-Hollywood myths and eager to prove their manhood, exactly what did they anticipate about this war, heroism, and their responses? Perhaps, the most pertinent way to answer this question and to describe the elements of the "John Wayne thing" is to examine briefly the 1967 film version of *The Green Berets,* in which John Wayne starred and which he co-directed.

In this film, elements of myth, romance, and propaganda come together. Incidents from Robin Moore's 1965 novel by the same name are conveniently altered to fit Kennedy's ideals for the Green Berets, Hollywood's traditional views of war, and Wayne's and the Defense Department's attempts to rally the American people behind the war effort in Vietnam. The result, according to Hellmann, is a film that "symbolized the rededication to the American errand, the reassertion of the virtues and imperatives of America's frontier mythos" (38). The result, according to movie critics, is a film filled with cliche, propaganda, unintentional humor, and the plot and values of many previous John Wayne westerns and World War II movies. As Michael Herr says in typically cryptic fashion, "That [*The Green Berets*] wasn't really about Vietnam, it was about Santa Monica" (188).

What we find in the film is that Sgt. Stryker, Wayne's character from the W.W. II movie *Sands of Iwo Jima*, has been resurrected, had his domestic problems eliminated, and is now a colonel fighting with the Green Berets in Vietnam. The setting is different from Wayne's W.W. II movies, and the Viet Cong have replaced the Japanese. But the message, characters, and portrait of conflict remain the same. This film, promoting a patriotic, simplistic view of a complex war, contains clear distinctions between right and wrong, "good guys versus bad guys," and humanitarian acts contrasted with brutal attrocities directed against civilians. Absent, for the most part, is an honest attempt to probe the realities and ironies of war in general and Vietnam in particular. Perhaps, this misleading view is best epitomized by one soldier's naive assessment of the war, "Kill stinking Cong and go home." As a result, missing are the difficult moral issues involved with war; the moments of self-revelation on the battlefield; the confessions of fear, brutal instincts, frustration; and the questions of personal responsibility. Unlike characters in the best of war literature, the American soldiers in *The Green Berets* are not changed by their war experiences. At the end of the film they have not moved beyond the first stage of innocent idealism into a serious consideration of their experiences.

Instead, present in the movie are unquestioning American soldiers fighting to preserve democracy at home and in Southeast Asia, and, as one soldier says, fighting "Communist domination of the world." The South Vietnamese, as worthy allies, welcome our involvement, look to us for protection, but also take an active and dedicated role in their own defense. At the end of the movie, Wayne (Colonel Kirby), walking into the sunset with the young Vietnamese orphan, Hamchung, delivers the real message of this film: "You're what this war is all about."

Within such a purposeful context, the American soldiers appear eager, confident, and heroic. They approach the war with loyalty and a missionary zeal as they bring technology and civilization to the country. Their sense of mission might be best portrayed by the following quote from Phillip Caputo describing the mission of his own Expeditionary Brigade entering Vietnam in 1965: "American lives and property had to be protected, a beleaguered ally helped, and a foreign enemy taught that the U.S. meant business" (44)—words right out of John Wayne's mouth. A similar sense of purpose leads the soldiers in *The Green Berets* to view death in combat as meaningful and heroic. Thus, after a Viet Cong attack on the Green Berets' forward camp ("Dodge City"), an American soldier, describing the death of the Vietnamese Captain Nimh, notes that Nimh "bought the farm, but he took a lot of them with him"— American praise of the highest order.

Of course, dominating the action and spirit of this film, as he had in his previous war movies and westerns, is John Wayne—the man and the myth. The roles and settings change from movie to movie, but the character remains basically the same—a character shaping the American male's image of toughness, courage, patriotic duty, honor, and glory. Above all, in his posture, movements, tone of voice, and commands, he exudes a pervasive sense of immortality and control—control of his destiny and the fate of those around him. During a difficult situation in the *Sands of Iwo Jima*, Stryker calms the fears of his squad with a simple "I'll be the mastermind here." In *The Green Berets* this self-assuredness and control also emerge in simple statements such as "Move Out," "The Mike Force is on the way," "Keep doing our jobs," and "We can move in there tomorrow: God willing and the river don't rise." Colonel Kirby reduces the war to simple terms (good versus evil), analyzes what needs to be done, and takes actions leading to intended results. His war has definite winners and losers, logic, progress, and even immortality. As a result, when his helicopter and later an observation tower are shot from under him, just like in the westerns, he brushes himself off and returns to the fight. Fear, doubt, or self-reflection have no part in this conflict.

In analyzing *The Green Berets*, we begin to understand the fundamental implications of the "John Wayne thing" for American soldiers and the potentially destructive influence of Hollywood's view of war. As Herr laments about naive American soldiers, "I keep thinking about all the kids who got wiped out by seventeen years of war movies before coming to Vietnam to get wiped out for good" (209). In reading the Vietnam narratives, we find that a few authors and characters never lose this superficial John Wayne-Hollywood view of war. Others, however, entering the war with this view, move beyond it. Certainly for Kovic, Caputo, and even Herr to a lesser degree, the romance, happy-warrior mentality, and jingoistic spirit left over from the John Wayne films soon turn into disenchantment with the brutality of war, questions about the meaning of the war, self-doubts, and feelings of helplessness. Each refers to this change in revealing ways. Kovic writes about his unheroic actions, "I would go off alone sometimes on patrol looking for the traps, hoping I'd get blown up enough to be sent home, but not enough to get killed" (210). Herr laments the end of one more movie fantasy:

"...and when the Cav sent an outfit to relieve the Marines on 471, it killed off one of the last surviving romances about war left over from the movies: there was no shouting, no hard kidding, no gleeful obscenities.... The departing and arriving files passed one another without a single word being spoken" (158).

And Caputo, learning of a close friend's death, articulates his disillusionment, " 'I guess the splendid little war is over' " (154).

Obviously, several of these Vietnam books do not follow the plot of a John Wayne movie, but instead chronicle soldiers' journeys into the moral, emotional and psychological ambiguities of a war fought in an alien environment and culture against an often unseen enemy. As the participants struggle with and ponder these experiences, their stories become antidotes to the simplistic tale found in *The Green Berets*. Many of the soldiers become disillusioned as they encounter the ironies of war mentioned by Fussell. Some honestly deal with the magnetism of combat (its intensity and exhilaration); others confess that concerns for survival quickly replace grandiose dreams of John Wayne heroism and self-sacrifice. But most eventually sense that the milieu of order, control, and progress present in a John Wayne film is absent in Vietnam. Tim O'Brien accurately describes this feeling among American soldiers in *Going After Cacciato:*

No sense of order or momentum. No front, no rear, no trenches laid out in neat parallels. No Patton rushing for the Rhine, no beachheads to storm and win and hold for the duration. They did not have targets. They did not have a cause.... They did not know good from evil. (320-21).

Consequently, much like Joseph Conrad's 1899 novella, *Heart of Darkness*, the best of the Vietnam narratives move beyond mere descriptive details—a diary of facts and events—and beyond the arrogant confidence and ill-conceived illusions of various characters. Rather, they explore the enduring psychological and metaphysical truths about individuals hesitantly confronting evil, violence, foreign culture, primal emotions, chaos, and savagery. My reference here to *Heart of Darkness* may seem obvious in light of its connections to the film *Apocalypse Now*, but the film's superficial treatment of the book only hints at the deeper relationships between this story and Vietnam narratives.

Several authors, once past detailing the initial effects of the John Wayne syndrome, address many of the same themes and issues found in *Heart of Darkness*. For example, they explore the nature of imperialism—particularly the "rapacious pitiless folly" associated with it; the impact of technology and civilization on nature and so-called primitive societies; individuals tested by alien experiences and a jungle environment; saving illusions; the dissolution of moral certainties; and evil's fascination and repulsion—Conrad's "the fascination of the abomination." Furthermore, these authors frequently focus on the inner conflict between savage and civilized behavior and the suddenness with which normal individuals can slip into the former. Therefore, as in Conrad's book, many of the best Vietnam narratives portray an individual's often unsuccessful struggle to maintain control—control of the dark, destructive emotions; control of the fear; and control of the creeping madness and chaos. A representative echo of this Conradian theme is the following passage from *A Rumor of War*. It reads like a modern version of a passage from *Heart of Darkness* describing the impact of the African jungle on European colonialists, in particular, Kurtz:

Out there lacking restraints, sanctioned to kill, confronted by a hostile country and a relentless enemy, we sank into a brutish state. The descent could be checked only by the net of man's inner moral values, the attribute that is called character. There were a few...who had no net and plunged all the way down discovering in their bottommost depths a capacity for malice they probably never suspected was there. (xx)[2]

In his perceptive commentary on *Heart of Darkness*, Ian Watt categorizes the responses of Conrad's colonialists to the fear, savagery, and primal emotions generated by the jungle: "those who respond to savagery and succumb like Kurtz; those who respond but possess 'a deliberate belief' which enables them to resist; and the fools who do not respond at all because they do not notice" (226). In striking ways, characters in the Vietnam narratives fall into the same categories. They range from the unreflecting fools—John Wayne figures, perhaps—to those individuals who are both attracted and repelled by the horrors of war. The latter fight, like Conrad's Marlow, through their work and a deliberate belief in their mission to maintain order in and control over their actions and psyches and to hold off atavistic regression. The best of the Vietnam books, then, become introspective plunges exploring the depths of character, and, as the Brussels doctor in *Heart of Darkness* tells Marlow while measuring his head, the changes that "take place inside."

Narrators and characters in these Vietnam narratives embark on psychological journeys as they proceed from the world of straightforward facts and John Wayne myths; through the literal and metaphysical darkness of the jungle; to some measure of truth, self-awareness, and judgment. Ultimately, what these soldiers confront is the self. Stripped of their protective John Wayne illusions about masculinity, war, and individual conduct, they suddenly find themselves confronting primal instincts, fears, and questions about responsibility for one's actions. Instead of remaining "unreflecting fools," many soldiers, in somewhat limited ways, ponder their response to these issues. The results are revealing as each reacts in a different way to his spiritual isolation, destructive impulses, and the disillusionment caused by the horrors of war. Kovic finds himself tormented by, what he believes to be, his accidental shooting of a fellow soldier and his involvement in the deaths of several civilians. Unable to cope with these thoughts and the war, he seeks a way out of Vietnam—a million dollar wound—that will send him home, but not severely wounded. Herr, on the other hand, finds that despite the horrors of combat, combat that as a journalist he can fly to and leave at will, he is fascinated with war. Herr certainly does not become a clone of the journalist in *The Green Berets* who readily accepts the military propaganda. But he is in Conrad's terms "fascinated by the abomination" as the visceral high of combat becomes a significant part of his Vietnam experience.

Finally, Caputo arrives at an important insight while evaluating his responsibility in the murder of two Vietnamese civilians. His response to this moral dilemma is, at times, evasive as he cites the war and military strategy as the principal causes of his actions. But he also probes the origins of his inner conflict between savage actions and civilized behavior. No matter what the cause, he acknowledges that he momentarily succumbed to the dark, destructive emotions within us all: "Perhaps the war had awakened something evil in us, some dark, malicious power that allowed us to kill without feeling" (309).

What we have then underlying much of the American literature about Vietnam is the motif of a John Wayne figure confronting a modern Heart of Darkness. Several characters and narrators in these books begin as naive John Waynes ready to act out their best movie fantasies about war and acts of heroism. Even after taking the physical and metaphysical journey from a world of straightforward facts and "B" movies into the moral, emotional, and psychological confusion of the Vietnam jungle, a few of the participants remain unchanged by their experiences—perhaps the worst of the tales. Many, however, in confronting the darkness are fascinated, repulsed, and inevitably changed by the experience—a story as old as war itself. The best of these tales become confessionals as characters confront their experiences, arrive at insights, and make judgments: Kovic's "All I could feel was the worthlessness of dying right here in this place at this moment for nothing" (222); Caputo's "I was finished with governments and their abstract causes"; Herr's fascination with the abomination; and the almost universal agreement in these books with Kurtz's "The horror, The horror."

But sadly, the John Wayne myth will not die easily. Already a new video generation is forming its own romantic illusions about war, both from Wayne's movies and the heir apparent to John Wayne—John Rambo. Perhaps indicating the progress we have made as a society and the distance we yet have to go are the contrasting responses to the Rambo films, especially *Rambo, First Blood Part II*. Most Vietnam veterans are outraged by its false treatment of war and heroism, while young people cheer on Rambo's exploits. Caputo, however, anticipated this perpetual conflict between generations in the following pessimistic assessment:

So, I guess every generation is doomed to fight its war, to endure the same old experience, suffer the loss of the same old illusions, and learn the same old lessons on its own. (77)

Notes

[1]This essay is based on a paper delivered at the 1985 Convention of the Modern Language Association for a special session on "Teaching the Literature of the Vietnam War." Background for this essay can also be found in my articles "Writing About Vietnam: A Heavy Heart of Darkness Trip" and "*Going After Cacciator:* The Soldier-Author-Character Seeking Control."

[2]This passage from Caputo's book echoes the following passage from *Heart of Darkness:*

You can't understand. How can you?—with solid pavement under your feet . . . how can you imagine what particular region of the first ages a man's untrammelled feet may take him into by the way of solitude, utter solitude without a policeman, by the way of silence—utter silence, where no warning voice of a kind neighbor can be heard whispering of public opinion? These little things make all the great difference. When they are gone you must fall back upon your own innate strength, upon your own capacity for faithfulness. (70)

Works Cited

Caputo, Philip. *A Rumor of War*. New York: Ballantine, 1978.

Conrad, Joseph. *Heart of Darkness*. England: Penguin, 1973.

Durden, Charles. *No Bugles, No Drums*. New York: Viking, 1976.

Ehrhart, William. "Why I Did It." *Virginia Quarterly Review* 56 (1980): 19-31.

Fussell, Paul. *The Great War and Modern Memory*. New York: Oxford UP, 1967.

The Green Berets. Dir. Ray Kellogg and John Wayne. Warner Brothers, 1967.

Hellmann, John. *American Myth and the Legacy of Vietnam*. New York: Columbia UP, 1986.

Herr, Michael. *Dispatches*. New York: Knopf, 1977.

Herzog, Tobey. "*Going After Cacciato:* The Soldier-Author-Character Seeking Control." *Critique: Studies in Modern Fiction* 24 (1983): 88-96.

————. Writing About Vietnam: A Heavy Heart-of-Darkness Trip." *College English* 41 (1980): 106-21.

Kovic, Ron. *Born on the Fourth of July*. New York: Pocket Books, 1976.

Lifton, Robert. *Home From the War: Vietnam Veterans*. New York: Basic Books, 1985.

O'Brien, Tim. *Going After Cacciato*. New York: Dell, 1979.

Smith, Julian. *Looking Away: Hollywood and Vietnam*. New York: Scribner's 1975.

Watt, Ian. *Conrad in the Nineteenth Century*. Berkeley; UC Press, 1979.

A version of "John Wayne in a Modern Heart of Darkness: The American Soldier in Vietnam" was delivered at the First International Conference on the Cultural Effects of Vietnam, Sept. 4-6, 1986, at Manchester Polytechnic.

'Old Kids': The Adolescent Experience in the Nonfiction Narratives of the Vietnam War

Jacqueline E. Lawson

There was an aura about the people who were over there. These guys were kids, but they weren't kids. There was something in their eyes that made them absolutely different. I was fascinated, mesmerized by these guys. I couldn't take my eyes off them. There was something very old about them, but I still felt like a kid. (Baker 62)

"The thousand yard stare," "eyes masked and dull like an old man's," "boys with men's faces"—these are the 'old kids,' chronologically the youngest group of veterans in America's history, experientially the oldest. The statistics are by now familiar: the average age of the American combatant in Vietnam was 19.2 years as compared with 26 years for the soldier in World War II, a chronological disparity that has led recent scholars to label Vietnam "the nation's first teen-age war" (Brende and Parson xi). These teenagers came home and immediately began recording their experiences. Veterans' accounts of the war began appearing as early as 1966-67. They continued to emerge throughout the duration of the war—a remarkable pluralization of a fledgling canon, helped along by the 365-day rotation which deposited new cadres of writers back in the States even as it was taking the future 'old kids' out—burgeoned in the mid-to late-70s, and have since proliferated into a canon of nonfiction works that have elicited almost unqualified praise.

Paradigmatic works in this genre are the oral histories—Ron Glasser's *365 Days* (1971), Mark Baker's *Nam* (1981), Al Santoli's *Everything We Had* (1981); full-length memoirs—Tim O'Brien's *If I Die in a Combat Zone* (1969), Ron Kovic's *Born on the Fourth of July* (1976), Philip Caputo's *A Rumor of War* (1977), John Ketwig's ...*And A Hard Rain Fell* (1985), W.D. Ehrhart's *Vietnam-Perkasie* (1983) and *Marking Time* (1986); and collected letters—*Letters From Vietnam* (1967) and *Dear America: Letters Home From Vietnam* (1985). The quality of these works is uneven, ranging from the most stylized to the most primitive. Some,

26

like Caputo's *A Rumor of War,* aspire self-consciously to literary greatness; others, like Kovic's *Born on the Fourth of July,* achieve it without really trying. The animating presence in all of these works is the 'old kid,' who tells the story of this war, his war, in a voice alternately brash, stricken, elegiac, and polemical, but always with the persuasive power of truthtelling that only the eyewitness can claim.

Admittedly, it is difficult to generalize about works forged from the highly personal experiences of individual veterans, most of whom had never engaged in literary pursuits more serious than an occasional letter, high school essay, or college term paper. Nonetheless, these works share certain structural and thematic elements that lend remarkable solidarity to the canon. So fungible are they, in fact, that they subvert their own narrative claims to singularity; after awhile, the stories all start sounding alike. Yet it is precisely in their intertextuality, in the commonality of the experience they describe, that their narrative power resides. Each veteran's account follows the contours of the *bildungsroman,* the narrative of education, at the heart of which is the 365-day tour.[1] This structural homogeny is the veteran's attempt to impose order on chaos, to concretize and thereby make comprehensible an experience which defied reason and logic. Thus, each veteran's overwhelming need to tell his story is superseded by the even greater need to understand what, exactly, had been done to him, to explain, in absolute terms, the inscrutable and subversive effect of having "a lifetime of experience compressed into a year and a half" (Caputo 4). The process of becoming an 'old kid' occurs in five distinct phases which, in turn, provide the infrastructure for the veterans' narratives.[2] For want of more concise terms, these phases may be labeled 1) the mystique of pre-induction, 2) the initiation into boot camp, 3) the dislocation of arrival in Vietnam, 4) the confrontation with mortality in the first firefight, and 5) the phenomenon of coming home, "nineteen-year-old bodies with thirty-five-year-old minds" (Baker 130).

Premature aging is a concomitant of all war. Yet the effect of sending adolescents into combat in the far-off jungles of Southeast Asia was particularly devastating because of the psychological immaturity of America's fighting troops. The nineteen-year-old, in the opinion of one psychologist, was "less mentally prepared for the carnage and terror that marked the Vietnam experience" (Brende and Parson 41) than the World War II soldier sent into combat in his mid-twenties. Most of the young Americans who went to Vietnam had never been away from home before, had never traveled further than the neighboring county or the next city block, had never interacted with those from different racial, ethnic, and socio-economic backgrounds—had never wanted to. Loneliness, homesickness, feelings of isolation and, later, of betrayal, were psychological burdens as debilitating for the nineteen-year-old as the fear that one would be killed and left in the jungle, or would come home horribly maimed. And who was the enemy of these teenaged warriors? The North Vietnamese soldier was in many cases even younger than his youthful American counterpart. As the war escalated in the late 1960s, the ranks of the North Vietnamese regulars and the Viet Cong were increasingly depleted, making it necessary to draft or otherwise enlist into active duty the youngest brothers and youngest sons of those killed in action. Thus, it was not uncommon to find adolescents—some as young as thirteen—as regulars in the NVA. Vietnam was a war fought by adolescents against adolescents, and in some cases, by adolescents against children. In other words, kids killing kids.

What was it that motivated American teenagers to head willingly, even eagerly, off to a war waged 10,000 miles from home in a country few could even locate on a map? Ron Kovic:

In the last month of school, the marine recruiters came and spoke to my senior class.... It was like all the movies and all the books and all the dreams of becoming a hero come true. I watched them and listened as they stood in front of all the young boys, looking almost like statues and not like real men at all.... As I shook their hands and stared up into their eyes, I couldn't help but feel I was shaking hands with John Wayne and Audie Murphy. They told us that day that the Marine Corps built men—body, mind, and spirit. And that we could serve our country like the young president had asked us to do.... I stayed up most of the night before I left, watching the late movie. Then "The Star-Spangled Banner" played. I remember standing up and feeling very patriotic, chills running up and down my spine. I put my hand over my heart and stood rigid at attention until the screen went blank. (Kovic 73-75)

No one is more susceptible to the seductive power of mythmaking than the young. Mythmaking is a crucial component of adolescence, for it is youths, with identities unformed, unactualized, who search most persistently for role models to emulate. The nineteen-year-old sees himself as the inheritor of myths, a *tabula rasa* yearning for an imprint of selfhood. Mythmaking is equally important to nations, for it is through our myths that we derive a sense of identity, a feeling of national pride and purpose. Without a collective national mythology, waging war would be a far more problematic proposition than it is, for war is dependent on the illusions held by one generation and passed down to the next. The war in Vietnam was conceived in the image of two mythic heroes, one celluloid and one real. John Wayne and John F. Kennedy are the two most frequently mentioned names in the veterans' accounts.[3] John Wayne provided America's youth with the prototype of valor, courage, maleness, invincibility, and immortality. This was the hero to emulate. Philip Caputo:

Already I saw myself charging up some distant beachhead, like John Wayne in *Sands of Iwo Jima*, and then coming home a suntanned warrior with medals on my chest. The recruiters started giving me the usual sales pitch, but I hardly needed to be persuaded. I decided to enlist. (Caputo 6)

The centrality of the John Wayne image to the veterans' narratives cannot be stressed enough. Psychiatrist Robert Lifton, a leading authority on the diagnosis and treatment of post-traumatic stress disorder, has isolated the syndrome, labeling it "the John Wayne thing," or simply "John Wayneism."[4] For the Vietnam generation, John Wayne became one of mass culture's most effective propagandists.

Even more alluring than the fictive exploits of John Wayne were the real-life heroics of John F. Kennedy, a decorated naval officer whose romantic adventures in the Pacific aboard PT-109 were touted and sensationalized by the media throughout the 1960 presidential campaign. Kennedy's authentic heroism lent added force to his highly-charged inaugural oration, "ask not what your country can do for you—ask what you can do for your country." This was the hero to follow, this was a living legend, in whose name a generation of young Americans were willing to "pay any price, bear any burden, meet any hardship...to assure the survival and the success of liberty" (Kennedy Inaugural Address, 20 January 1961). Caputo:

If he was the King of Camelot, then we were his knights and Vietnam our crusade. There was nothing we could not do because we were Americans, and for the same reason, whatever we did was right. (Caputo 66)

It was these mythic heroes, both larger than life, that in the early phase of the war propelled wave after wave of the nearly three million Americans who would eventually serve in Vietnam out of the nation's cities, suburbs, and farms and through the gates of military boot camp.

The thirteen weeks of basic training served as a rite of passage, the first step toward initiation into manhood. In the subversive cultural climate created by the Vietnam war, boot camp also became a key factor in the eventual creation of the 'old kid.' New recruits entered boot camp with their illusions intact, and while for some, the diabolical regimen of calisthentics, forced marches, sadistic drill instructors, and daily degradation proved crushing (there is invariably a fat kid in every veteran's recollection of boot camp, who either kills himself in the first two weeks or becomes the sentimentalized object of everyone's pity), for most, boot camp served as a personal test of individual mettle, a proving ground for one's adolescent machismo.

Turning an Iowa farmboy into a killer is a collusive process, requiring the young trainee to give up his identity while still retaining his illusions, his intractable belief in myth. Boot camp forced the complete abandonment of ego, the regression of personality to a primal, infantile state, effected in the earliest weeks of basic training through a combination of punishing physical exertion and emasculating rhetoric: " 'All right, ladies. You look like shit, so we're going to do a little PT now.... On your bellies. Get up, get down' " (Baker 39); " 'You no good fucking civilian maggots.... I want you maggots to know today that you belong to me and you will belong to me until I have made you into marines' " (Kovic 77). This simultaneous demystification and remystification of manhood—destroying one's masculinity in order to make one a man— allowed for the eventual restructuring of the personality into nothing but the mythic identity: the super patriot, the noble warrior, the killing machine. John Ketwig:

We were pushed, pulled, beaten, screamed at, humiliated, and emasculated.... Up at five, train till six...Always aching, always cold, always scared; never secure...Exhaustion. Depression. Over a thousand days. Hand-to hand combat. Charge a dummy with a mock bayonet. "What's the spirit of the bayonet?" "Kill! Kill! Kill!" (Ketwig 25)

Boot camp impelled adolescents toward a fictive manhood as illusory as the flickering image of John Wayne on the TV screen. Basic training enforced and validated all the lofty, romantic notions of war held in boyhood, even as it hardened and toughened its boys into men. Becoming a man in the military meant accepting the loss of a youth that one hadn't yet lived. The nineteen-year-old doesn't know who he is, much less who he will become. He becomes John Wayne. Mark Baker's *Nam:*

By the time you get to the end of that whole process you feel like you're the baddest thing that ever walked the earth. When they call you Marine in the graduation ceremony, there's tears in your eyes. You are thoroughly indoctrinated. (Baker 40)

Arrival in Vietnam was a dislocating experience. Having appropriated a mythic identity fabricated out of wholly illusory notions of honor, courage, and maleness, the new arrivals regarded themselves as warriors—soldiers, infantrymen, marines, 'men'—the status officially conferred on them by the military at their graduation exercises. Each believed he had a purpose in coming to Vietnam: "to assure the survival and the success of liberty" (JFK Inaugural) through the swift and sure eradication of communism. America's young soldiers arrived in-country with an exalted sense of patriotism, honor, duty, and the rightness of America's cause. Many also harbored a glorified view of the war zone, seeing it as an exotic locale, an adventureland holding out the promise of heroic deeds and extraordinary acts of bravery. Vietnam, in the abstract, would be their Iwo Jima, the place they could point to with pride after the war, saying, *"this* is where I became a man." In sum, they perceived themselves as a monolithic conflation of John Wayne and John Kennedy, the mythic embodiment of America's muscular patriotism. The gulf between illusion and reality was chasmic, making the disillusion that followed all the more shattering. Nearly every veteran recalls his first moments in Vietnam as bewildering, disorienting, but ultimately revelatory—a jolt into reality. Mark Baker's *Nam:*

As soon as we hit the airfield they open the doors and tell us to get out.... You smelled the napalm and you smelled the human flesh burning.... We ran out through that smell into the bunkers and waited for the rockets to stop. After it was all over, they brought us out and lined us up for an orientation. In front of us is this lieutenant, a guy from the field. His uniform is filthy, all raggedy with the grenades hanging off of it.... You look into the guy's eyes and you saw that there was no joy there. Everybody I saw at the air base was in a zombie type of world. (Baker 81)

Vietnam was no adventureland: it was a pestilent, degraded inferno baked by a killing sun, crawling with leeches, rats, and snakes, littered with decomposing corpses, and inhabited by an army of the walking dead, the 'old kids,' those seasoned veterans whose glassy eyes and filthy, tattered uniforms gave the lie to John Wayne's theatrics and Kennedy's hyperbole. The grim reality of Vietnam exposed the hollowness of American jingoism, the ruinous belief—propagandized by the media, mouthed by the politicians, perpetrated by the military, and disseminated by mass culture—that "whatever we did was right." "Winning hearts and minds," "killing to save lives," "burning the village in order to save it," "peace with honor"—these were the oxymoronic *codae* used to wage, escalate, and ultimately justify a war that even the greenest recruit knew was lost from his first moments in-country. Mark Baker's *Nam:*

One of the first things you realized when you got to Nam was that you weren't going to win this war. There was no way we could win doing what we were doing. After the first month, me and everybody else over there said, "I'm going to put in my twelve months and then I'm getting the fuck out of here. It's not worth it." (Baker 112)

Survival thus became the only goal, the 365-day tour the only certainty in a war fought by the book but never by the rules, where the enemy was elusive, cunning, and victorious, where success was measured in body counts and kill ratios, and defeat was the sight of your buddy blown to bits in front of your eyes. Death occurred in Vietnam with alarming frequency, always unpredictably and always at random. Despite the tonnage of napalm and defoliants dropped on Indochina by U.S. forces, the war in Vietnam was fought chiefly on the ground. It was a guerrilla war of mines and booby traps, designed for the death of one and the demoralization of many. By the period of the Tet Offensive (1968), mines and booby traps were claiming more American casualties than ground

fire and air strikes combined. The anti-personnel nature of the war
(literally, "against persons") had the paradoxical effect of personalizing
the experience of dying for each soldier. Mark Baker's *Nam:*

We had constant attrition from booby traps, seven out of ten casualties a month
were traumatic amputees.... You're watching every place you step wondering who's
going to hit it. You know someone is going to...*Boom!* Just like that and a guy
is missing a foot.... Everything hits slow motion, like you're in your own movie.
You try to be cool, calm, and collected, and you are...kind of. You certainly ain't
John Wayne. (Baker 100, 101)

The average nineteen-year-old cannot conceive of death, his own or that
of his peers. Teenagers regard themselves as invincible, immortal, and
eternally virile. Caputo:

The possibility that I might not return did not occur to me. I was...in superb
condition, and quite certain that I would live forever. (Caputo 41)

American adolescents are raised on a steady diet of dying, killing,
and maiming, though always the sanitized version offered up by Saturday
matinees, TV adventure shows, and Sunday morning cartoons. The
anesthetizing effect of media violence and its concomitant glorification
by pop culture icons like John Wayne made the war in Vietnam possible.
It also made it unwinnable. American teenagers were willing to die an
idealized, media-hyped version of death (quick, clean, painless, glorious);
they were patently unwilling to play out the fantasy once they had seen
death up close.

     The first firefight—the actual combat experience—debunked the
myth, purveyed by the imposter hero John Wayne, that dying for one's
country is an ennobling experience, the ultimate act of patriotism, the
rite of passage into manhood. Ketwig:

Dying, or being disfigured, is not a patriotic act. It is a waste, an unnatural and
abhorrent affront to human decency. It is painful, and you can't change a channel
selector and make it go away. (Ketwig 166)

The war in Vietnam exposed the fallacy of America's belief in its own
mass-culture propaganda even as it destroyed the illusions of its teenaged
warriors. "John Wayne" does die and when he dies, he cries out for
his mother. Kovic:

Men are screaming all around me. "Oh God get me out of here!" "Please help!"
they scream. Oh Jesus, like little children now, not like marines, not like the posters,
not like that day in the high school, this is for real. "Mother!" screams a man without
a face. "Oh I don't want to die!" screams a young boy cupping his intestines with

his hands. "Oh please, oh no, oh God, oh help! Mother!" he screams again. (Kovic 16, 17)

Thus, the initiation into manhood ends, paradoxically, with a de-nitiation back into boyhood. A nineteen-year-old can't 'die like a man' if the manhood he seeks is fraudulent. Neither can he appropriate the identity of the 'noble warrior' if the war he is fighting is not noble. Sergeant Douglas McCormac, Company C, 5th Special Forces Group:

I think perhaps this experience is changing me.... Of course, Americans are dying, and I would not belittle anyone who served "with proud devotion" and faith in this enterprise. It may not have been a terribly wrong theoretical idea at one time. But the foreign, introduced offensive, the consequent corruption and then the contempt that developed between people and groups—it makes a mockery of the "noble" words used to justify this war. It belies the phony enthusiasm with which those words may be delivered. It's now a war of survival...(Dear America: Letters Home From Vietnam 216)

Despair was America's real enemy in Vietnam. As American platoons continued to suffer heavy losses—forcing Lyndon Johnson and, later, Richard Nixon to escalate the war—order among the troops began to break down. Exhausted and demoralized, American soldiers began to turn against themselves, each other, their officers, and ultimately the war. Drug use soared, incidents of fragging, self-inflicted wounds, racial conflict, and insubordination mounted as the war dragged on. An overwhelming sense of rage, frustration, and especially betrayal informs the narratives of those veterans who served in the later years of the war's escalation phase. Particularly striking in these accounts is the growing disillusion on the part of our adolescent soldiers with America's leaders and its people. W.D. Ehrhart:

I knew at last that nothing I had ever done in Vietnam would ever carry with it anything but shame and disgrace and dishonor; that I would never be able to recall Vietnam with anything but pain and anger and bitterness; that I would never again be able to take pride in being an American. And the rage and sorrow and tragedy of it all was overwhelming. (Ehrhart, Marking Time 247)

The explosion of the 'noble warrior' myth, coupled with the inordinate stress and anxiety that were daily realities in Vietnam (the "certain uncertainty" of stepping on a mine or tripping a booby trap) helped create the phenomenon of the 'old kid' and may go far in explaining the alarmingly high incidence of post-traumatic stress disorder among Vietnam-era veterans. Caputo:

I came home from the war with the curious feeling that I had grown older than my father, who was then fifty-one. It was as if a lifetime of experience had been compressed into a year and a half.... I had all the symptoms of *combat veteranitis:*

an inability to concentrate, a childlike fear of darkness, a tendency to tire easily, chronic nightmares, an intolerance of loud noises—especially doors slamming and cars backfiring—and alternating moods of depression and rage that came over me for no apparent reason. Recovery has been less than total. (Caputo 4)

Marine lieutenant Ron Kovic, the boy who pledged allegiance to the TV screen on his last night as a civilian, did not die in Vietnam. He did, however, come home with the one wound everyone dreaded most. Ron Kovic went to Vietnam in quest of a fictive manhood to match John Wayne's and John F. Kennedy's. He returned a "sexlessman," paralyzed from the waist down by the bullet that severed his spinal cord. Kovic:

It is over with. Gone. And it is gone for America. I have given it for democracy. It is okay now. It is all right. Yes it is all right. I have given my dead swinging dick for democracy. It is gone and numb, lost somewhere out there by the river where the artillery is screaming in. Oh god oh God I want it back! I gave it for the whole country, I gave it for every one of them. Yes, I gave my dead dick for John Wayne and Howdy Doody, for Castiglia and Sparky the barber. Nobody ever told me I was going to come back from this war without a penis. But I am back and my head is screaming now and I don't know what to do. (Kovic 112)

Kovic's emasculation is a hideously apt metaphor for the cultural castration that marked America's failure in Vietnam. Like the other 'old kids,' his was a movement, not from innocence to experience but from naivete to cynicism, a difference in degree and kind. The lesson held out by the 'old kids' of Vietnam is that myths are as illusory and disposable as the image of the rough and ready cowboy flashing across the big screen. That we continue to recycle our myths is less a reflection of American foreign policy than of the current generation of high school students, Iowa farmboys, and college sophomores.

Rambo has replaced John Wayne, America's youngest president has been supplanted by America's oldest, and media coverage of Vietnam, Laos, and Cambodia has given way to nightly press reports from Nicaragua, El Salvador, and Honduras. It would be premature to attempt to gauge the success of the nonfiction narratives of the Vietnam War, since veterans are still busily engaged in publishing their accounts. I can, however, speak to the failure of this canon. The works by the 'old kids' of Vietnam will have failed if the next generation of veterans—the 'old kids' of Nicaragua, perhaps—produce a canon of war literature indistinguishable from theirs.

Notes

[1]The structural similarity of the veterans' narratives to the *bildungsroman* follows the convention of previous war literature, whereby a young man attempts to trace the process of his maturation from childhood to adulthood. In the case of the Vietnam narratives, however, the traditional structure of the *bildungsroman* undermines the myth that war is somehow a pivotal experience in a young man's education, a line of demarcation between boyhood and manhood. That the myth of manhood is exploded in nearly every veteran's account underscores the highly subversive nature of the Vietnam experience, a war which robbed the veterans of their youth rather than serving as a signpost on the road to manhood. The concept of a lost or truncated youth is central to the 'old kid' phenomenon. For mention of the *bildungsroman* structure in the Vietnam narrative see John Clark Pratt's Forward to W.D. Ehrhart, *Vietnam-Perkasie: A Combat Marine Memoir* (Jefferson, N.C.: McFarland and Co., 1983), pp. ix, x.

[2]Virtually every veteran's account is divided, either overtly or implicitly, into distinct categories or phases. Even the oral histories and collected letters are organized by descriptive sub-headings, chronologically arranged, denoting either topics, themes, or stages of the war. For example, Mark Baker's *Nam: The Vietnam War in the Words of the Men and Women Who Fought There* (1981: New York; Quill, 1982), is organized under the headings Initiation, Operations, War Stories, and The World; Al Santoli's *Everything We Had: An Oral History of the Vietnam War by Thirty-Three American Soldiers Who Fought It* (New York: Ballantine Books, 1981), is similarly divided into five "chapters," Gathering Clouds, Sand Castles, Peaks and Valleys, Barren Harvest, Operation New Wind; *Dear America: Letters Home From Vietnam*, ed. Bernard Edelman (New York: Pocket Books-Simon and Schuster, 1985) contains eight sections, arranged chronologically from " 'Cherries' ": First Impressions to the posthumous Last Letters. The use of chronological phases, following the *bildungsroman* structure of the narratives themselves, has been adopted by scholars for organizing critical studies of the Vietnam texts. Individual scholars have devised their own categories; see, for example, Lloyd B. Lewis, *The Tainted War: Culture and Identity in Vietnam War Narratives*, Contributions in Military Studies 44 (Westport, Connecticut: Greenwood Press, 1985), who identifies four phases of structure and meaning in the Vietnam narrative: Propaedeutic, Initiation, The Retreat from Meaning, and Walking Wounded. Lewis's categories are comparable to the five phases I have identified in that they attempt to replicate the complete Vietnam chronology, from pre-induction to the war's aftermath.

[3]See, for example, Philip Caputo, *A Rumor of War* (New York: Ballantine Books, 1977), pp. 6, 66; Ron Kovic, *Born on the Fourth of July* (New York: Pocket Books-McGraw Hill, 1976), pp. 54, 55, 71, 74, 91, 112; John Ketwig,...*And a Hard Rain Fell: A GI's True Story of the War in Vietnam* (New York: Pocket Books-Simon and Schuster, 1985), pp. 7, 10, 61, 159; Ehrhart, *Vietnam-Perkasie*, pp. 8, 187, 247 and *Marking Time* (New York: Avon Books, 1986), pp. 170, 244; Baker, *Nam*, pp. 33, 34, 40, 83, 101, 311. This is only a partial and representative listing.

[4]Robert Jay Lifton, *Home from the War: Vietnam Veterans, Neither Victims nor Executioners* (1973; New York: Basic Books, 1985), pp. 219-263; also see Lewis, pp. 21-37.

Works Cited

Adler, Bill. *Letters From Vietnam.* New York: Dutton, 1967.

Baker, Mark. *Nam: The Vietnam War in the Words of the Men and Women Who Fought There.* 1981. New York: Quill, 1982.

Brende, Joel Osler and Erwin Randolph Parson. *Vietnam Veterans: The Road to Recovery.* New York: Signet-NAL, 1985.

Caputo, Philip. *A Rumor of War.* New York: Ballantine Books, 1977.

Edelman, Bernard, ed. *Dear America: Letters Home From Vietnam.* New York: Pocket Books-Simon and Schuster, 1985.

Ehrhart, W.D. *Marking Time.* New York: Avon Books, 1986.

_____. *Vietnam-Perkasie: A Combat Marine Memoir.* Jefferson, N.C.: McFarland and Co., 1983.

Glasser, Ronald. *365 Days.* New York: George Braziller, 1971.

Ketwig, John. *...And A Hard Rain Fell: A GI's True Story of the War in Vietnam.* New York: Pocket Books-Simon and Schuster, 1985.

Kovic, Ron. *Born on the Fourth of July.* New York: Pocket Books-McGraw Hill, 1976.

Lewis, Lloyd B. *The Tainted War: Culture and Identity in Vietnam War Narratives.* Contributions in Military Studies 44. Westport, Connecticut: Greenwood Press, 1985.

Lifton, Robert Jay. *Home from the War: Vietnam Veterans, Neither Victims nor Executioners.* 1973. New York: Basic Books, 1985.

O'Brien, Tim. *If I Die in a Combat Zone, Box Me Up and Ship Me Home.* 1969. New York: Delacorte Press, 1975.

Santoli, Al. *Everything We Had: An Oral History of the Vietnam War by Thirty-Three American Soldiers Who Fought It.* New York: Ballantine Books, 1981.

" 'Old Kids': The Adolescent Experience in the Nonfiction Narratives of the vietnam War;" was presented at the 1987 meeting of the PCA in Montreal, March 24-26, 1987.

MIAs, Myth, and Macho Magic: Post-Apocalyptic Cinematic Visions of Vietnam

Louis J. Kern

He commits himself to the forest primeval; there, so long as life shall be his, to act upon a calm, cloistered scheme of strategical, implacable, and lonesome vengeance. Ever on the noiseless trail; cool, collected, patient; less seen than felt; snuffing, smelling—a Leather-stocking Nemesis.... The Indian-hater is good as gone to his long home, and "terror" is his epitaph.

Herman Melville, *The Confidence Man* (1857)

But you have there the myth of the essential white America. All the other stuff, the love, the democracy, the floundering into lust, is a sort of by-play. The essential American soul is hard, isolate, stoic, and a killer. It has never yet melted.

D.H. Lawrence, *Studies in Classic American Literature* (1923)

For many of those who awaited the return of America's warriors in our longest, most unpopular, and most divisive war, there was a feeling of frustration, a sense of an almost insurmountable barrier to understanding the Vietnam conflict. While our national preoccupation with the war was accurately reflected in Michael Herr's epitaphial words— "Vietnam, Vietnam, Vietnam, we've all been there (260)—it remains true that our cultural vision of that wartime experience has remained fragmented and seriously flawed.

Extensive media coverage of the war provided but little insight into the broader context of America's involvement in Southeast Asia. Instead, the media provided a series of discrete, disconnected images that became powerful symbols evoking deep emotional responses in the public mind, but no wider vision of the war's significance, no apparent justification for its seemingly senseless waste and brutal prosecution. Individual visions of the war abounded, but the communal mind, while deeply moved by its visual and ideological symbols, found no coherent, integrative, reconciliatory outlet for the powerful emotions stirred by the Vietnam experience. The war remained enigmatic for most Americans; they were

37

confused, disoriented by it, and finally profoundly alienated from the traditional national mythos.

The most fundamental unresolved enigma that emerged in the troubled post-war American psyche revolved around the brute fact of America's loss of the war. Col. Harry G. Summers described this incongruence between perception and reality when he wrote of a conversation he had with a North Vietnamese counterpart after the fall of Saigon. "You know you never defeated us on the battlefield," Summers said. "That may be so," Col. Tu replied, "but it is also irrelevant" (21). The winners can afford to treat the accidents of history as irrelevancies, but for the losers explanations that restore national self-confidence and provide scapegoats for public disgrace are avidly sought. It would be in the cultural undergrowth of socio-historical myth that Americans would fight the symbolic battles to recapture a coherent sense of national identity and to achieve historical exoneration. This paper will examine the transformation of traditional social myths undertaken to justify America's participation in and conduct of the war that has been most self-consciously expressed in an enormously popular series of films— the MIA-POW/Avenger-Vigilante sub-genre.

Typically, a healthy cultural mythos functions as a subliminal reinforcement of national character and identity, and provides a gloss on a people's historical experience, simultaneously stretching backward and forward to link the present with the past and future. The classic expression of American mythic consciousness is the call to a divinely ordained mission, a heroic trial against threatening external forces, the success of which depends on internal resources and periodic outbursts of purgative violence directed outwards. The corollary of this focus on America's special sense of mission is the belief that the strength of national character has always been such as to insure triumph in the holy quest. On the level of mythic consciousness, then, Americans have traditionally believed that as a people they are an exception to history.[1]

American experience in Vietnam, however, profoundly shattered the foundations of the national myth and shook public faith in the traditional terms of the belief in American uniqueness. The soldiers who fought in Southeast Asia were both the instruments of a national reenactment of the myth (an embodiment of the popular mythic consciousness), and symbolically surrogates for America's confrontation with the dark ambiguities at the heart of the myth. The men in the field were simultaneously fighting a war against the prescriptive external enemy and the internal demons of doubt about commitment to national ideals. The breakdown of the familiar mythic organizing principles that had historically sustained America's self-image meant that the Vietnam War was not simply a struggle for Asian "hearts and minds," but for our own as well. The Vietnam experience was a national *crise de conscience*; American ideals were perilously at risk.

In the jungles of Southeast Asia, American fighting men were the latest in a long line of macho heroes who incarnated the nation's archetypal self-image. In the popular mind that heroic line stretched unbroken back to our origins as a distinctive people, and found its classic expression in the figure of the Frontiersman/Indian Fighter. He lived amidst scenes of death and destruction and was the agent of the advance of civilization through his mastery and exercise of the special skills of savage warfare, a war of extermination. As distinguished from "civilized" conflict, savage warfare has perennially provided the basis for an "American mythology of violence...[which] continually invokes the prospect of genocidal warfare and apocalyptic, world-destroying massacre..." (Slotkin, *Regeneration* 61). To preserve civilization (i.e., the American way of life), the mythic Indian Fighter becomes a living sacrifice, an embodiment of the collective popular will. He emerged as an ambivalent, paradoxical figure—a savage instrument of civilization, who had "developed a monomania for vengeance; who dedicated his life to destroying Indians; left civilization and became a savage himself, and perhaps even went insane; who, in any case, was cut off by his monomania from all proper contact with family, home, and the good society" (Pearce 111).

As the archetypal American hero, the Indian Fighter/Vigilante, the paladin of civilization, has figured most prominently in a Crisis-Annihilation-Restoration myth cycle. The language of crisis has typically been hyperbolic, apocalyptic. As Harvey Cox described this state of mind, "apocalyptic creates a mood of world negation, fatalism.... Rational action is useless because powers outside history and beyond human control will quickly bring the whole thing to a blazing end" (qtd. in Russell 22). The figure who can face this terrible ordeal by fire is a man of instinctual action and brute violence; a man whose plenitude of natural virtue places him above history and whose purity frequently sets him apart from the political world—the Vigilante/Avenger. His function is to destroy the external threat, restore public faith, and re-establish the traditional values of the community.

The most prominent apocalyptic crisis for Americans since World War II was the Vietnam conflict. Some sense of the perceived seriousness of the threat posed to ideology and geopolitical hegemony, and to the idealized national self-image by events in Southeast Asia is conveyed in a book entitled *Vietnam Crisis* published just as the U.S. undertook primary responsibility for the prosecution of the war. "Vietnam demands," its authors maintained, the close attention of the entire world today. It is of the utmost concern both to those who are still free, and to those who are already behind the Iron and Bamboo Curtains. The outcome of the Vietnamese war will not only decide the fate of people in that area, it can greatly affect the rest of Asia as well as Africa and Latin America.... Europe's fate may also depend on the outcome of Viet Nam. (Pan and Lyons v)

We fail to realize that if we compromise in Vietnam...it will be the beginning of the end of the United States as the leader of the free world, and that without a leader, it will be the beginning of the end of the free world itself. If we lose Viet Nam we will suffer the greatest defeat in all of our history. The repercussions will reverberate around the world. (Pan and Lyons xiv-xv)

In the end, of course, we did lose Vietnam. As a nation we had failed in the critically decisive crusade; the national mood was post-apocalyptic. It was symbolically reflected in the million refugees that fled southward before the victorious NVA troops, the frenzied struggles to clamber aboard the evacuation vehicles, and perhaps most graphically in the abandonment and destruction of American helicopters by USN personnel during the final evacuation of Saigon on April 29-30, 1975. The loss of Vietnam threatened the very core of American identity: it contradicted the lessons we had drawn from historical experience; it mocked the structures of belief that maintained the myth of a unique national mission; and it seriously undermined the essential elements of our world view.

American films of the post-1975 period attempted to come to terms with the crisis of confidence, the pervasive sense of longing for a world of lost ideals, the paranoic conviction that the mythic code had been cravenly betrayed that gnawed at the tranquility of the national psyche. Although collective amnesia and denial frequently characterized the public and official response to the war during the decade after the fall of Saigon, the box-office success of cinematic considerations of the war suggested that what was consciously denied on a political level was of paramount concern in the subliminal world of myth.

Indeed, the two most popular as well as critically acclaimed "Vietnam" films of this period, Michael Cimino's *The Deer Hunter* (1978) and Francis Ford Coppola's *Apocalypse Now* (1979),[2] are really about the isolate, individual hero's confrontation with the ambiguities and contradictions at the heart of classic American mythology in the context of a Southeast Asian jungle setting. In this archetypal savage landscape to which Americans come bearing messianic dreams of omnipotence, they find themselves trapped; surrogates of a nation sucked into an Asian quagmire and "held captive and forced to confront the full implications of its own impulses" (Hellmann 182). As Robin Wood observed in his perceptive study of the films of this era, *The Deer Hunter* "is centrally concerned with the way in which the invasion of Vietnam (a country) by America is answered by the invasion of America (an experience, a symbol, a state of mind)" (276-77). The tone of the film conveys a pervasive sense of loss, while its plot underlines the failure of traditional macho heroics and national ideals of the war.

The very title *The Deer Hunter* resonates with the power of traditional mythic consciousness in its echo of the title of Cooper's 1841 novel *The Deerslayer*. Its protagonist, Michael (Robert DeNiro), a member of a middle-America, working-class, ethnic community, embodies the heroic qualities of the macho Hemingway hero. His power resides in his closeness to nature, in his savage, instinctual skills as a woodsman, and in the purity of his devotion to a masculine code of honor. His symbolic character is summed up in the fetish of "one-shot," an obsession with control, an almost mystical union of eye, hand and weapon that enables him to bring down his prey with a single bullet, thus sanctifying the ritual of the hunt. The motion of the film, which moves us with brutal abruptness from the world of pseudo-savagery of the deer hunt to the horrors of Vietnam, pits the power of self-control against utter unreasoning destructiveness.

The failure of "one-shot" in the crucible of the Vietnam experience is graphically illustrated by the fate of Michael's best friend, Nick (Christopher Walken), who is psychically destroyed by the war. The American mythology of regeneration through trial in the wilderness is mocked in the scene portraying Nick's recuperation from wounds in a Saigon hospital. From his bed he can see the rows of body bags and the plastic coffins into which they are to be loaded. Dominating the foreground of this shot is an American flag that dwarfs the field of the dead. Nick ultimately falls victim to the horrors of the war and suffers a paralysis of belief in national ideals. He drifts into the decadent Saigon criminal underworld, becoming a drug addict and a professional Russian roulette player.

Michael returns to Vietnam after the war, finds Nick and tries to convince him to return home. In the climactic scene of the film, Nick puts the gun to his temple and kills himself. The code of "one-shot" has been inverted by the Vietnam experience. After Nick's death, when Michael returns to the woods, although he has a buck in his sights, he cannot fire. American mythic ideals, and the macho code of self-control expressed as "one-shot," Cimino suggests, have clearly failed us in Vietnam. And their viability in the symbolic landscape of the American mind has been overwhelmed by impotence, the objective correlative of which is Michael's inability to shoot the buck. America's defeat in Vietnam is imaginatively conceived here as a fall from grace.

The trauma of that fall is portrayed even more powerfully in *Apocalypse Now*. The world of *Apocalypse* is a self-consciously mythic one. The protagonist, Capt. Benjamin Willard (Martin Sheen), is the traditional hero on a quest. Since his mission is ostensibly to locate and "terminate with extreme prejudice" the renegade Green Beret Col. Walter E. Kurtz (Marlon Brando), he takes on all the overtones of the traditional American hero cum Indian Fighter/Vigilante. But his unspoken agenda is an interior mission—into the savage heart (or more properly the bowels)[3] of the violent core of American identity. This reading of the film is reinforced by the studied shot in which the viewer gets a glimpse of Kurtz's occasional reading matter—James Frazer's *The Golden Bough* and Jesse L. Weston's *From Ritual to Romance*. The latter particularly calls our attention to the heroic quest for the sacral vessel. But here the terms of the ritual have been cruelly inverted. The original champion has betrayed the trust and a lesser knight has been sent to assassinate him. The grail quest has been abandoned as obsolete by the shadowy powers that conduct the war by remote control; their goal now is to destroy the evidence of their failure.

This vision of the meaning of the film for American consciousness is reflected from a more oblique perspective in the character of the appropriately label-named Col. Kilgore (Robert Duvall). His link to the mytho-heroic past is symbolized by his non-regulation headgear—a nineteenth-century U.S. Cavalry hat. Kilgore is the self-anointed hero of his own fantasy movie, playing out the terms of the hero as genocidal killer in the Southeast Asian terrain dubbed "Indian Country" by American "grunts."[4] The film's macabre echo (both in Kilgore's exultant destruction of an apparently peaceful village, and even more centrally from a mythic perspective, in Willard's ritualistic murder/sacrifice of Kurtz) of an American commander's statement that "we had to destroy the village in order to save it," provides a powerful commentary on the grotesque irrelevancy of American ideals to Vietnam. The film, in Coppola's own words, was intended to portray "the moral dilemma of the Vietnam war" (Adair 161).

While both *The Deer Hunter* and *Apocalypse Now* were apocalyptic cinematic visions (as the latter's title explicitly attested) of America's experience in the symbolic landscape of its own internal Vietnam, contemporaneously a post-apocalyptic response to the war emerged in the Hollywood imagination—the POW-MIA/Avenger film. On one level these films were rooted in a more explicitly ideological position grounded in the doctrinaire right's interpretation of the war: there had been mistakes by American leaders in its conception and execution; there had been a failure of will on the part of the American people; and there had been self-imposed limitations that had prevented its vigorous prosecution, and thus an American victory. Yet, if we had seized defeat from the jaws of victory, two of the most coherent discussions of the American failure in Vietnam reached a paradoxical conclusion—despite our defeat, the system had worked. Leslie H. Gelb and Richard K. Betts in *The Irony of Vietnam* (1979) argued that the political/bureaucratic system had performed as expected, while Col. Harry Summers in *On Strategy* (1982) argued that from the point of view of tactics and logistics the military system had worked to perfection. The belief in fundamental systemic soundness fed into what Richard Hofstadter has called the "paranoid style of politics." As Hofstadter argued, those most profoundly alienated by the course of historical events, those who feel dispossessed of their traditional symbolic/ideal heritage, conclude that "history *is* conspiracy," that

America has been largely taken away from them and their kind, though they are determined to repossess it and to prevent the final destructive act of subversion. The old American virtues have already been eaten away...the old national security and independence have been destroyed by treasonous plots, having as their most powerful agents not merely outsiders and foreigners but major statesmen seated at the very center of American government. (Hofstadter 23-24)

The feeling that internal enemies had acted in concert with the external Asian menace to precipitate the debacle in Vietnam hauntingly echoed Walt Kelly's wartime line from *Pogo*—"We have met the enemy, and he is us." The national ambivalence toward the war, the simultaneous desire to deny its horrors and consequences, and the impulse to atone for collective sins of omission, provided a hospitable climate for the cinematic evolution of the Avenger hero so central to the POW-MIA films. The Avenger Vet evolved in the context of the wave of exploitation films produced in the latter half of the 1960s and the early 1970s, that although coterminous with the course of the war, were part of the phenomenon of psychic denial and collective amnesia about Vietnam that characterized American consciousness during that era. These films might most properly be called "Vetsploitation"[5] films. Like the network television shows of the era, they were not directly about the war, but instead focused on returning servicemen "as freaked-out [losers] who replayed the Vietnam war by committing violence against others or themselves. Vets were time bombs waiting to go off, a new genre of bogeymen" (Gibson 3).

These films were typically loosely attached to one sub-genre or another—motorcycle/violence, women-as-victims, etc.—and reified the war through the depiction of vets as moral monsters who literally brought the war home to America. Representative of these films were Bob Clark's *The Night Walk* (a.k.a *Deathdream* or *Dead of Night*, 1972), in which a young K.I.A. is willed back to life by his mother and returns to his home town. He comes back to the "World" as a zombie, sustained by human blood, who avenges himself on the society that sent him to war (Wood 133).[6] *Don't Answer the Phone* (1980), directed by Robert Hummer, deals with a psycho vet as rapist in Los Angeles, who strangles his victims with Vietnamese coins tied up in a stocking.[7]

The profoundly disturbed, alienated anti-heroes of these films represented a fictional acting out of the collective national trauma of the war. The link between these exploitation films and the POW-MIA/ Avenger series of the 1980s is evident in two films—*The Losers* (1971) and *Rolling Thunder* (1977). John Flynn's *Rolling Thunder* is the story of an ex-POW who monomaniacally pursues the killers of his wife and son. In *The Losers*, five Hell's Angels-style bikers are recruited by the CIA to sneak into Cambodia to rescue a presidential advisor held captive by the Red Chinese. The press release for the film pretentiously asserted that "the result of their attempt and the mission provide a capsule [sic] of what the Vietnamese conflict is all about for confused Americans— from fighting the unseen enemy to living with the results of a battle too costly to be called a victory, and too complex and frustrating to result in the human glory that comes from having won" (Adair 87).

The immediate cinematic source of the POW-MIA/Avenger sub- genre, however, was Ted Post's *Good Guys Wear Black* (1977), which starred Chuck Norris as John T. Booker, a vet who is recruited by the CIA during the final negotiations for a cease fire in Paris in 1973. His mission is to rescue POWs still held in captivity in Southeast Asia. Booker and his Black Tiger team are betrayed—there are no POWs at the camp they attack, and the expected helicopter to lift them out of the jungle never arrives. Booker later discovers that the man who set him up was the then Under-Secretary of State, Morgan, who is now scheduled to become head of the State Department. Maj. Minh, a loyal Vietnamese ally during the war, turns out to be one of Morgan's most trusted henchmen. Booker takes revenge on Morgan by taking the place of his chauffeur and driving him to his death at the bottom of the river, asking rhetorically, "How would you like to be MIA?"

Good Guys Wear Black established most of the plot conventions for the formulaic POW-MIA/Avenger series that was to become prominent in the next decade: use of a small rescue team of highly specialized mercenaries, all vets, frequently former POWs; cynicism about the government manifested in depictions of bureaucratic negligence and incompetence, and the betrayal (of both POWs and their potential rescuers) by high-ranking officials; racist portrayals of the Vietnamese as a faceless Asian menace (including the perfidy of former ARVN allies); explicit criticism of the way Americans fought the war; and the emergence of an implacable vigilante hero, the reassertion of the efficacy of the tough-guy hero of an earlier era for the post-Vietnam era.

What made this ideological reading of the war so attractive was the way it fit so neatly into the political preoccupations of the resurgent right in the Reagan era, and the way it so perfectly meshed with the primary symbology of national heroic mythology manifested in the Indian Fighter/Avenger. MIAs were a "hot" issue, a patriotic way of approaching a most unpopular war. In the opening scenes of *Good Guys Wear Black*, for instance, we see the Eiffel Tower, while the voice-over radio announcer tells us that negotiations for a peace treaty are going on (June 1973) "against the background of what to do about the release of American POWs. In the U.S., sentiment is running high for a complete accounting of all the POWs and MIAs before any treaty is signed." Despite "Operation Homecoming" (May 1973), many Americans still believe there are live POWs in Southeast Asia, that the U.S. government has not done all it could to secure their release, and has, in fact, conspired to prevent the public from verifying their existence.[8]

The continued viability of the POW-MIA issue has spawned a whole series of MIA-POW films during the last few years that unite the theme of sacred quest with the frontier mythology of the Indian Captivity/Hunter-avenger cycle. They express a self-consciously cathartic vision of atonement through suffering and purgation through violence. They portray Southeast Asia, and by extension America's wartime experience, as an arcane, hermetic universe, whose secrets are legible only to the initiate. This belief that there are specialists in savagery, who are at once projections of our fears of seduction by barbarous decadence and our hopes for the righteous destruction of the external evil threat, is as old as our central formative mythology. Mary Rowlandson, who penned one of the earliest and certainly the best known of the Indian captivity narratives in 1682, expressed it best when she observed that "as none knows what it is to fight and pursue such an enemy as this, but that they have fought and pursued them; so none can imagine what it is to be captivated, and enslaved to such...but those that have tryed it" (qtd. in Van Der Beets x). The roles of captive and hunter, so familiar to the American frontier experience, have been taken on by the MIA-POW and the Avenger-Vigilante hero in the contemporary transformation of the myth. The emotional power of the cinematic version of this myth lies both in its links with traditional national mythic self-perceptions and in its relevance to modern historical experience.

The first of the POW-MIA films was *Uncommon Valor* (1983), whose Col. Jason Rhodes (Gene Hackman) expressed the heroic quest for the reclamation of national honor in his very name. In 1984 Col. James Braddock (Chuck Norris, again) busted American POWs out of prison camp in *Missing in Action*. In the prequel, *Missing in Action, II: The Beginning* (1985), his own earlier escape is detailed.[9] *POW-The Escape*, with David Carradine as Col. Cooper, followed in 1986. But the most popular and arguably the most powerful of these films was *Rambo, First Blood, Part II* (1985). This film was not only enormously popular in the U.S.—it grossed $75.8 million in the first twenty-five days of its release—but broke box-office records abroad (specifically in the Philippines and Beirut) as well. Indeed, the Rambo phenomenon became a national craze that was variously dubbed the "Rambo Syndrome" and "Rambomania."[10]

The Rambo version is at once the most pretentious of the POW-MIA films and the purest embodiment of their mythic roots and their obsessively macho mystique. Its enormous popularity and archetypal status require its more detailed consideration. Rambo is portrayed from the outset as a messianic demigod, quite literally a Christ figure. In the opening shots of the film, we see John Rambo on the rock pile of a maximum security prison's quarry. This Dantesque vision of the lower rings of Hell is reinforced by the film's dialogue. Col. Trautman, Rambo's former Green Beret commander, who is trying to recruit him for a POW-reconnaissance mission, says: "I'm sorry they sent you to such a Hell-hole." Rambo is figuratively raised from Hell amidst the title sequence displaying his name in flames.

When Rambo is captured by the Vietnamese later in the film, he is twice tortured in mock crucifixions. First, he is suspended in the water tied to posts in a spread-eagle position. Then, he is subjected to electric shock while tied to the inner-springs of a bed by the more technologically advanced Soviets, who for some inexplicable reason, seem to run this Vietnamese POW camp. Reinforcing this messianic portrayal of Rambo are the words of salutation with which Marshall Murdock, the bureaucratic Judas of this morality play, greets him upon his arrival in Vietnam—"So you're the chosen one." Although we are clearly intended to identify Rambo as the nation's savior, his soteriological doctrine is an inversion of Christian precepts. He is more demon-destroyer than god.

This aspect of the Rambo character is clear from the earlier *Rambo, First Blood* (1983), which depicts him as an enraged vet wreaking vengeance on an ungrateful American society that is unappreciative of his sacrifice. In the POW sequel, Rambo, an outcast, a deracinated loner, comes "home" to Vietnam. As the personified Vietnam vet, he has been rejected by his country; he is returning to a landscape where his life has some meaning. As Col. Trautman describes the Rambo psychology to Murdock, "What you choose to call Hell, he calls home." Later, when Rambo has been captured, Murdock says, "He went home."

As Robin Wood has observed of the similarly macho "buddy" films of the late 1960s and 1970s (like *Easy Rider*, 1969), the absence of home as an emotional center is striking in the POW-MIA films. " 'Home,' here," he wrote, "is of course to be understood not merely as a physical location but as both a state of mind and an ideological construct, above all as ideological security" (Wood 228). The motion of the Rambo cycle brings the POWs home, but also brings America back home in the sense of restoring its faith in the fundamental mythic elements of American identity.

Rambo and the whole cycle of POW-MIA films as vehicles for fantasy-wish-fulfillment provide a psychic redemption of America's historical experience. Their simplistic understanding of the Vietnam experience offers an ideological justification of American participation in the war; a denial of the individual soldiers' role in the defeat; and a potent paranoic vision of betrayal—by the American government, by American institutions, and by the failure of American nerve and faith. In the post-apocalyptic universe produced by a crisis of overwhelming proportions, the solution these films offer is trust in the retribution of the pure in heart.

The individual, purged of sin and sanctified by suffering (this is the mythic function of the torture scenes in these films), having atoned for his society's failures and betrayals during the war, becomes the projection of collective consciousness (albeit a false consciousness), a National Nemesis. As a vessel of purified hate, the Avenger/Vigilante figure is an ideal instrument of vengeance; he has been apotheothized as the dehumanized (or superhuman) hero, the mechanized killer, the apocalyptic monster. The Avenger/Vigilante hero is at once an agent of retribution for our sins of omission, and an implacable destructive force against those responsible (both internally and externally) for the unbearable burden of national guilt over Vietnam. These films function as rituals of both purification through cataclysmic violence and exorcisms of guilt through suffering. By recreating a cathartic myth cycle, their goal is to restore America to its "real" self from which the Vietnam experience so effectively alienated it. They vigorously echo the political shibboleth of the Reagan era—"bringing America back."

MIAs are the central political symbol of our commitment to that restorative process. The Vietnam experience suggested the need for serious soul-searching and reconsideration of the role of the U.S. in international affairs. Yet, symbolically, the MIAs in the cinematic consideration of this issue, represent the smaller nations in thrall to Communism. Our refusal to abandon the MIAs means that we have not forgotten them, either. Our claim to the traditional moral cachet as "leader of the free world" thus seems legitimized.

In the convoluted logic of fantasy, the mythic thread that leads out of the labyrinth of the Vietnam experience requires a reversal of history. In a marvelous, thaumaturgic transformation, the American Avenger/Vigilante hero takes on all the attributes of his wartime enemy the Viet Cong guerrilla fighter; symbolically the Indian Fighter must become the Indian in order to redeem historical experience. The heroes of these films are at home only in the jungle (their very savagery excludes them from the ordinary peacetime, workaday world of "home"); they are usually bereft (often through betrayal) of the advantages of superior hi-tech weaponry and high-speed transportation (the failure of helicopters in these films is phenomenal); and they operate in a shadow world between legality and criminality. To "win" the war we are symbolically re-fighting on the screen, to reverse the verdict of history, we must be transformed into our enemies (who won in the "real" world), while they are transformed into us.

This aspect of the POW-MIA films is most clearly shown in *Uncommon Valor,* where those preparing for the rescue mission eat nothing but Vietnamese food so they will smell like the Vietnamese. John Rambo is significantly half Indian. He cuts away his advanced equipment during his parachute drop before he begins his mission, and uses as his primary weapons his knife and a bow and arrows equipped with explosive tips that are reminiscent of the fire arrows with which generations of Hollywood Indians attacked wooden stockades. Like those wooden stockades, Vietnamese reed huts and "hooches" are highly flammable, and the Vietnamese are uniformly depicted as immobile, holed-up in camps and fortresses that are vulnerable to guerrilla infiltration. They are typically depicted as brutal butchers, who massacre women and children, and as debauched sex fiends alternately raping and whoring.

American heroes in these films retain their purity largely through abstention. They are isolate male figures who have almost no contact with women. For example, Co, Rambo's female Vietnamese guide, functions briefly to confirm him in his dedication to the code of pure destruction; she is a catalyst (as if any were needed) for his transfiguration into the pure embodiment of will, the distilled personification of force. As Rambo expresses it, "To win war, you got to become war." The homo-erotic, proto-fascist nature of the POW-MIA version of the national myth is deeply underscored in the shots of Rambo's body glistening with sweat, shown in extreme close-up. We see only parts of that body that suggest strength—biceps, forearms, pectorals. These shots are intercut with shots of affectionate fondling of weapons—the survival knife, the bow, the arrows.

If these films are representative of a far-right fantasy, it is a kind of anarchistic, survivalist fantasy.[11] Their broader appeal, however, is suggested by the chronology of their release. They came out simultaneously with the end of society's denial of the experience of the war. In November 1982 the Vietnam Veterans' Memorial was dedicated in Washington, D.C. In February 1983, the University of California sponsored "Vietnam Reconsidered: Lessons From a War," the first major academic conference on the war. In the Fall of 1983, PBS presented its thirteen-part documentary series *Vietnam: A Television History.* Finally, on Memorial Day, 1984, the unidentified remains of a Vietnam vet were buried in the Tomb of the Unknown Soldier at Arlington National Cemetery (Gibson 6). After a decade, it was at last possible to begin the process of the symbolic rehabilitation of the Vietnam vet and to exorcise the image of the demon vet, if not perhaps as yet to accept the harsh historical verdict of the war itself.

On another level, *Rambo, First Blood, Part II* is a blatant call (as are such other 1985 vehicles as *Red Dawn* and *Invasion America*) to return to the true faith. As Sylvester Stallone put it in an interview with the *New York Times*: "I'm not right-wing, I'm not left-wing. I love my country" (qtd. in Hoberman 60).[12] Unfortunately, the emotional appeal, the enormous popularity of the POW-MIA films,[13] and their reflection of a mindless acceptance of the political agenda of the militant right, has done little to reconcile the nation to the historical reality of the Vietnam experience. Instead, it has promoted the rehabilitation of the vet as heroic figure while prescribing only a powerful soporific to the national conscience. The effect has been to legitimize the national amnesia about the meaning and consequences of the Vietnam war and to make a more aggressively militaristic stance around the world more acceptable to the American people. Indeed, these films use the Vietnam experience as a bridge to link traditional American values and policy, and national symbology to the future. Perhaps the clearest examples of this function of "Rambomania," as the most popular version of the Avenger/Vigilante mythology, can be seen in the realms of children's cartoons and toys.

In the wake of the phenomenal success of the two Rambo films, Carolco International (the same company that distributes Stallone's adult ventures), began a cartoon series featuring the Rambo character, in which he fights the forces of S.A.V.A.G.E. (the Secret Army of Vengeance and Global Evil), comprised of Arab terrorists, Soviet militarists, and the punk-rocker "garbage" (as they are called in one episode) of our city streets. Against the powerful alliance of internal and external enemies our freedom is in danger, but, the voice-over at the end of each episode informs us, "with Rambo and the Force of Freedom, justice and liberty will never surrender, no matter what the odds."

The cartoon Rambo, unlike his celluloid progenitor, is not limited to action in Vietnam, but frequently operates in Latin America, the Middle East, and Central Asia. A whole line of action figure toys and plastic replicas of Rambo's M-60 machine gun and survival knife have been produced by enterprising toy manufacturers that provide a direct link between the ideological level of the adult films and the psyche of the rising generation.[14] These toys are sold under the inscription "If the Army can't, Rambo can! He's unequaled in courage, unfailing in patriotism."

For the American psyche, Vietnam was a traumatic fall from grace. The post-apocalyptic cinematic response to that fall was the initiation of a heroic quest, a symbolic return to the heart of that experience to exorcize through rituals of reenactment the horrors of defeat, to expunge the failure of ideology, and to redeem the national soul. The imaginative journey we have taken through this nightmarish historical landscape, however, has not reconciled us to experience, but has instead provided us with a macho hero who has tried to subdue experience by sheer force of will and distilled violence; who has conjured up for an alienated post-Vietnam American consciousness "an 'ideal world,' a 'mythic anti-history' designed to 'halt, to stem the tide of the ongoing process itself' " (Warren Susman, qtd. in Bercovitch 181). James C. Wilson has aptly described this fantasy as "derealizing Vietnam" (96).

But it is a dangerously delusory and meretricious consciousness that seeks to convince us that we must interchange history and fantasy in order to preserve our sense of national honor. The post-apocalyptic cinematic vision of Vietnam may well represent a triumph of the will, but it is the specious triumph of the narcissistic will of a childish tantrum, not a triumph rooted in the self-mastery and reasoned control of a more mature consciousness. In the cinematic darkness of movie houses across America, we are fighting (and losing) our second Vietnam war. Again, we are winning all the battles and losing the war. In the symbolic battle for our own "hearts and minds," we are finally overwhelmed by the Leatherstocking Nemesis, that relentless specter, that has so long haunted our mythic consciousness.

Notes

[1]Cf. Richard Slotkin's *Regeneration Through Violence: The Mythology of the American Frontier, 1600-1860* (Middletown: Wesleyan UP, 1973), Chapter I, "Myth and Literature in a New World" 3-24; his *The Fatal Environment: The Myth of the Frontier in the Age of Industrialization, 1800-1890* (New York: Athaneum, 1985), Chapter II, "Myth and Historical Memory" 13-22; and John Hellmann, *American Myth and the Legacy of Vietnam* (New York: Columbia UP, 1986), " 'An Angry Dream': The Cold War, Southeast Asia, and the American Mythic Landscape" 3-40.

[2]Both *The Deer Hunter* and *Apocalypse Now* were among the top twenty films in total earnings for 1979; each brought in over $20 million in profit that year. *Apocalypse Now* was also among the most expensive films ever made ($31.5 million). *Apocalypse Now* won the 1979 Cannes Film Festival award for best film. Both films appeared, respectively in 1978 and 1979 on the *New York Times* annual best ten lists. *The Deer Hunter* won the Academy Award for best picture in 1978; Michael Cimino was selected best director and Christopher Walken best supporting actor by the Academy that year. Michael Cimino won the Golden Globe Award as best director of 1978 as did Coppola in 1979. Nevertheless, as of 1980, no Vietnam war film was among the top ten money-making American war films. Nine of the ten were about World War II. The only Vietnam film on the top twenty list was *The Green Berets*

in twelfth position. Cf. Cobbett S. Steinberg, *Film Facts* (New York: Facts on Film, 1980).

[3]The Do Lung Bridge is described by an off-camera voice as "the asshole of the world." Since it is the gateway to Kurtz's world, this reading of the symbolic level of the film seems justified.

[4]The scene of the bombing of the village by the Americans under Kilgore's command, which is accompanied by an ear-splitting sound track playing Richard Wagner's "The Ride of the Valkyries" (from *Die Walküre*, second of the operas comprising the Ring cycle) to "scare the shit out of the slopes," (who are also explicitly referred to as "fucking savages" by Kilgore), makes a clear statement of Coppola's point of view. Kilgore is seen as a thorough-going racist and proto-facist. Cf. Gilbert Adair, *Vietnam on Film: From The Green Berets to Apocalypse Now* (New York: Proteus, 1981) 152-54. The operatic allusion also underscores the mythic dimensions of the main story line of the film. The heroic Walsüng twins of the opera, offspring of Wotan and therefore demigods, have been separated since childhood. The opera deals with their reunion and the growth of passionate love between them. In the film, the two heroes are reunited so that one may destroy the other. Yet, Willard recognizes much of himself in Kurtz, he understands that they are both products of the same national ideals, and that those ideals have in some sense been betrayed and perverted in the course of this brutal war. The use of the Wagnerian operatic motif here underscores the film's ironic and schizophrenic stance toward traditional American myth and belief.

[5]They existed side by side with Blaxploitation, Femsploitation, and Teensploitation films in the world of "B" cinema.

[6]The story is a "rip-off" of William Wymark Jacobs' tale "The Monkeys Paw." The theme of zombie vet as retributive force meting out justice in kind to a society that had callously condemned its young men to the carnage of jungle warfare and then renounced them when they returned home is also present in the surrealistic *Tracks* (1976). In this film, a U.S. Army sergeant (Dennis Hopper), accompanying the body of a Black comrade back to his hometown for burial, encounters only indifference and hostility from the civilian population. At the interment, Hopper leaps into the open grave and emerges in full battle dress. The avenger vet has risen from the dead, crying "You want to go to Vietnam? I'll take you there!" He has brought the war home with a vengeance. Cf. James C. Wilson, *Vietnam in Prose and Film* (Jefferson: McFarland, 1982) 82. Even more graphic were the cannibalistic vet zombies of the *Invasion of the Flesh Hunters* (1982). Here, cannibalism is portrayed as the result of the torture and starvation of American POWs in Southeast Asia. When they return to the U.S. they bring the contagion of a decided predilection for human flesh with them. In fact, an epidemic of cannibalism breaks out, spreading from the zombie vets to their formerly indifferent friends and neighbors. Although all the vets are killed by the end of the film, the curse of Vietnam has been passed on to the next generation, for two children have become "flesh hunters" through "biological mutation due to some psychic alteration." Not only do the zombie vets wreak horrible (if somehow appropriate) vengeance on American society here, but they effectively pass on the utter horror of their experience to the innocent and naive— the rising generation. The dark vision of this film suggests that America may never really be free of the "legacy" of Vietnam, that it will eat at our collective vitals until it destroys us.

[7]For descriptions of these films, see Richard Meyers, *For One Week Only: The World of Exploitation Films* (Piscataway: New Century, 1983), and Michael Weldon, *The Psychotronic Encyclopedia of Film* (New York: Ballantine, 1983). *Poor White Trash, II* (1976) and *Stanley* (1972) are two examples of general, vet-as-psycho-freak films, while *The Black Six* (1974) is a Blaxploitation, vet motorcycle film. *Angels From Hell* (1968), *Satan's Sadists* (1969), *The Hard Ride* (1970), and *Chrome and Hot Leather* (1971) were segregated, all-White films of this type. The utterly tasteless *Black Frankenstein* (a.k.a., *Blackenstein,* 1973), involves a parapalegic Black vet who receives an arm and leg graft from Dr. Frankenstein. He is betrayed by a rival for his fiancee's affections, however, and is transformed into a monster who preys upon women. The Billy Jack cycle—*Billy Jack* (1971), *The Trial of Billy Jack* (1974), and *Billy Jack Goes to Washington* (1977)—about a half-breed vet who struggles against social evil and political corruption, is a more polished Vetsploitation venture. Despite the titular echo of Frank Capra's 1939 populist parable in the last film of the trilogy, they convey a more sinister message—that violence is the only solution to our socio-political problems. The Billy Jack character (played by Tom Laughlin) had been introduced in one of the Vetsploitation motorcycle epics, *The Born Losers* (1967), which Laughlin had also directed.

[8]Cf. the BBC-produced documentary *We Can Keep Them Forever—MIAs,* which aired on public television in January 1987. Of the 3500 MIAs at the end of the war, some 2400-2500 are still unaccounted for. Only 500 Americans came home in May of 1973 after the peace accords were signed. A viewer survey taken at the end of the program that compiled telephone responses from 31,151 callers indicated that 89% believed there are still live Americans held against their wills in Southeast Asia. The NBC television movie *In Love and War,* which aired in March 1987, underscores the current interest in the MIA issue. In the light of the ideological dimensions of the MIA-POW films, it is interesting to note that this presentation of the experience of Naval Commander James Stockdale and his wife Sybil reinforced the paranoic vision of the actions of the U.S. government both during the war and in its response to the POW-MIA issue. Under government duress, Mrs. Stockdale kept quiet about the torture of POWs in Vietnam for four years. Stockdale's capture in 1965 is directly attributed to the duplicity of President Johnson in his escalation of the air war over Vietnam in the wake of the Gulf of Tonkin Resolution.

[9]There is a tantilizingly suggestive link between the MIA-POW/Avenger-Vigilante cycle of the Vietnam era and earlier American heroic myth here in that James Fenimore Cooper wrote his "Leatherstocking Tales" backwards, too. The last volume of the saga, *The Pioneers,* which depicts Natty Bumppo's later years, was published in 1823. *The Deerslayer,* which is the story of his early years was not published until 1841. The hero of *POW—The Escape* (1986) is a Col. Cooper. Reviewers have repeatedly linked the POW-MIA films with the Indian-captivity Westerns, especially John Ford's *The Searchers* (1956).

[10]The figures are from Richard Zoglin, "An Outbreak of Rambomania," *Time* 25, 24 June 1985: 72. The term "Rambomania" was also used in a *Macleans* article (July 29, 1985), and *Newsweek* identified the syndrome in its January 20, 1986 issue.

[11]Cf. the cover of the 1987 U.S. Cavalry (a para-military supply house) catalog. Beneath the cover photograph of Sylvester Stallone as Rambo, is an ad for the "Rambo Survivalist Pack." For $649, the Pack includes a take-down compound bow, one dozen arrows with bullet tips, a half-dozen broadhead arrows, and a "Jungle King II" survival knife. The 1960s left also had fantasies of achieving political change through a symbolic alteration of American historical experience involving a reliving

of the past in the inverted role of Indian instead of cowboy. Cf. Hellmann, *American Myth* 75, and 81-82; and Slotkin, *Regeneration* 17. Rambo's long hair and his ubiquitous headband suggest both his symbolic link with the Indian tradition (the earlier Billy Jack tradition is also invoked here), and the perception that the character owes something to the Hippie culture of the 1960s.

[12]Stallone claimed that the message of the film was that "frustrated Americans [were] trying to recapture some glory. The vets were told wrong. The people who pushed the wrong buttons all took a powder. The vets got the raw deal and were left holding the bag. What *Rambo* is saying is that if they could fight again, it would be different" (qtd. in Zoglin, "Rambomania" 73).

[13]As of this writing there are at least twenty of this sub-genre of film circulating in videotape format. Though many of them confine themselves to a Southeast Asian setting, like *Tiger Joe* (1985) or *Code Name Wild Geese* (1986), they are by no means always about POWs-MIAs in Vietnam. Several deal with the war at one further remove, metaphorically expressing the American obsession with Vietnam as drug addiction. *American Commandos* (1985) and the aforementioned *Code Name Wild Geese* fall into that category. Others are more clearly mercenary films, in which the heroes provide simplistic solutions to a whole host of thorny international problems—*Delta Force* (1986), with Chuck Norris, deals with the hijacking of a plane by terrorists in Beirut, while *Killer Commandos* (1986) details the overthrow of a White-supremacist leader of a Black nation. An interesting peripheral group of films deals with female avengers, who rescue enslaved women prisoners from their brutal male captors, usually in a vaguely Latin American jungle setting. Films such as *Savage Island* (1985) and *Caged Fury* (1985) belong to this type. The continued box-office viability of the MIA-POW film is attested by the fact that several new films are scheduled for release later this year—*Hanoi Hilton, Braddock: Missing in Action, III, Rambo III* (rumor has it that it will be set in Nicaragua and will deal with the anti-Sandinista crusade), and *Eye of the Eagle*. The Russians, realizing the Cold War propaganda value of such a dynamic figure, have produced a "Rambo" of their own in *The Detached Mission*, directed by Mikhail Tumsanishivilli.

[14]Adult "toys" spun off from the Rambo films include "Rambo Vitamins," a "Rambogram" (in New York City), in which a Stallone-look-alike delivers the message of your choice; a U.S. Army recruiting poster (with the caption "America's Hero Wants You!"); and a porn stud—Dick Rambone, who appears in what is billed as "porn's first action serial"—*Rambone the Destroyer* is presumably part one. There are, in fact, real-life Rambos like James G. "Bo" Gritz, who planned to use Thailand as a base to stage a raid deep into Laos in search of POWs. The classic embodiment of the type, however, is Robert K. Brown, mercenary pundit and founder of *Soldier of Fortune* magazine, who was called "Uncle Rambo" in a *Newsday* article (19 January 1986, Sunday Magazine). A group of congressmen who have denounced the Reagan administration's MIA policy has been labelled "Rambo Congressmen" by the press. In fact, the President took pains to closely associate himself with the Rambo image. For his pains he was lampooned in the underground poster depicting him as "Rambo Ronnie." Both Ronald and Nancy Reagan have a direct thespian relation to the POW issue. He played a Korean War POW who is mistakenly accused of being a Communist on his return to the U.S., and Nancy (Davis) played his wife in *Prisoner of War* (1954).

Works Cited

Adair, Gilbert. *Vietnam on Film: From the Green Berets to Apocalypse Now.* New York: Proteus, 1981.

Bercovitch, Sacvan. *The American Jeremiad.* Madison: Wisconsin UP, 1978.

Gibson, James W. *The Perfect War: Technowar in Vietnam.* New York: Atlantic Monthly, 1986.

Herr, Michael. *Dispatches.* New York: Avon, 1968.

Hellmann, John. *American Myth and the Legacy of Vietnam.* New York: Columbia UP, 1986.

Hoberman, J. "The Fascist Guns in the West: Hollywood's 'Rambo' Connection." *Radical America* 19.6 (1985): 53-62.

Hofstadter, Richard. *The Paranoid Style in American Politics.* New York: Knopf, 1966.

Meyers, Richard. *For One Week Only: The World of Exploitation Films.* Piscataway: New Century, 1983.

Pan, Stephen and Daniel Lyons. *Vietnam Crisis.* New York: East Asian Research Institute, 1966.

Pearce, Roy Harvey. "The Metaphysics of Indian-Hating: Leatherstocking Unmasked. *Historicism Once More: Problems and Occasions for the American Scholar.* Princeton: Princeton UP, 1969: 109-36.

Russell, David S. *Apocalyptic: Ancient and Modern.* Philadelphia: Fortress, 1968.

Slotkin, Richard. *The Fatal Environment: The Myth of the Frontier in the Age of Industrialization, 1800-1890.* New York: Athaneum, 1985.

———— *Regeneration Through Violence: The Mythology of the American Frontier, 1600-1860.* Middletown: Wesleyan UP, 1973.

Smith, Julian. *Looking Away: Hollywood and Vietnam.* New York: Scribner's, 1975.

Steinberg, Cobbett S. *Film Facts.* New York: Facts on File, 1980.

Summers, Harry G. *On Strategy: A Critical Analysis of the Vietnam War.* New York: Dell, 1982.

Van Der Beets, Richard, ed. *Held Captive by the Indians; Selected Narratives, 1642-1836.* Knoxville: Tennessee UP, 1973.

Weldon, Michael. *The Psychotronic Encyclopedia of Film.* New York: Ballantine, 1983.

Wilson, James C. *Vietnam in Prose and Film.* Jefferson: McFarland, 1982.

Wood, Robin. *Hollywood from Vietnam to Reagan.* New York: Columbia UP, 1986.

Section II:
Differences and Debts

Words and Fragments:
Narrative Style in Vietnam War Novels

Nancy Anisfield

This is not a settled life. A children's breakfast cereal, Crispy Critters, provokes nausea; there is a women's perfume named Charlie; and the radio sound of "We Gotta Get Out Of This Place" fills me with a melancholy as petrifying as the metal poured into casts of galloping cavalry, squinting riflemen, proud generals, statues in the park, roosts for pigeons. My left knee throbs before each thunderstorm. The sunsets are no damn good here. There are ghosts on my television set. What are we to do when the darkness comes on and we wait for something to happen, as Huey, who never even knew she shared her name with a ten-thousand-pound assault helicopter, sprawls on the floor with her sketchbook, making pastel pictures of floating cities, sleek spaceships, planets of ice, and I, your genial storyteller, wreathed in a beard of smoke, look into the light and recite strange tales from the war back in the long ago time. (Wright 8)

As readers dependent on language and our trust in the written word, we read or hear a paragraph like this and feel a subtle but certain urge for connections. The images are strong, but the connections are confusing. The simple point here is that the same was true of the Vietnam War.

If we are going to look to the literature for help in understanding what happened, both here at home and over there, perhaps the first step—if you agree that language shapes reality—is to put ourselves in a linguistic environment that resembles the war as closely as possible.

The attempt to have language and narrative style themselves convey the confusion and absurdity of war is not new or unique. In the literature of nearly all wars there are texts whose style could be called fragmented. World War I gave us the easily read narrative of Ernest Hemingway's *A Farewell to Arms*, but it also produced Dalton Trumbo's surreal, stream-of-conscious *johnny got his gun*. World War II inspired the correct chronology of Norman Mailer's *The Naked and the Dead* and James Jones' *The Thin Red Line*, but also spawned Joseph Heller's *Catch-22* and Kurt Vonnegut's *Slaughterhouse-Five*. The Vietnam War is no exception. The novels to come out of this war so far have a similar division in stylistic approach. There are the more traditional narratives of John Del Vecchio's *The 13th Valley*, David Halberstam's *One Very*

Hot Day, and James Webb's *Fields of Fire*, but also the fragmented styles of Tim O'Brien's *Going After Cacciato*, Stephen Wright's *Meditations in Green*, Nicholas Profitt's *Gardens of Stone*, and Rob Riggan's *Free Fire Zone*.

Although the 365 day insertion which characterized the average soldier's tour of duty in Vietnam seems to lend itself to a sequential narrative, the thematic concepts which usually accompany such a narrative don't work in writing about this war. The rites-of-passage novel where the young boy matures through his war experience into wise manhood seems inappropriate when dealing with Vietnam. Here the characters may mature, but too often also end up drug addicts, psychopaths, dead, or too alienated from society to function normally. The gradual development of male camaraderie frequently found in combat novels is also inappropriate here. Frequent transfers and no continuity of military operations or personnel eliminate male bonding as an acceptable focus. And, finally, the Vietnam War novel can't be a political novel if it seeks to accurately portray a war in which political ambiguity—as well as moral ambiguity—was pervasive.

Indeed, the novel in which time jumps back and forth, fantasy mixes with reality, and isolated incidents are depicted with unusual intensity is better qualified to represent the American soldiers' feeling of confusion and alienation. Such a novel shows the psychic dislocation of fighting in a war where the lines of combat were constantly changing, where there was no welcome and no debriefing, where drugs were prevalent, where the jungle environment was hostile, and where small squads and platoons were the functioning units rather than battalions and regiments. Thus, in works like *Meditations In Green* and *Going After Cacciato*, the narrative becomes a mimetic presentation of the soldier's experience during and after the war.

Before looking at those novels more closely, the characteristics of what I am terming "fragmented" novels should be explained. First of all, these novels contain rapid shifts in time and mood. The tone can switch from serious/tragic to absurd/humorous within a sentence. Understatement is combined with overstatement, and the reader learns to adapt to quick change. Similarly, the cataloguing of events, which seems to give an overview of the war experience, is often set against the heightened realism of minute details and focused description.

These novels also contain a nervous energy which is conveyed through the rhythm of the language and the images presented.

Overload was such a real danger, not as obvious as shrapnel or blunt like a 2,000-foot drop, maybe it couldn't kill you or smash you, but it could bend your aerial for you and land you on your hip. Levels of information were levels of dread, once it's out it won't go back in, you can't just blink it away or run the film backward out of consciousness. (Herr 65)

This passage is from Michael Herr's *Dispatches*, which, although it is non-fiction, is one of the first and finest examples of fragmented narrative to come out of the war. It is typical of the energetic pacing and startling combination of military images with abstract images that characterize these writings.

This combination of images might be considered surreal. If surrealism is defined as above or out of realism, with the desire to be freed from logic and reason, these works could certainly be considered surreal. Furthermore, surrealism can be considered the attempt to express the language and images of the subconscious mind. What better way could there be to try to make sense of an event than by approaching it from inside the minds of those involved?

The two final elements to be found in all the fragmented novels are a vehicle for the time shifts and a culminating event that pulls all the fragments together. Some mode of transition is necessary to flow from one fragment to another. That mode may be the description of a drug-induced state, a written format (such as a journalist's dispatches) or a movement of the imagination. In addition, there must be climax around which the narrative revolves. In *Going After Cacciato* the squad's final charge on the grassy hillside is not only the focal event, but it is enacted twice, once in real time (42 pages into the novel) and once in Paul Berlin's imagination (at the end). The night James Griffin's base is overrun and he is wounded is the event toward which *Meditations In Green* moves. If plot were entirely abandoned there would be no parameters for any character change, so the fragments must have some direction.

The use of time shifts, tone changes, heightened detail, energetic pacing, and transitional modes are not new. What is unique here is the concentration, the frequency, in which these elements are found in the novels of the Vietnam War. There is one other element that must be considered, however—the language. In the fragmented novels, language is intensified beyond the colloquialisms found in standard narratives.

The world of the U.S. soldier in Vietnam is conveyed through the use of various jargons. The words are mixed, mutated, and piled upon each other to enhance the confusion and create an overload guaranteed to send a jolt through the reader's linguistic circuits. First, there are the military acronyms and the slang identifying the U.S./Vietnam environment, for example: LZs, ground fire, choppers, REMFs, FNGs, I Corps, frag, hootch, arclight, the World, LURPs, and a two-digit midget. Second are the 60s slang, rock lyrics, and drug lingo exemplified by: "it made you feel Omni," "he's a control freak at the crossroads," or "really a dude who shot his wad." And, finally, there are the euphemisms and epigrammatic phrases which attempt to emotionally distance the speaker from the pain of the situation, such as: "There it is," "It don't mean nothin'," or getting wasted, zapped, blown away or greased. The importance of this language is indicated by the number of works, fiction and non-fiction, which contain glossaries. With the exception of science fiction, perhaps, no other genre or sub-genre of literature has such a self-conscious need to define its own terms.

The combination of the fragmented style and the in-country tone create a fictional environment which not only shows the physical and psychic atmosphere of the war, but gives the writer more dimensions through which to comment on the war.

Tim O'Brien explores the potential of the imagination through the triple structure of *Going After Cacciato*. The novel is divided into real time—the boredom and anxiety of Paul Berlin's midnight watch at the observation post, memories—flashbacks of the brutal and confusing events he'd witnessed in Vietnam so far during his tour, and imagination—his dream quest in which he and his squad pursue Cacciato to freedom. At first these times are divided, but there are parallel episodes, one often leading into another. For example, during the imaginary journey, when Berlin looks into Li Van Hgoc's periscope he sees, then enters, a flashback of the tunnel episode when Frenchie Tucker and Bernie Lynn got shot. Similarly, when he is ordered to frisk the passengers on the imaginary Delhi Express, he enters a flashback of frisking children and an old man along the Song Tra Bong.

This interplay between memory and imagination forefronts the association between the two. We imagine only with the material furnished by our memories, and we remember only through the pull of our imaginations. Both are as important and powerful as 'real time' thought.

...back for an instant in his observation tower by the sea-awake again, this wasn't a madman's fantasy. Paul Berlin was awake and fully sane. Not a dream, he thought, nothing demented or unconscious or fanatic about it.... Didn't everyone do it, one way or another, more or less? Imagining how to spend freedom... (O'Brien 322)

O'Brien is showing us the importance of the imagination in survival and in establishing the framework of hope necessary for coming to terms with war. Berlin's imaginary journey helped him cope with the terror inside him and with the nightmarish reality of combat. It also allowed him to disassociate himself from the war and the parts of it he couldn't understand. More important, however, his imagination was a manifestation of man's survival instinct in a nihilistic environment.

In the end of the novel, Berlin's imagination fails on its own and he is forced to face the reality that breaks through when memory and imagination are finally joined. The breakthrough is violent, but he does come to terms with his fear and the horror around him, as we perhaps do, along with him.

Meditations In Green is a network of experiences James Griffin has as a veteran and heroin addict living in New York after the war; flashbacks of Vietnam which are drug-induced; and 'meditations'—poems whose overriding plant imagery encompasses the lushness of the jungle, defoliation, dope, and the survival of all organic life. Not only does the time jump back and forth, but the point of view switches from first person to third throughout the novel.

Stephen Wright establishes a tone which is on the edge of hysteria with *Catch-22* style exaggeration and overstatement. He intensifies some details:

...the helicopter, suffering a compound fracture lay in an uneven heap along a ridge of broken rock, the rocks and surrounding grass littered with hundreds, thousands of variously shaped and sized pieces of bright metal, one window on the pilot's side having survived the plunge completely intact, reflected a square of blinding sun back up into the sky(279)

and sends others swirling into a maelstrom of poetic images:

...the fascinating realm of carpet bombing, lost among the oddities of the weave: the not uncommon crater within a crater, Chinese boxes of destruction; the lone untouched tree at the center of a field of matchsticks, the bomb distribution games of connect-the-dots and see a smiling fish, a happy flower; and through it all the long winding road, a living organism of strength and guile, slithering among the damage, easily skirting the small holes...(57)

Thus the war experience becomes a catalog of images and people; time and emotion become lost to language.

Neither Griffin nor the reader are completely lost at the end of this novel, however. All the fragments are brought together in one image which combines the experience of dope, death, war, and the act of writing about them into a tribute to those who served and those who remember.

...the transformation of this printed sheet twisted about a metal stem for your lapel your hat your antenna, a paper emblem of the widow's hope, the doctor's apothecary, the veteran's friend: a modest flower. (342)

Michiko Kakutani's April, 1984, *New York Times Book Review* article quoted Stephen Wright as saying:

It was a struggle to find a form for writing about Vietnam... What I tried to do was simply put down the experience as well as I could. You couldn't take a definite moral outlook, so instead of holding up signs as to what's proper and what isn't, I tried to leave it up to the reader to decide. I tried to convey the specific feel of

Vietnam with the texture of the language. There was a kind of dislocation I tried to get in there—a constant nervousness and jumpiness. (40)

Though there are those who say a fragmented narrative is too complex to persuade or affect the average reader, it seems important not to lose an accurate representation of what it was mentally and physically like to be there, and the surreal novel may be the best suited to such a task. Furthermore, if we've gone from *M*A*S*H* and "Alice's Restaurant" to Rambo and "Born in the USA", and if the literature offers such extremes as *The Green Berets* and *Born on the Fourth of July*, then we have to look for an alternative literary approach to reach a middle ground and thereby try to understand the effect this war had on our generation and our country.

If the fragmentation of time, in-country language, and surrealistic suggestions of the effects of war on the psyche can accurately remind us of what the Vietnam experience was like, then, and only then, do we have the best possible chance, through literature, of assimilating this experience, as Paul Berlin and James Griffin did in the end of these two fine novels.

Works Cited

Herr, Michael. *Dispatches*. New York: Avon, 1978.
Kakutani, Michiko. "Novelists and Vietnam: The War Goes On", *The New York Times Book Review*. April 15, 1984.
O'Brien, Tim. *Going After Cacciato*. New York: Dell, 1975.
Wright, Stephen. *Meditations In Green*. New York: Charles Scribner's Sons, 1983.

"Words and Fragments: Narrative Style in Vietnam War Novels" was presented at the 1986 meeting of the PCA in Atlanta, April 2-4.

Vietnam Fiction and the Paradoxical Paradigm of Nomenclature

Owen W. Gilman, Jr.

In the twentieth century the war novel has come into its own as a distinct genre, moving steadily away from the province of historical fiction where writing about war was concentrated through much of the nineteenth century. As we all know, Stephen Crane had a major role in propelling war narratives far beyond the confines of historical record and on to the forefront of the American literary landscape. A little later John Dos Passos helped to strengthen this development with *Three Soldiers*, chiefly by reinserting the political/moral dimension that Crane had omitted from *The Red Badge of Courage*. War served as a kind of home base for Ernest Hemingway throughout his career. Norman Mailer made his first significant mark with a war story, and James Jones found war crucial to his imagination. More recently the Vietnam War has served as a nexus to sustain the life of this genre in our time. In fact, the abundance of fiction related to Vietnam may mean the emergence of a new genre: the Vietnam War novel. It is my purpose here to explore that possibility and its significance for American culture.

However, before I delve into the specific characteristics of Vietnam fiction and sketch out the paradoxical paradigm of nomenclature which gives war writing of this era certain unique features, I wish to consider the general standing of genre fiction. By genre fiction I mean particularly those categories of creative enterprise wherein the writer develops a design known in advance to readers—readers who are faithful and devoted. Bookstores across the land cooperate in this enterprise, with whole sections devoted to science fiction, westerns, detective mysteries, spy thrillers, horror stories, sagas of fame and fortune, and the ever-popular romances. James Michener has a place to himself. And perhaps, should things continue as they have been going, we will soon regularly see a section established for Vietnam War novels.

But what is the meaning of these genres? They clearly do well at the marketplace, we know that. Yet when these texts pass for review by the arbiters of high cultural standards, commercial success becomes a certain liability. The academy frequently adopts the judgmental posture of Hawthorne in his famous caustic observation about the work of those domestic sentimentalists whose output (and sales) swamped his own. Hawthorne today might well indict that "damned mob of word processors" who have their digital resources firmly clamped on the pulse of the middle-brow and low-brow reading public in American life.

At times I am sympathetic with such an indictment, and yet it should be part of our business to attend to the constitution and the impact of these genres which have a formulaic or recipe quality about them. We can doubtless profit from efforts to determine their significance in reader-response terms; Janice A. Radway's *Reading the Romance: Women, Patriarchy, and Popular Literature* (1984) provocatively illuminates the romance genre in this regard. I suspect that studies of the readership patterns related to Vietnam literature will help us understand the forces governing the evolving production of texts where the subject is Vietnam. The sooner we get discriminating audience studies (Dove Readers/Hawk Readers?), the better.

Nevertheless, we must also scrutinize the internal or formal characteristics of these genres, to look closely at what makes them structurally cohesive, to determine what techniques and patterns inhere in them—and finally, to find what kind of language vitalizes them.

To get the search for common ground in the Vietnam War novel genre started, we might consider an initial, trivial linkage; almost every novel that has been reviewed can claim the distinction of being labeled "the best piece of original fiction yet to come out of the Vietnam era." This judgment has been reached so many times it is meaningless. It is clear we do not have a genre of several hundred brilliantly original texts about the Vietnam War.

A slightly more potent dimension of commonality concerns the brooding darkness that shadows Vietnam fiction. As the keynote speaker for the Asia Society's 1985 Vietnam conference, James Webb worried at length about the causes for this darkness. Toward the end of his address, reproduced in Timothy Lomperis' *"Reading the Wind": The Literature of the Vietnam War* (1987), Webb zeroed in on the pernicious—in his mind—pressure of the writer's community, the "Academic-Intellectual Complex" (18) that compels the writer to adopt anti-establishment (i.e., government) positions, hence leading to a dangerously constrained literature, which, due to these constraints, seems to come from one source. Webb suggested that all of this was part of publishing realities in the post-war era. Other participants at the conference took Webb sharply to task for this assertion, and I am not yet ready to accept his view as a salient means of defining the cohesiveness of the Vietnam War novel genre.

On a deeper level, however, we can discern qualities of prose texture, style, and word use which establish a core of likeness. These qualities would enable us to pull a passage from one Vietnam novel and place it in another novel without causing noticeable disruption. I suspect that most of us are instinctively uncomfortable with that sort of situation. We are thoroughgoing romantics in this regard. Style swells out of the individual, and each writer's work flowers most fully in its stylistic uniqueness. We know Hemingway through one style, Faulkner through another; Twain via one voice, James in a different voice altogether. Melville in *Moby Dick* would not be confused with Hawthorne in *The Scarlet Letter*. All of this we know from our training in literature, and we vigorously promote the virtues of stylistic difference to our students as we teach the texts of these American writers.

But when we examine the fictions of the Vietnam War, we find infinite points of similarity in language, certainly enough to allow the substitution exercise I mentioned earlier. How can we live with that? What does it signify? Does this core of likeness, which I soon will call a paradigm of nomenclature, mean that the Vietnam fiction genre is second-rate...or worse?

Of the other popular genres, science fiction falls closest to Vietnam fiction on the matter of language. The science fiction writer faces the immediate task of creating a separate world, one which is knowable (and unique) through a particular set of terms. Only a new set of terms can lead to the revelatory kind of foresight afforded by projection of time through the one human element where progress is steady: science.

Vietnam and science fiction converged directly in a recent text, *In the Field of Fire* (1987), a volume of short stories by science fiction writers, both well-established veterans of the genre and some newcomers. Introducing the collection, Jeanne Van Buren Dann and Jack Dann focus on the Post-Traumatic Stress Disorder issue in relationship to the future as it might be known to Vietnam veterans. They suggest that science fiction and fantasy are well suited to exploring the "fears and nightmares" (14) that are derivatives of the Vietnam experience. In reviewing this collection for the *New York Times*, the novelist David Bradley drew out the science fiction angle even more bluntly: "What *In the Field of Fire* says is that Vietnam *was* science fiction" (49).

While the sci fi world is always meant to mirror some earthly and human dilemma, it does so in outrageously fresh terms. Writers in this genre have to be quick and good at word coinage, ready to make us feel a difference on the first page; they faithfully follow Ezra Pound's injunction to "make it new"—at least on the surface—and this pattern of newness appeals to many readers, quite a few of whom probably major in computer science.

Yet science fiction never appealed to me, mainly because I get bogged down in all the exotic new names for things. It seems unnecessarily tedious, all this surface newness and difference. I become preoccupied with translation, that urge to reformulate all I am reading in terms of significance for the earth I know. Many of my students have the same grievance with poetry. I don't. It's only with science fiction that I find this radical newness unsatisfying.

However, I confess to having had something of the same reaction to Vietnam War fiction when I first began to read through it. I had read enough earlier war fiction to know that our modern wars have each spawned a new lingo, so I should have been prepared. For example, Henri Barbuse's *Le Feu (Under Fire,* 1916) is difficult to read because of all the slang; Barbuse's efforts to speak of the first world war necessitated extensive use of idiomatic French, the language coinages of men who knew the war through the horror of combat.

But something more than a set of slang phrases seemed to be operating in Vietnam War fiction, and at first, that ingredient put me off. I was looking then for a novel which would both get to the savage heart of the whole Vietnam era and stand as a lasting commentary on the human condition, a text that was viscerally real and symbolically potent. I found pungent and searing reality in almost every word, but that constancy of emphasis on the particulars of combat reality put the larger reach toward the symbolic out of focus. The obligatory devotions to reality— all done in a tumbling succession of set piece scenes tied up with the same recurrent phrases and linguistic notions—were overwhelming. The language of other wars was not applicable. The war demanded that it be told in its own language.

This situation varies greatly from the one involving science fiction peculiarities in language. These terms were not *made up* to project some visionary fantasy; they came directly—untranslated—from the miasmal ooze of the war itself. A host of writers had mental tape recorders running throughout their encounter with the Vietnam War. They heard the war; they knew it through its language, its idiom. And when they pushed the war into narrative form (whether through realism or through fantasy— or through something between realism and fantasy), it only made sense in that language. The fiction of Vietnam, then, is built on a paradigm of nomenclature.

I choose the word nomenclature both for its specific meaning related to the bedrock, fundamentalist spirit of the military training manuals used to prepare soldiers for combat and for its potential meaning: nomenclature becoming inclusive of all the terms, phrases, and expressions generated by the participants—as well as any allied stylistic tendencies. In this broader sense, nomenclature serves as a handle for describing a whole epistemological system, one essentially shaped and controlled by a frantic word generation impulse, an impulse set in motion by the basic training ritual of coming to "know your nomenclature."

In training people for the role of combat soldier, the military works hard to establish behavioral patterns quite separate from those associated with civilian life. Freedom of action is exorcised in the name of command authority: individual separateness is spurned in favor of unit identity and *esprit de corps*; common or general terms are replaced by an ever-growing set of precise new names. Time after time the trainee is directed to iterate the steps of an action or parts of equipment with strict military precision, always involving use of the correct words.

A classic example—if infamous—involves the referential term for the basic personal weapon of the infantryman—a rifle. Pity the poor trainee who would mistake his rifle for a gun. The military patois introduces a perverse sexual allusion to make the rifle/gun distinction clear, with "gun" signifying the male sex organ. From this effort to establish correctness of nomenclature ensues a mnemonic ditty: "This is my rifle and this is my gun, one is for killing and one is for fun." This bit of gross word play might well happen in day one of basic training, and it typifies the wide-ranging effort to form an ethos where violence of any kind is accepted as an assumed norm. While that kind of orientation has been part of military training throughout this century, during the Vietnam era it became especially salient, a development documented equally well in memoir (for example, Tim O'Brien's *If I Die in a Combat Zone, Box Me Up and Ship Me Home*) and fiction (for example, Gustav Hasford's *The Short Times*). Recognizing this development makes it easier to understand the wild outer limits of word coinage and concept formulation that served to define the nature of the war experience. It also makes it somewhat harder to understand why there were not *more* atrocities like the My Lai massacre; after all, the language system was predicated upon debasement of human life, the terminology leaned hard in that direction, and the combat conditions exacerbated tendencies toward a nihilism where everything was "UNREAL."

To provide support for these general observations, I would offer passages from Stephen Wright's *Meditations in Green*, a 1983 novel which won the Maxwell Perkins Prize. If we place Vietnam fiction on a continuous line—with a left polarity represented by the surrealistic, fantastical black humor of William Eastlake's *The Bamboo Bed* (1969) and a right polarity represented by the gritty naturalism of Larry Heineman's *Close Quarters* (1974) or Winston Groom's *Better Times Than These* (1978)—then Wright's text, both in narrative technique and in rhetorical intensity, falls well over to the left, somewhere near Tim O'Brien's *Going After Cacciato* (1978). It is worth noting that the examples to the left are all in the lineage of Melville; the war is taken up as an enormous subject (far beyond ordinary experience), one demanding the utmost in visionary idiosyncrasy and wordplay. These writers and their texts aspire to reach beyond the bare facts, a challenge clearly endorsed by Tim O'Brien in his remarks at the Asia Society gathering when he refused to accept the limits of superficial historicity.

The visionary dimension thrusts these narratives toward some higher, universal truth—however terrifying that may be—but the idiosyncratic features and lyric impulse of the wordplay fixes the action in a unique moment of cultural time. The resultant paradigm is thus paradoxical, for an invitation to make connections with what went before and with what will follow (with meaning for humans in eternal time) is coupled to—or contingent upon—dazzlingly unique, one-time expressions. That's one way of phrasing the paradox. Here's another that may be helpful for showing what I'm getting at. I've managed to squeeze it into epigramatic form: "The greatest *depth* in Vietnam War fiction is all on the *surface.*"

The stamp of originality is boldly placed on *Meditations in Green*; this text does not appear initially to be in any way a carbon copy of other fictions of the war, one made original only by random shuffling of pages and rearrangement of essential *topoi*. The narrative structure is fairly complex, proceeding along multiple time lines, with interpolated poetic meditations on plant life (beginning with marijuana, of course) spacing the action scenes. Several after-the-war experiences of the protagonist, Specialist James Griffin, are interwoven with during-the-war combat scenes. This technique dramatically implies that, for veterans at least, all time is synchronous, all centered on the Vietnam period. Certain terms make it this way, certain dispositions toward language. If we think of life as an act of languaging, then the languaging action peculiar to the Vietnam War orders and directs the life of those who lived through it.

Midway through the first chapter, Griffin, who serves as our "genial story-teller" (6), asserts the general malaise of his condition after the war, declaring simply, "This is not a settled life" (5). As he quickly illustrates, language contributes massively to the unsettled quality of his existence:

A children's breakfast cereal, crispy critters, provokes nausea; there is a women's perfume named Charlie; and the radio sound of "We Gotta Get Out Of This Place" (The Animals, 1965) fills me with a melancholy as petrifying as a metal poured into casts of galloping cavalry, squinting riflemen, proud generals, statues in the park, roosts for pigeons. (6)

The past rides hard on Griffin. We learn in the first chapter that while he has formed a relationship with a young woman, a part-time social worker, Huette Mirandella, even this possible hope for the future carries with it a ghostlike presence in the guise of her nickname, Huey—an abbreviated form of reference to "a ten-thousand-pound assault helicopter" (6), one bit of nomenclature which everlastingly sets the Vietnam War apart from others in American history no matter how it may be memorialized in other ways.

The particularizing nomenclature of the war appears frequently throughout Wright's novel. Griffin comes home from the war wounded. His wound is in the tradition of Henry Fleming and Frederic Henry and Jacob Barnes, but the physical pain of his injury lingers on through his return to civilian life, thus forcing upon him some sort of imaginary escape. When walking is hard for his battered leg, he dreams of moving with ease—and this immediately opens the door to a rush of nomenclature from his past: "Imagine commandeering a tank, one of the big ones, forty-seven tons of M48, cast steel hull, 90mm gun, 7.62 MG coaxially mounted in the turret, and running down the boulevard.... Imagine the snap, the crackle, the pop" (4). Much of this dream vision originates in precise military nomenclature of basic training manuals. While outsiders might be content with the simple, generic notion of a tank, not so with the insiders, those who experienced the war. Their reference point is infinitely more specific. When they speak—or think—they do so with language which sets them apart. Even the concluding portion to Griffin's rhapsodic speculation shows the particularizing tendency of Vietnam War language patterns. In this case, an advertising slogan for breakfast cereal is linked spontaneously to the sounds of combat equipment in action, carrying with it the crisp incisiveness so desired by military men. The result of this layering, the mix of words from one realm with the experience of another, is often an irony which cuts quickly and deeply. Linguistic surprises burst upon us like illumination rounds—and we are shocked to a new awareness.

Another example of the shock value to the nomenclature of the war comes from a scene devoted to Griffin's combat adventures. Some prisoners have been captured by Griffin's unit. A character named Kraft is talking with a kid who is known as a "good killer." While they chat about ways in which the kid has killed the enemy, others in their unit tie packages of C-4 explosive to the chests of prisoners. The passage ends with the narrator's summary of action in the background: "Behind them came the shock and echo of a huge explosion. Then another. Gookhoppers" (78).

Gookhoppers. A unique coinage, but one born of the same naming impulse which produced the M48, cast steel hull, 90mm gun, 7.62 MG coaxially mounted tank. A new world is being discovered, and it must be named. The situation is thoroughly Adamic. Once the naming pattern was initiated, anything was fair game. In this case, language is right at the cutting edge of reality. "Gookhopper" is full of life. Imagination is inherent in this manifestation of nomenclature, as is the vitality which ensues from moments of human perception—fresh, original perception. The fiction of the Vietnam War is full of new word coinages (even the soldiers assumed typecasting monikers when they arrived in-country), and it may well be that we are drawn to it—fascinated by it—because of the intensity of language supplied by texts derived from that experience. Gookhoppers...a word full of snap, crackle, and pop.

Perhaps for a moment we might consider the usual sources for new words in English today. Much of the newness comes from scientists (who find previously unknown sub-atomic particles to name), social scientists (who fabricate new concepts to keep themselves in business, too frequently without any regard for the real needs of our language), and most recently, the computer wizards (who try to keep the English language in touch with the various languages of the computer). Politicians and the media gang help in this business mainly by borrowing or adapting new words for the sake of efficiency. As can be discerned from any five minutes of exposure to contemporary political discourse, we've come a long, long way from the Renaissance, where the addition of words to the language was in the province of people whose business it was to produce literary texts—Shakespeare and company.[1]

Various other subcultures also contribute to language change. Those of us in the humanities occasionally introduce new terminology, although since our work is fundamentally conservative, most of our new slants involve borrowings of one kind of another; for example, the appropriation of contemporary continental philosophical terms and key words in rabbinical hermeneutics has fed the fires of the deconstruction school of literary criticism for the last decade. More important, however, are social subcultures—Californians, ghetto dwellers, and youth. In this category we should also place the Vietnam veterans and those who have spun webs of fiction out of the war.

Why exactly was language innovation essential to this group? As I have already suggested, part of the impetus came from basic training rituals. Military life is indeed "another world." But the combat situation in the war was vitally important in keeping the spirit of nomenclature going strong. In a word, the war was "UNREAL." It's unreal, man, fucking unreal. Remember how often we heard that idea. It originated with the war, but it quickly spread to become a convenient label for anything remotely painful or difficult—like final exams. The war was truly bad, however, so perplexing and puzzling, so terrifyingly nonsensical and idiotic as it went on for year after year, that the participants needed special coping mechanisms. One of the means of sustaining the human spirit in the face of abysmal nothingness was to have a language that was alive. The soldiers of Vietnam could not play it safe; they could not be conservatives. Their solution was to play out their roles right at the brink of apocalypse. The language that ensued was full of breathtaking intensity. It was alternately superheated and supercool. As I work toward my conclusion, let's listen in to a passage from the middle of Wright's novel—a passage that, with one name change, might be placed equally well in many other fictions of the war:

Higher up in the sky, between Griffin and the sun, a flight of F-4s came streaking in, bodies camouflaged in splotches of brown and green paint, wings and tails cut to resemble shark fins. Griffin's ears filled with cool professional voices so near their owners might have been jammed into this cockpit with him.

"Good morning, Spud, how are you?"

"Looking good, Bluebird, what size eggs you got to lay for me today?"

"Five hundred pounders, four rocket tubes, some twenty mike mike, all that good shit."

"Make me happy."

There's heavy fire coming from the tree line. The village has got a damn stone wall around it. I count about a dozen structures, same-same bunkers, spider holes, looks like a tunnel system all through it, I think they're in there pretty tight."

"Need some loosening, huh?"

"The province chief says the whole place is lousy with VC so knock yourselves out. Don't bother with the phosphorous. Figure you can line it up on the road and work your way in along that axis."

"Affirm."

One by one the F-4s peeled off and came swooping down in over the tree line. Griffin could see shock waves along the ground as clear as the rings in a pond of water when a rock is tossed in. Columns of smoke lifted into the blue sky.

"Oh boy!" shouted someone in Griffin's ear. "Oh fucking boy!"

The separate columns of smoke joined together in one solid wall rising high and thick from the combustion below. Palm trees swayed in the fire, turned black and shrank. The burning hootches became visible, collapsing in slow motion into the flames. There was no sign of life anywhere on the ground.

"Shit hot, Bluebird, that's a one-oh-oh. Six structures, at least twenty KBAs. Thank you very much."

"Hold one, Bluebird. There's a definite unfriendly scooting out the back door. Can someone handle that?"

"Roger."

Griffin could see a speck moving along a brown road.

One of the jets knifed swiftly downward, swept in over the road. Its black nose twinkled. A dust cloud rose up. The speck stopped moving.

"Right on. Thank you, Bluebird, it's been a pleasure working with you."

"Any time, Spud."

The F-4s soared into the haze.

"Wonderful," said Griffin.

"See all the fun you office boys miss out on," said Mueller.

Their plane climbed a spur of jagged mountains and entered a valley of the moon, barren earth pounded into dust and pocked with craters more numerous than skin pores, a bowl of holes, depressions in an ashtray.

"What the hell was down there?" asked Griffin.

"Nguyen's Pizza and Hamburgers, Commie Community Drive-In Theater, who knows? I think what we're looking at here is actually a site of random mineral exploration. Chop up the ground with explosives, see what rises to the surface. Damn country's loaded with tungsten, you know. For filaments, light bulbs. Bombing this place is really keeping our homes back in the world clean and well-lit." (199-201)

There it is—a passage of prose which leaps off the page. Bizarre twists of nomenclature aplenty. The language scintillates: weird lingo that transforms the brutality of American technology at work into something quite acceptable in its context, just what one might expect from the strangely composed mythological griffin inherent in the protagonist. We are treated to lots of metaphoric play that mocks the humdrum quality of the work-a-day world in every delicious turn of phrase—and thanks to Wright's literary sensitivity, something not uniformly distributed through the Vietnam War fiction genre, a considerable dose of irony. In juxtaposition to the devastation brought by those bombs, think of the cordiality of the closing ("Thank you very much...Glad to be of service")—how often we might hear those phrases in our daily affairs. And "Bluebird"—the bluebird of happiness, I suppose. The last line from the passage takes us back to Hemingway country, that "clean and well lighted place" of which he wrote to explore "nada."

The style is relentlessly running, with the pace accelerated by fragments. There is too much intensity here, too much loco-motion, too much zest for peeling off in language as those F-4s do against the sun in the sky, swooping in so as to nail the reader-target dead between the eyes, too much explosiveness for prose that waits. This is not a world meant for periodicy, for that stylistic structure requires a balance and control alien to the elemental conditions of war in Vietnam. Constraints of that order were not operative there, so we are given over to the "shake'n bakes," "short-timers," allegorically named characters like "Trips" from Wright's novel—"trips" as in "he's tripping," or "it was a bad trip, man"—and to a succession of wildly frenzied moments. Nomenclature...a world apart...says it all.

Not surprisingly, it is not the fiction alone which displays these linguistic features. Michael Herr's new journalistic reportage in his book *Dispatches* has all the same qualities regarding word coinage and style. Surprisingly, some of the best literary criticism devoted to texts of the Vietnam War seems positively inspired by the essential language of the combat experience. I think particularly of Philip Beidler's *American Literature and the Experience of Vietnam*, but you can often hear traces of that phenomenon from papers on Vietnam literature at academic conferences. It may be, in one more strange twist of irony, that the Vietnam War will be the best thing to happen to literary criticism for decades.

Don't we need, perhaps, an occasional burst of rhetorical excess to keep us going strong?

And now to final considerations: What will be the net result of the radical newness of language found swirling in the fiction of Vietnam? In the first place, an abundance of self-referential nomenclature singularizes the Vietnam War, serves to make it unique. Surely many of the writers of this era heard the voice of Crane, or Hemingway, or Mailer, or Heller, or Vonnegut talking to them at some point, but more importantly, they listened to the war itself. So we have a war that becomes unique in its literature. Possibly there is a hidden motive in all of that uniqueness: the war is *so* unique, and we are never allowed to forget that fact, we are thus given encouragement not to repeat the experience. The war must remain unique, never to be duplicated in part or in whole. I am suggesting, then, that a subtle anti-war bias may be at work in this literature at the language level.

Such a possibility represents the bright side of where Vietnam fiction might fit into the long reach of history. But just as the language use is two-sided—and paradoxical in its doubleness—so too is the possible impact of it. There is a dark side. Although the 1980s have brought a certain return to normalcy, with campuses almost funereal in their quietude, and while the business of everybody seems to be business, it still seems fair to say that "this is not a settled life." The matter of Vietnam is certainly not settled, and more people than just the veterans, whose needs to resolve the past are acute, have been kept prisoner of the war's enigmatic mystery. Could it be possible that the intensely bright flame of language burning within the fiction of the war will draw readers as fascinated moths ever closer to it, closer and closer until the urge to join with the fire leads us toward the source of that intensity—and doom? I admit to being troubled with that possibility.

Darkness has always been the strong suit in American literature. Apocalypse stands perennially ready to greet the end of the American dream, and the parade of writers who have known the enchantment of doom is both long and estimable. D.H. Lawrence brilliantly exposed this preoccupation (and its attendant violence) early in this century. The dark romanticists of the last century—Poe, Hawthorne, and Melville—have been matched stroke for stroke by the dark naturalists—Mailer and Hemingway—of our time. As a point for my closing, Mailer's case is worth particular scrutiny.

Norman Mailer's career has been built on one deplorably bad and disgusting idea—that violence is some kind of therapeutic answer to the anxiety and alienation of modern life, but he is such an astounding stylist that his repackaging efforts have kept him widely read. And maybe, just maybe, the idiocy of his theory has escaped us. At the least, we have allowed him to keep us enthralled. We need his language so much—

to keep ourselves from falling into a deep, stultifying sleep—we accept him lock, stock, and barrel. Oh...the snap, the crackle, the pop.

And so, possibly, it may be with the reception of Vietnam War fiction in American Culture. Even as we gorge ourselves on the language of Vietnam, in 1987 finally brought to the movie screen in Stanley Kubrick's *Full Metal Jacket* (based on Gustav Hasford's *The Short-Timers*), our hunger grows, and we consider a return to the source. Well, the alternatives are several. Sometime, surely not too far in the future, an answer will come. If not today, tomorrow...or the day after. We can only wait.

Notes

[1]For both the substance and tenor of these comparative observations, I am indebted to Anne Drury Hall's ongoing reflections about Renaissance rhetoric. For an example of her esteem for seventeenth-century wordplay, see her "Epistle, Meditation, and Sir Thomas Browne's *Religio Medici*," PMLA 94 (1979): 234-46.

Works Cited

Beidler, Philip. *American Literature and the Experience of Vietnam*. Athens, Georgia: University of Georgia Press, 1982.

Bradley, David. "War in an Alternate Universe." Rev. of *In the Field of Fire*, ed. Jeanne Van Buren Dann and Jack Dann. *New York Times* 3 May 1987, Book Review section: 25, 49.

Dann, Jeanne Van Buren, and Jack Dann, eds. *In the Field of Fire*, New York: TOR/ St. Martin's Press, 1987.

Eastlake, William. *The Bamboo Bed*. New York: Simon and Schuster, 1969.

Groom, Winson. *Better Times Than These*. New York: Summit Books, 1978.

Hall, Anne Drury. "Epistle, Meditation, and Sir Thomas Browne's *Religio Medici*." *PMLA* 94 (1979): 234-46.

Hasford, Gustav. *The Short Timers*. New York: Harper and Row, 1979.

Kubrick, Stanley, dir. *Full Metal Jacket*. With Matthew Modine. Warner Bros., 1987.

Lomperis, Timothy. *"Reading the Wind": The Literature of the Vietnam War*. Durham, N.C.: Duke University Press, 1987.

O'Brien, Tim. *Going After Cacciato*. New York: Delacorte Press, 1978.

If I Die in a Combat Zone, Box Me Up and Ship Me Home. New York: Delacorte Press, 1973.

Radway, Janice A. *Reading the Romance: Women, Patriarchy, and Popular Literature*. Chapel Hill, N.C.: University of North Carolina Press, 1984.

Wright, Stephen. *Meditations in Green*. New York: Charles Scribner's Sons, 1983.

A version of "Vietnam Writing and the Paradoxical Paradigm of Nomenclature" was presented at the MLA Convention in Chicago, Dec. 27-29, 1985.

From the DMZ to No Man's Land: Philip Caputo's *A Rumor of War* and its Antecedents

Cornelius A. Cronin

The Vietnam War was the event which politicized, even radicalized, a good part of an entire generation of Americans. Indeed, so intense did the political debate over the war become that the war itself became of secondary importance to that debate. However, the growing body of literature produced by participants in the Vietnam War tends, with rare exceptions, to find the politics of the war irrelevant; what these writers connect their combat experiences to is not the political debate which surrounded their war but the experiences of other men who fought in earlier modern wars and wrote about doing it.

The work which has appeared so far on American literature from the Vietnam conflict tends to see that literature and the events which produced it as unique in the American experience and largely unconnected to earlier combat literature. Tobey Herzog uses Conrad's *Heart of Darkness* as a metaphor for the journey into the darkest reaches of the self which he sees the most successful writers of Vietnam literature taking. Peter McInerney sees fiction, or *story* taking the place of *history*: "Fiction can identify what was 'hiding under the fact-figure crossfire' there, because it can tell 'a secret history.' Literature of the Vietnam War is a casualty of 'History's heavy attrition,' and one consequence is the breakdown and transformation of the historical imagination itself" (187-8). And Gordon O. Taylor, while mentioning in passing that Vietnam novels "assume a continuity of literary enterprise between the war in Vietnam and earlier American conflicts," emphasizes that Vietnam literature generally represents a case "of literary method in relation to a subject resisting definition by literary precedent," and that the novelists "continue to reconnoiter in relatively new literary terrain," while the writers of memoirs and personal narratives embark on a "quest for alternative form" (294-5). Philip D. Beidler conceives of his book *American Literature and the Experience of Vietnam* as "a case study in literature and literary

74

consciousness considered in relation to the larger process of cultural myth-making" (xi), and he is not concerned with the relation of this literature to earlier combat literature. John Hellmann, in *American Myth and the Legacy of Vietnam* "first traces the relation of America's mythic heritage to its experience in Vietnam. It then explores the legacy of Vietnam, the awful place it has come to occupy in American myth" (ix). Thus, all five of these writers emphasize the uniqueness of the Vietnam experience and either deemphasize its relations to other combat experiences and other combat literature or place it in a context in which those relations seem unimportant.

Vietnam was, of course, unique in the sense that all events are unique, but the uniqueness that these critics posit infers a kind of ontologically privileged status for the Vietnam War which will not stand up under close scrutiny. In fact, the real uniqueness of literature written by participants in the Vietnam War can only be appreciated when that literature's profound connectedness to earlier twentieth-century combat literature is understood.

Philip Caputo's memoir, *A Rumor of War*, illustrates both the debt which Vietnam literature owes to earlier combat literature and the ways in which it represents a new development in that tradition. One of the central themes of *A Rumor of War* is the journey from innocence to experience which Caputo makes during his thirteen months in Vietnam. Throughout the book, in references in the text and in nine of the book's twenty-four epigraphs, Caputo refers to, alludes to, and quotes from several English writers of World War I whose works recreate the same journey from innocence through experience to disillusionment. Caputo uses these writers, principally Wilfred Owen and Siegfried Sassoon, for two purposes: first, as a point of reference which anchors his book firmly in a recognized literary tradition, and, second, as a point of departure against which he contrasts the different, and, as he perceives it, more self-destroying experience of the Vietnam War.

Seen one way, *A Rumor of War* is simply a factual account of one marine's experiences in Vietnam, and this is the concept of the book advanced most strongly by the author:

This book does not pretend to be history. It has nothing to do with politics, power, strategy, influence, national interests, or foreign policy; nor is it an indictment of the great men who led us into Indochina...it is a soldier's account of our longest conflict...as well as a record of a long and sometimes painful personal experience. (p. xi)

But the book is not nearly so simple nor so artless as this disclaimer suggests. There are at least three Philip Caputo's in the book. The avatar of Philip Caputo who tells the story uses a cynical tone and a self-consciously retrospective point-of-view which distances him from the young Philip Caputo who grew up finding "flint arrowheads in the muddy creek bank" in the ersatz pastoral landscape of suburban Chicago and who "wanted to find in a commonplace world a chance to live heroically" (5). The cynical narrator describes the young Philip Caputo's enlistment in the Marine Corps in this way: "THE MARINE CORPS BUILDS MEN was another slogan current at the time, and on November 28 I became one of its construction projects" (7). Much later in the book the would-be marine hero and the cynical narrator come together. "And there was that inspiring order issued by General Green: Kill VC. In the patriotic fervor of the Kennedy years we had asked 'What can we do for our country?' And our country answered, 'Kill VC' " (230). And there is a third Philip Caputo, the student who regrets being unable to take his books to Vietnam (43), and who, less than a year before finding himself in Vietnam "was discussing the relative merits of *Tom Jones* and *Joseph Andrews* in a seminar on the English Novel" (47). This third Philip Caputo is in both of the other two. The young marine has "read all the serious books to come out of the World Wars, and Wilfred Owen's poetry about the western front. And yet, [he] had learned nothing" (81). The narrator scatters twenty-four epigraphs through his book, all concerning war, Hemingway, and the British World War I poets Siegfried Sassoon and Wilfred Owen.

The epigraphs from Owen and Sassoon carry on a dialogue with the narrator. Part One tells of Caputo's Marine training and his first few months in Vietnam including his first combat experiences. The first and last chapters of this initial section of the book have epigraphs from Wilfred Owen—two lines from "Arms and the Boy" and four lines from "Apologia Pro Poemate Meo" which speak to the young Marine Caputo's sense of closeness with his platoon and company, and remind the reader that Caputo and that platoon have not yet tasted much of "war's hard wire." Part two tells of Caputo's five months of staff duty, counting corpses as Regimental Casualty Reporting Officer; most of the epigraphs are taken from Sassoon's angrier poems, particularly "The Effect" and "Base Details," and they tend to reflect Caputo's growing alienation and self-loathing. Part Three deals with Caputo's last five-and-a-half months in Vietnam, after he has returned to a line company, and it is framed by epigraphs from Sassoon and Owen. The first, taken from Sassoon's poem "Dreamers," reaffirms Caputo's sense of brotherhood with the World War I poets; the second, from Owen's "Apologia Pro Poemate Meo," emphasizes the ways in which Caputo sees his Vietnam experience as fundamentally different from the World War I experience.

The epigraphs taken from the British World War I poets constitute an important connection between *A Rumor of War* and the literature of World War I, but the tripartite structure of the book provides an even more important connection, one which highlights the complexity of that relationship. The structure of *A Rumor of War* echoes two of the most common structures in British World War I officer memoirs. The first paradigm is described by Paul Fussell:

The "paradigm" war memoir can be seen to comprise three elements: first, the sinister or absurd or even farcical preparations...second, the unmanning experience of battle; and third, the retirement from the line to a contrasting (usually pastoral) scene, where there is time and quiet for consideration, meditation, and reconstruction.... Movement up the line, battle, and recovery become emblems of quest, death, and rebirth. (130-31)

There is a second, contrasting three-part paradigm in British World War I memoirs, exemplified by Siegfried Sassoon's *The Memoirs of George Sherston* and Guy Chapman's *A Passionate Prodigality*, in which the progression is first, training and initiation into battle; second, separation from the unit and removal to a safe place (a hospital, or staff duty); third, return to the front. This pattern also involves quest, death and rebirth, but, significantly, death is associated with removal from battle and from one's comrades in arms and rebirth with a return to the front.

Actually, *A Rumor of War* encompasses completely the first paradigm just in Part One. Illustrating Fussell's first stage, "the sinister, or absurd or even farcical preparation," Caputo describes the Marine officer candidates pre-meal chant at Quantico: " 'Sir, the United States Marines; since 1775 the most invincible fighting force in the history of man. Gung ho! Gung ho! Gung ho! Pray for War!' " (12)—and at the Jungle Warfare School in Malasia—"Sergeant: ' *can't hear you, marines.' Class, this time in unison: 'AMBUSHES ARE MURDER AND MURDER IS FUN' "* *(36)*. By Chapter Six, Caputo's company is going out on operations and undergoing "the unmanning experience of battle:"

But we saw enough to learn those lessons that could not be taught in training camps: what fear feels like and what death looks like, and the smell of death, the experience of killing, of enduring pain and inflicting it, the loss of friends and the sight of wounds. We learned what war was about, "the courses of it and the forms of it." We began to change, to lose the boyish awkwardness we had brought to Vietnam. (95)

Caputo's "retirement from the line to a contrasting...scene where there is time and quiet for consideration, meditation, and reconstruction" comes with the return to base camp after his first long combat operation when he reflects on what has happened to his company:

I only know what I had acquired a great deal of affection for those young marines, simply because we had been through a few things together. They were the men with whom I had shared the heat and dust, the tense, watchful nights, the risks of patrolling some desolate jungle trail. There were more admirable men in the world, more principled men, and even men with finer sensibilities, but they slept in peaceful beds. (137)

The tone of this reflection is almost elegaic, and the reader must remember that the narrator is reporting the thoughts of the young Philip Caputo who is about to learn more about combat than he expected and a good deal more than he wanted.

The second paradigm, the paradigm of exposure to battle, removal to the rear and return to the front, is the World War I paradigm which *A Rumor of War* follows most closely in its totality. Part One sounds like a British World War I memoir with its Owen-like description of "the intimacy of life in infantry battalions, where the communion between men is as profound as any between lovers" (xv).

Part II begins as an unremarkable memoir of life on the regimental staff, but quickly becomes a reification of the phantasmagoric world of Sassoon's "The Effect," which provides two of its epigraphs. Although Caputo's main duty on staff is assistant adjutant (administrative officer), his whole account of his time on staff centers around his secondary duties as Regimental Casualty Reporting Officer. In this capacity, his official duties consist of taking and filing casualty reports, verifying identification and the cause of death of bodies at the base hospital, and updating the colonel's "scoreboard" daily.

One episode in particular underscores the air of macabre absurdity which comes to surround Caputo's job. The bodies of four dead Viet Cong are brought in on a trailer and dumped in the regimental area on the orders of the colonel, who wants the headquarters troops to march by them "to get used to the sight of blood" (173). The troops march by "like visitors passing before an exhibit in a museum" (174). Since the bodies are starting to decompose in the tropical heat, Caputo has them trucked off, only to be told that he must get them back for the benefit of a visiting general from MACV (Military Assistance Command, Vietnam). Sending a driver off to retrieve the corpses, Caputo returns to his desk, "where, in the spirit of the madness in which I was taking part, I made up a new title for myself. I wrote it on a piece of cardboard and tacked the cardboard to my desk. It read: 1LT P.J. CAPUTO. OFFICER IN CHARGE OF THE DEAD" (175).

The corpses, which are now in pieces, are returned, and Caputo has them washed off. His new self-awarded title sounds like typical youthful irreverence, but his internal response as the visiting general and his entourage walk past the corpses is neither so innocent nor so simple: "I saluted sharply as they walked past me to my freshly washed corpses. I thought of them as mine; they were the dead and I was the officer in charge of the dead" (177). We are almost completely in the world of Sassoon's "The Effect" here ("Who'll buy my nice fresh corpses, two a penny?''), and if Caputo seems only to be playing at getting lost in the madness of war, his madness becomes more frighteningly real as he begins to obsess over his dealings with the dead, ultimately taking command of a corpse platoon in his dreams:

That night I was given command of a new platoon. They stood in formation in the rain, three ranks deep. I stood front and center, facing them. Devlin, Lockhart and Bryce were in the first rank, Bryce standing on his one good leg, next to him the faceless Devlin, and then Lockhart with his bruised eye sockets bulging. Sullivan was there too, and Reasoner, and all of the others, all of them dead except me, the officer in charge of the dead. I was the only one alive and whole, and when I commanded "platoon, rye-eet FACE! Sliing HARMS! For-WARD HARCH!" They marched along, my platoon of crippled corpses, hopping along on the stumps of their legs, swinging the stumps of their arms, keeping perfect time while I counted cadence. I was proud of them, disciplined soldiers to and beyond the end. They stayed in step even in death. (199)

When Caputo awakens he is profoundly afraid, and the image of his new platoon stays with him, until, horrifyingly, his vision of the dead as living is transformed into a vision of the living as dead:

It was a kind of double-exposure. I saw their living mouths moving in conversation and their dead mouths growing the taut-drawn grins of corpses. Their living eyes I saw, and their dead eyes still-staring.... Asleep and dreaming, I saw dead men living. Awake, I saw living men dead. (201)

As Caputo grows more horrified and unbalanced by his constant dealing with the dead, he also grows more dissatisfied with his existence as a staff officer. Near the beginning of Part Two the reader hears the cynical, retrospective narrator observing his younger self and his fellow staff officers as they ignore indications of a coming attack on the Da Nang airbase: "No, level-headed professionals that we were, we did what staff officers usually do: nothing" (184). A little later the narrator shows his bookish side as he describes, in a way reminiscent of World War I line-staff hostility, the staff officers gathered in the TOC (Tactical Operations Center, or command post) during the attack: "We were all crowded in there, along with a number of radio operators and message clerks. A single shell could have wiped out half the regimental staff, and I'm sure there were some line officers who hoped one would" (186).

Finally, the themes which structure Part II come together when the narrator simply reports the thoughts of the young Philip Caputo after his terrifying dream of the platoon of the dead: "I had acquired a hatred for the scoreboard, for the very sight of it. It symbolized everything I despised about the staff, the obsession with statistics, the indifference toward the tragedy of death, and because I was on the staff, I despised myself" (210-11).

Caputo is ready for a return to the line, to wash the bad taste of staff life out of his mouth by returning to the battalion. But he cannot return; the batallion is leaving without him, and he is about to cease to be a brother to Wilfred Owen and Siegfried Sassoon and to become the representative Vietnam soldier.

British World War I literature almost universally defines combat as essentially a group experience. The individual draws strength from the group; he is able to engage in life-threatening actions long past the time when he is animated by any sense of patriotism or even of mission. The people he counts on are the people who count on him. Men fight in modern wars primarily through coercion; the sure penalties for refusing to fight seem more frightening than the possibility of death or injury on the battlefield. The group, whether platoon, company or battalion, is the universe of the combat soldier: from it he draws his strength and a sense of identity; to it he gives his loyalty and possibly his life. Sassoon's George Sherston, a thinly disguised avatar of Sassoon himself, abandons his pacifist protest and returns to the line not because he has regained his belief in the war, but because he feels guilty that he is safe in the hospital while the men of his unit continue to risk their lives in the trenches (*Sherston's Progress* 75-82). When the war is over Guy Chapman remains in the army only so that he can stay with his batallion (274-81).

The fact that Caputo's battalion, the first Battalion, Third Marines (1/3) is shipping out for Camp Pendleton, California, to be completely reorganized becomes a crucial transition point in the dialogue between Caputo's book and earlier combat writers with whom he has identified. The U.S. Army and Marine Corps have traditionally kept units intact, moving whole units in and out of the line and to the rear, using individual replacements only to fill holes left by deaths and serious casualties. In Korea a point system for rotation was instituted, but the real change of policy came in Vietnam when a soldier's tour of duty was fixed at one year. A division which spent four years in Vietnam would have had four complete changes of personnel, as well as replacements for losses. Probably the effect of this policy on unit efficiency was detrimental; the effect on individuals was psychologically debilitating.

Because of the one-year tour and the individual replacement policy, the American soldier in Vietnam was denied at least part of the supportive effects of identification with the unit. He arrived alone, he left alone, and he spent his year as a member of a unit each of whose members was primarily concerned with surviving until the end of his own 365 days. In a sense, Caputo's experience was even more isolating. He arrived with a unit and his unit left him. His company commander, a marine he admires, and who, he remembers, "instilled in me a lasting fear of criticism and, conversely, a hunger for praise" (35), "summed up Charlie

Company's collective feelings one night shortly before the battalion shipped out. 'Phil,' he said to me over a beer in the HqCo mess, 'We've been shot at and missed and shit on and hit, and now we're getting out of this hole' '' (215-16). The Marines, or at least Philip Caputo's piece of the Marines, have landed and are leaving, having decided that this is no war for them. When the battalion which is to replace them, the first Battalion, first Marines (1/1) arrives, Caputo sees them through the eyes of a cynical, disillusioned veteran:

It was a big, fine-looking battalion, and when I saw them I felt as an old man does when he sees someone who reminds him of his youth. I thought of the way we had been six months before. I was both charmed and saddened by their innocent enthusiasm—charmed because I wished I could be that way again; saddened because they didn't really know what they were getting into. I did. (217)

The last two words of this quote imply that the young Philip Caputo feels he has nothing more to learn; they are the culmination of a tendency he has shown to see himself as a French soldier in Vietnam before Dienbienphieu, cursing the climate and the jungle and developing the *cafarde*, the thousand-yard stare. But the statement also reflects a change in the narrator's tone, from a cynical, irreverent irony to a deeper, sadder irony; for he knows, writing almost ten years after the fact, that Philip Caputo is going to learn more about his own potential for evil than he can even dream as he watches the new battalion arrive.

Part Three primarily recounts Caputo's second stint as a line officer, as a platoon leader in C Company, First Battalion, First Marines (C/1/1). He returns to the line at his own request for a variety of reasons.

The paramount was boredom...I cannot deny that the front still held a fascination for me...the fear of madness was another motive...there would be very little time to think in a line company. That is the secret to emotional survival in war, not thinking.... Finally, there was hatred, a hatred buried so deep *that I could not then admit its existence*... Revenge was one of the reasons I volunteered for a line company. I wanted to kill somebody. (230-1. Emphasis mine)

This analysis is retrospective; as the narrator tells us, he could not at the time have admitted the existence of his desire for revenge. But he does recognize it after the fact, and it is precisely in this recognition that he again parts company with his World War I brethren, who tend to see themselves as passive sufferers who are acted upon, in seeing himself as personally guilty, as somehow responsible for the acts he performs and ultimately for an act he only wills.

The central trope of the typical Vietnam memoir or novel is the atrocity, and *A Rumor of War* has its atrocity, in the last chapter of Part Three. Throughout the book the narrator has worked to make the reader aware of the special complexities of fighting a guerrilla war with regular troops. The order "Kill VC" (230) is a lot simpler to carry out than its prerequisite, "Identify VC." Caputo's marines are fighting an enemy indistinguishable from the rest of the population, and in order to protect the population the marines operated under an elaborate set of "rules of engagement." These rules essentially required that marines patrol without ammunition in the chambers of their weapons unless contact was imminent (an almost meaningless concept in a war of ambushes). Also, no unarmed Vietnamese was to be fired on unless he was running. When the platoon leaders are given this information before Caputo's first operation, they are disturbed and confused. They are not eager to kill civilians, but they are no more eager to be courtmartialed for a decision made in the heat of combat. The captain reassures them by relaying the battalion command's rough-and-ready interpretation of the rules: " 'Look, I don't know what this is supposed to mean, but I talked to battalion and they said that as far as they're concerned, if he's dead and Vietnamese, he's VC' " (74).

As the war grows in intensity, the distinction between VC and *the people* becomes harder for line troops to maintain. They are not informed about, do not understand, and probably would not be interested in the complex life of a Vietnamese village, and they show no awareness of the difficulty the villagers would have keeping the VC out even if they wanted to do so. All the marines know is that when they come under fire from a village, or consistently run into booby traps near a village, they see that village as the enemy, often with disastrous results for the village. In Part One, Third platoon, C/1/3 goes berserk after being ambushed from the Hamlet of Giao-Tri (3) and burns it to the ground. Caputo later reflects on what has happened: "It is then that I realize that the destruction of Giao-Tri was more than an act of madness committed in the heat of battle. It was an act of retribution as well" (110). Caputo stops short of feeling any real guilt here; neither he nor his platoon is involved. But he does not attribute what happened at Giao-Tri to "the war." He sees it as an action performed by men who, even though they are soldiers, are responsible for what they do.

In Part Three, Caputo's platoon, which is involved in a particularly furious helicopter assault and subsequent firefight, burns down the village of Ha Na after finding some VC supplies there, an action which Caputo describes as arising "out of some emotional necessity...a catharsis, a purging of months of fear, frustration, and tension" (305). But as he reflects on the action, he is overwhelmed by his own sense of individual guilt:

I felt sick enough about it all, sick of the war, sick of what the war was doing to us, sick of myself. Looking at the embers below, at the skeletons of the houses, a guilt weighed down on me as heavily as the heaviest pack I had ever carried.... Yes, the later deliberate destruction had been committed by men *in extremis*; war was a state of extremes, and men often did extreme things in it. But none of this wisdom relieved my guilt or answered the question: *"Tau Sao?"* Why? (305-6)

In the last lines of this quote Caputo raises and dismisses the argument, implicit in most combat literature from world Wars I and II, that "the war," or "the government" or some similar abstract, impersonal concept is responsible for the actions of the individuals involved in it. All guilt is collective according to this argument. Caputo feels guilt personally at least in part because he is also conscious of how captivated he is by war, and he documents this attraction throughout the book. In the Prologue he argues that any combat soldier in Vietnam was attracted to the war: "Anyone who fought in Vietnam, if he is honest with himself, will have to admit he enjoyed the compelling attractiveness of combat" (xv). Early in his stay in Vietnam, watching from the vantage point of a hilltop outpost as another company goes on an operation, he longs for combat: "More than anything I wanted to be out there with them. Contact! That event for which so many of us lusted. and I knew then that something in me was drawn to war. It might have been an unholy attraction, but it was there and it could not be denied" (71). After returning home he is reticent when asked about his combat experiences, lying when asked how he felt going into combat for the first time for fear of being thought a war lover, for "The truth is, I felt happy" (81).

His attraction to war is not, however, one-sided. The complexities and paradoxes inherent in it become clear when he explains his return to the front in Part Three: "I cannot deny that the front still held a fascination for me. Perhaps it was the tension of opposites that made it so, an attraction balanced by revulsion, hope that warred with dread." (230) His attraction to war exists in tension with a revulsion for the war and for himself as warrior, a tension which causes him to see combat as a "violent catharsis [he] both seeks and dreads" (294), but the attraction still exists and is consistently acknowledged.

Caputo's self-consciousness about this tension is reflected in his tendency to self-observation and introspection, a tendency which becomes steadily more evident as his increasing dread of combat conflicts with his undiminished desire for combat. And this tendency to self-observation and introspection finds its own cathartic release when he sends a patrol out to make a strictly illegal night-time raid on a hamlet named Giao-Tri (2) and kidnap two young men identified as VC by an informer. Although Caputo's decision to order the capture of these two men arises from deep introspection and an "irresistible compulsion," the men who are to go out on the patrol immediately divine his unspoken thought that "I wouldn't mind if they summarily executed both Viet Cong" (317).

"Yes, sir," Allen said, and I saw the look in his eyes.... In my heart I hoped that Allen would find some excuse for killing them, and Allen had read my heart. He smiled and I smiled back, and we both knew in that moment what was going to happen. (317)

When the patrol returns they have, indeed, killed both men, and further investigation reveals that one of the men they took from the village was the wrong man—they snatched and killed their own informer. Since the return of the patrol the air has "seemed charged with guilt" (320), and the discovery of the terrible mistake clarifies Caputo's sense of guilt:

They had killed the wrong man. No, not they; *we*. We had killed the wrong man. That boy's innocent blood was on my hands as much as it was on theirs. I had sent them out there. My God, what have we done? Please God, forgive us. What have we done? (320)

A complaint is lodged by the villagers of Giao-Tri (2) and Caputo and his men are indicted for murder. Caputo feels guilty, but it is a personal, ethical guilt he feels, not a legal one. He sees his court-martial as a device by which the military intends to absolve itself of all blame:

If we were found guilty, the Marine Corps' institutional conscience would be clear. Six criminals, who, of course, did not represent the majority of America's fine fighting sons, had been brought to justice. Case closed. If we were found innocent, the Marine Corps could say, "Justice has taken its course, and in a court-martial conducted according to the facts and rules of evidence, no crime was found to have been committed." Case closed again. Either way the military won. (323)

Caputo has long debates with Lt. Sam Rader, his defense counsel. He feels guilty that he has, in a sense, killed the boy, but not guilty of murder: "because half the Vietnamese killed in this war have been murdered" (329). He sees himself as a *killer*, not as a murderer. His conception of himself resembles Robert Jay Lifton's conception of the "socialized warrior," the modern corruption of the myth of the warrior-hero. The worth of the socialized warrior "comes to be measured by concrete acts of killing, and by a still more concrete 'body count'.... The socialized warrior thus becomes a distorted, literalized, and manipulated version of the Hero as Warrior. The larger purpose of the heroic quest gives way to a cultivation of skill in killing and surviving" (Lifton 28-9).

American soldiers in Vietnam were not the first socialized warriors, but those who write about their experience tend to see themselves in those terms more clearly and more self-consciously than their predecessors from other wars. Philip Caputo does not see himself as a murderer, but he does see himself as evil: "Something evil had been in me that night....

There was murder in my heart.... And yet I could not conceive of the act as one of premeditated murder. It had not been committed in a vacuum. It was a direct result of the war" (326).

Radar, being a lawyer, sees murder in a more technical sense, and he is not interested in the truth; he is interested in the facts. What matters is what Caputo *said*, not what he thought. The first trial, of Crowe, one of the men on the patrol, results in an acquittal, and the Corps drops all charges against Caputo except the minor one of making a false statement. The facts have set him free, but the truth keeps him a prisoner of the war. While awaiting trial he has decided that he will take whatever comes: "I would not break. I would endure, and accept whatever happened with grace. For enduring seemed to me an act of penance, an inadequate one to be sure, but I felt the need to atone in some way for the deaths I had caused" (332).

Caputo's atonement does not take the predictable form of involvement in the antiwar movement. He joins the Vietnam Veterans Against the War after his discharge and sends his campaign ribbons to Richard Nixon, but his "grand gesture" proves "futile" when the medals are returned to him along with a curt and vaguely threatening note. He cannot participate wholeheartedly in the antiwar movement because he is "both opposed to the war and yet emotionally tied to it" (342). His resolve to atone gets mixed up with the continued attraction war holds for him, and when discharged from the Marine Corps in May, 1967, he "felt as happy as a condemned man whose sentence has been commuted, but within a year I began growing nostalgic for the war" (xiv).

Impelled by this nostalgia, Caputo becomes a foreign correspondent for the *Chicago Tribune*, and in that role he becomes a kind of "ancient mariner" of war, traveling from war zone to war zone and writing about what he has seen. At one point he underlines the continuing tension between his attraction to war and his revulsion toward it when, describing the universality of the stench of death he uses the occasion to parade his credentials as an *aficionado* of war:

...if two people have been dead for the same length of time and under the same conditions, there will be no difference in the way they smell. I first made that observation in Vietnam in 1965, when I noticed that the stench of a dead American made me just as sick as that of a dead Vietnamese. Since then, I have made it again and again in other wars in other places, on the Golan Heights and in the Sinai Desert, in Cyprus and Lebanon, and, coming full circle back to Vietnam, in the streets of Xuan Loc, a city much fought over during the North Vietnamese offensive in 1975. All those dead people, Americans, North and South Vietnamese, Arabs and Israelis, Turks and Greeks, Moslems and Christians, men, women, and children, officer and enlisted, smelled equally bad. (170)

Philip Caputo's post Vietnam career as a war correspondent keeps him tied to his war, but it also renews his connection to other warriors, past as well as present. Unable to put his war experiences behind him he uses them as a fixed base from which he explores the wars of the 1970s, and to which he returns in 1975 at the fall of Saigon. Acutely aware both of what connects him to combat veterans of other times and other wars and of what separates him from them, he and his book help us to begin to map the complex terrain of Vietnam War literature.

Works Cited

Beidler, Philip D. *American Literature and the Experience of Vietnam*. Athens, Georgia: The University of Georgia Press, 1982.

Caputo, Philip. *Rumor of War*. New York: Holt, Rinehart and Winston, 1977.

Chapman, Guy. *A Passionate Prodigality: Fragments of an Autobiography*. New York: Holt, Rinehart and Winston, 1966.

Fussell, Paul. *The Great War and Modern Memory*. New York: Oxford University Press, 1975.

Hellmann, John. American Myth and the Legacy of Vietnam. New York: Columbia University Press, 1986.

Herzog, Tobey C. "Writing About Vietnam: A Heavy *Heart of Darkness* Trip." *College English* 41 (1979-80): 680-695.

Lifton, Robert Jay. *Home From the War: Vietnam Veterans, Neither Victims Nor Executioners*. New York: Simon and Schuster, 1973.

McInerney, Peter. " 'Straight' and 'Secret' History in Vietnam War Literature." *Contemporary Literature* 22 (1981): 187-204.

Sassoon, Siegfried. *Sherston's Progress* in *The Memoirs of George Sherston*. New York: Doubleday, Doran & Co., 1937.

Taylor, Gordon O. "American Personal Narrative of the War in Vietnam." *American Literature* 52 (1980): 294-308.

Section III:
Craft and Techniques

Fact, Fiction, and Metafiction in James Park Sloan's *War Games*

Robert M. Slabey

"And I thought *Catch-22* was fiction"—Philip Caputo

"Where now? Who now? When now?"—Samuel Beckett

When in the 1978 film *Coming Home* Bob (Bruce Dern) is asked what it is like in Vietnam, he answers, "I don't know what it's like. I only know what it is. TV shows what it's like. It sure as hell don't show what it is." A career marine officer, he experienced the shock that the reality of war bears no resemblance to its depiction in books. He is devastated by the gap between reality and language; and he lacks the imagination to describe what it's like. More recently the young protagonist of *In Country* Sam Hughes, the posthumous daughter of a Vietnam casualty, is obsessed with finding "what it was like to be at war over there" (Mason 48). For her, history books are inadequate just as for the Vietnam generation, Walter Cronkite's "the way it was" did not tell the "real" story of the American experience there.

This year many reviewers hailed *Platoon* as *The* Vietnam film because of its authentic depiction of jungle warfare. Nearly everyone agrees that the film is absolutely "real" in recording a time and place: 1967 on the Cambodian border. But over three million Americans served in Vietnam, with the war varying in different areas of the country, even from unit to unit, and the nature of the war changed over time (Karnow 464). Moreover, 86% of Americans never saw combat (Baritz 297). Everyday reality would probably be some Spec 4 shuffling papers in Qui Nhon or some "grunt humping through the boonies" (Leepson 10). After he surveyed some one hundred and thirty novels, John Clark Pratt concluded that *"the* Vietnam novel has yet to be written" (Lomperis 42) and may in fact be an impossibility.

Vietnam was many experiences and had many political interpretations, from Ronald Reagan's "noble crusade" to Daniel Ellsberg's "heinous crime." The depiction of America's longest, strangest war required new devices, structures, styles, even a new language to tell it "like it is." In this essay I will be concerned with the problem of the writer: finding words and strategies to describe places, persons, actions, feelings—both actual and imaginary. The Vietnam writer, moreover, writes in a literary context as well as a historical era, with Vietnam books inevitably sharing elements with postmodernist writing: reflexivity, collage, moral uncertainty, individual "reality," and fictions becoming metafictions. As Vietnam changed the way Americans thought about war, it changed the way Americans wrote about war. "Conventional journalism," Michael Herr wrote, "could no more reveal this war than conventional firepower could win it" (232), and "reveal" is, I think, the operative word for Vietnam writing.

For my purposes, *War Games* (1971) by James Park Sloan is an exemplary work. The nameless protagonist's intelligence condemns him to a desk job as headquarters clerk in Fourth Corps at Can Tho in the Mekong Delta. He will never be in combat (except only once and then only as an observer). The ambience is that of the early years with American "advisers." Sloan, like his surrogate, a college dropout, served in the midsixties, but as a paratrooper. His protagonist did not go to Asia principally to encounter "life" but to gather material for "the definitive" novel of Vietnam: "I thought I might call it *A Small War*. In order to gather material I would disguise myself. I would pretend to be a soldier like everybody else. It wasn't hard" (9-10). As preparation he reads and studies *A Farewell to Arms, All Quiet on the Western Front*, and *The Red Badge of Courage*, thinking that if he reads enough he can shape his life "more like a story." And it "is important only to find out which model of the war novel applies and to write that novel with a maximum of local color from Vietnam" (10). From the start, the reader sees that he lives at a distance, seeing "reality" in terms of literary, film, and television stereotypes.

He finds, however, that Vietnam does not fit models from the past. While his narrative reveals his familiarity with texts from the classics in literature and philosophy to contemporary popular culture, he does not mention three writers whose influence is apparent: Jorge Luis Borges, Franz Kafka, and Joseph Heller.[1] Like Borges his aphoristic prose is ironic and bookish. His nickname had been "Books," and though he survives his tour unscathed, his cherished books suffer mildew. When looking for a Vietnamese "mistress" he naturally selects a librarian. Like the Kafkan antihero, he is isolated, ambivalent, and separated from traditional values.[2] Though he does not include *Catch-22* among his readings, Sloan's satire of the military mind and the military bureaucracy resembles Heller's.[3] For example, the protagonist's request for combat duty is frustrated by his superior's "Catch-22": "Wars . . . are reserved for those who do not want to go" (103).

In addition, Sloan includes many absurd-comedy details. There is a former aide to the commander who becomes a hero: "While a company commander, he called in napalm on his own position. To save face, the army gave him the medal of honor" (188). And mail from home crosses the ocean twenty-seven times before final delivery. Then there is the Christmas entertainment (though it is not Christmas). The protagonist's punishment for asking to be excused from the mandatory attendance order is to carry the star's bags. The comedian, however, thinks that he is a "combat hero who had won under fire the privilege of being his valet," (52) a misapprehension that the general certifies. The protagonist performs some Yossarian-like protests, by not boiling the water for coffee (giving the men diarrhea) and by urinating in the swimming pool. Unlike Yossarian, whose motive is to stay alive, Sloan's protagonist wants to see combat and to have the opportunity to kill. Finally, he receives the Cross of Gallantry for his sole combat experience in which he massacres a squad of South Vietnamese rangers. In this incident he also plays the god-like Author destroying his creatures when they display the brutal impulses that he has been keeping under control.

Furthermore, the general element of "play" is recurrent in *War Games*. The war is played like Monopoly: "They held Pennsylvania Avenue. We've got Park Place. They have the Reading and one other railroad..." (116). A colonel has mock battles with model airplanes. And Major Rachow works out strategy modeled on famous battles: *"Nelson at Trafalgar...Horatio at the Bridge...Stonewall at Chancellorsville"* (155), and, bored with Vietnam, plans an invasion of Canada. In Sloan's vision, life is a game, the playing of roles and the wearing of masks, just as that famous Christmas comedian always plays for money and popular esteem. The elusive protagonist hides behind the disguises of soldier and novelist; his motto is "devise the play, then act in it" (15).

Besides black humor, Sloan recycles stereotypical elements from the Military Novel: boot camp inspections, venereal disease and prophylactics, transoceanic journeys, finicky officers, the military's misuse of language, and (for Vietnam) the invisible enemy and the Vietnamese as mysterious and alien. But unlike most war fictions, the book is metafictive. Instead of directly reporting the action, the narrator watches himself in the process of creating the fiction, calling attention to his pallet of literary tactics and to his playing an invented role in a plot of his own devising. At one point he speculates, "Have I begun inventing things? A man who goes to a war should return with tales to tell. God knows, I would like to take part in tellable stories. Is my life merging with my imagination?" (133). And "Implausibility is my enemy. My life must remain believable, I kept thinking. Will M. buy this?... Would a person if he read about it? I feared that I was tramping, step by step, in the direction of the implausible. Was it possible that my life was becoming like that of a literary device? An actor in a novel, or perhaps a memoir?" (138). And "I'm telling of my experiences as they seemed to me. Later I shall go back and read between the lines" (185).

On one level, his military experience is a self-inflicted psychological joke: "I am here to demonstrate the possibility of my being here" (34). He constantly speculates and contemplates how things could be or might have been. His often-mentioned alter-ego "M" may be, he finally admits, "only a straw man... A figment drawn up inside my head" (185), just as all the people in the book are imagined. "Inside his head" is, ultimately, the only setting and the only reality, as in the novels of Samuel Beckett. On one occasion, he imagines the speech he will give at his homecoming celebration: "There were Indians to the left of me, Indians to the right of me...."(102). Thus in future retrospective, Vietnam will become a cliche Western but in the rhythms of Tennyson's Balaclava—a poem within a myth within a fiction. He almost boasts of the advantage of his aloofness, "living fifteen layers deep beneath the skin" (72).

One of the hero's assignments is to prepare a map of war sites for a visiting congressman. He is proud of his achievement, especially because nothing is black or white, only shades of gray. But his single field experience takes place in a village *not* on his map. Sloan's analogy is between mapping the territory graphically and finding the language to describe "reality," the gulf between words and acts. Of course, the narrator's job as clerk writing combat reports parallels the novelist's situation. Here he develops a paradigm for his reports. In "monthly" reports he merely changes the "names and dates. My premise is that the facts are interchangeable.... I have standardized the statistics as well. No one really reads the reports" (91-92). His "One-of-a-kind" reports, however, require "singularities, innovative mistakes, windfalls, inventions." He improvises not to please the brass—a common practice (Baritz 284)—but for his own pleasure and to impose his design on "reality." Thus facts become fictions that are then accepted as factual. He applies a similar strategy to his personal correspondence with a model letter (like "model" letters from earlier wars): *"Dear—How are you? I am fine. The war, too, is fine. You will pardon me for not writing. I have been the victim of a recurrent—"* (48).

As for the "characters" in the book: most of them are not given names, only letters—Sergeant R, Major DeL *et al.* (an obvious parody of an archaic literary device). And the only persons accorded much human depth are the Quixotic Colonel Rachow and his black assistant K.C. Rachow, who flies helicopters with his eyes shut, carries in his head a textbook of military tactics. Instead of the usual macho motto *(e.g.* "Big Dick from Boston"), he has inscribed on his helicopter lines from

Yeats: "Those that I fight I do not hate/those that I guard I do not love." And like Yeats' poetic "Airman" Rachow "foresees his Death" "Somewhere among the clouds above" (Yeats 135). Some—maybe all?—of K.C.'s colorful life-stories were probably fabrications. Fictions within a fiction. The Rachow sections are the most concrete and lively within an otherwise abstract narrative. At the moment when the narrator sees that K.C. plays Sancho to Rachow he is inspired to see himself as another Cervantes. However the stories of Rachow's and K.C.'s are second-hand and "dubious," but Rachow is accorded an Arthurian finale since his body is never recovered. The Vietnamese characters lack individuation, viewed with condescension as "midgets." He treats his childlike mistress Lwan like "a most desirable toy," misleading her regarding his intentions. But at their last meeting he wonders if it were "Possible that behind her myth of using me she had loved me all along. Possible that behind my myth of using her, I had loved her as well" (82).

Having come to Vietnam to write a combat novel and frustrated by his office job, he contemplates deserting for the battlefield, making, as he says, a "private war," the reverse of that familiar "separate peace" sought by Frederic Henry, Yossarian, and others. His desire to see action is finally fulfilled when he accompanies South Vietnamese rangers to the site of a recent Viet Cong attack. This at last gives him the opportunity to write a vivid description of carnage and devastation. But the episode becomes a descent via helicopter into his Vietnam heart-of-darkness when he annihilates the Allies. The killer emerges from beneath the civilized self, the primitive hate and anger that he had kept hidden, except for a few spiteful eruptions. The incident, like many in Vietnam literature, illustrates how war nurtures the inherent seeds of brutality. But again Sloan gives us a variant on the recurrent village-massacre scene: here those killed are not innocent peasants but venal and vulgar ARVN, and the perpetrator, with his anesthetized conscience, feels neither guilt nor remorse.

As in many realistic narratives, Vietnam again does not permit one to play the role of traditional hero in a noble cause. And on his last day in-country the protagonist avoids the final opportunity to be a "legitimate hero" (184). And, unlike many others, he never experiences enlightenment. His tour was not what he expected nor what he intended. And in the circular conclusion during his return to America on board a trans-Pacific flight he feels only boredom and numbness, as the book comes to its entropic conclusion with the writer running out of words.

Structurally, the book's short chapters are divided into short, sometimes discontinuous, elements. One repeated structural entity is the narrator's visits to the dentist. "The dental bill of rights" described is partly a military joke: "When the army repairs a tooth, it is obligated to care for that tooth for the rest of your life. The adjacent ones as well...by the end of my tour the government is going to be legally responsible for my entire mouth." And partly an ontological problem: is "reality" what happens between dental work or are dental visits "reality"? In addition, his toothaches might be twinges of guilt, with decay a metaphor for the loss of innocence (a device possibly borrowed from Thomas Pynchon). Anyway, not since Poe's "Bernice" and Norris' *McTeague* has there been such dentiphilia! The book is a collage of memories, reflections, dreams, illusions, facts, fictions, the believable and the implausible, all melding into each other, all equally "real," equally "unreal." As a metafiction, it comments on its own fictionality, on the reality of fiction, and on the fictions of identity and reality.

In fine, while *War Games* has many limitations, especially the cynical and nasty protagonist who manipulates people for his private amusement, it is eccentric *and* representative, exemplifying both the perils of fiction and the limits of metafiction in writing about an experience that was itself ambiguous, circular, fragmentary, entropic. *War Games* tells "how it is" by telling it "like it is," experience presented *like* a novel (but not a novel) with a protagonist-narrator who is neither the traditional hero in a war novel nor the traditional narrator of a realistic novel. His single combat encounter is *like* his recurrent dreams of mass murder— or is it a dream? The venerable Chinese *Chuang Tzu* tale is also reprised within the text: A man "dreamed he was a butterfly, and when he woke up, he thought perhaps he was a butterfly who had dreamed he was a man" (83). A reviewer hailed the book as "the *Catch-22* of the 1970s" (Andrews 3926). But lacking Heller's exhuberant inventiveness and affirmation of human values, *War Games* might be rated a "Catch 8½."[4]

Notes

[1]Except for reviews in periodicals, only Philip Beidler has commented on *War Games;* he finds that Sloan "came close for the first time to bringing off a Vietnam metafiction that actually seemed to work" (87).

[2]Sloan's second novel *The Case History of Comrade V* (1972) is even more Kafkan and more Borgesian. Its protagonist, a schizoid monomaniac confined to an institution in a totalitarian state, is provided with a "Case History" that is later exposed as a fiction.

[3]In a 1985 PCA Conference paper William J. Searle explored "The Inspiration on Heller's *Catch-22*" on Sloan's book among other Vietnam novels.

Works Cited

Andrews, Charles R. "Portrait of the Artist as a Young Civilian-Soldier." *Library Journal* 95 (1970): 3926.

Baritz, Loren. *Backfire* 1985. New York: Ballantine, 1986.

Beidler, Philip D. *American Literature and the Experience of Vietnam*. Athens: U of Georgia P, 1982.

Herr, Michael. *Dispatches*. 1977. New York: Avon, 1978.

Karnow, Stanley. *Vietnam: A History*. 1983. New York: Penguin, 1984.

Leepson, Marc. "*Platoon*: The Praise, the Backlash, The Message." *V V A Veteran* 7.3 (March 1987): 10-12.

Lomperis, Timothy J. *"Reading the Wind:" The Literature of the Vietnam War*. Durham, N.C.: Duke UP, 1987.

Mason, Bobbie Ann. *In Country*. 1985. New York: Perennial, 1986.

Sloan, James Park. *War Games*. 1971. New York: Avon, 1973.

Yeats, William Butler. *The Poems: A New Edition*. Ed. Richard J. Finneran. New York: Macmillan, 1983.

"Fact, Fiction, and Metafiction in James Park Sloan's *War Games*" was delivered at the 1987 meeting of the PCA in Montreal, March 24-26.

When Buffalos Fight It Is The Grass That Suffers: Narrative Distance in Asa Baber's *Land of a Million Elephants*

James Quivey

Especially among the early works, no quality in novels of the Vietnam War more clearly separates the few from the many than narrative distance. Whether by artistic choice, because they remained overwhelmed by the experience, or because they felt a moral/social obligation to reveal the worst, most writers remained close to the action; and the resultant you-are-there realism with its accoutrements of heat, blood, death smells, and traditional if sometimes redefined motifs of heroism, cowardice, initiation, racial tension, lifer/draftee conflict, etc. became the standards of Vietnam fiction. The relatively few early novels employing other than realistic modes are therefore refreshing and are, further, individually significant as guidons for the variety and richness that ultimately has come to the genre.

In many respects the best of the exceptions among those early works and certainly the most appealing in tone is Asa Baber's 1970 *Land of a Million Elephants*,[1] a novel that seems more reasonably a product of post-war reflection than of mid-conflict intensity. Set in the mythical kingdom of Chanda—analogue for Laos, a nation descended from the ancient kingdom of Lan Xang, the Land of a Million Elephants—Baber's book evolves from conditions and events leading up to, culminating in, and immediately following Kong Le's 9 August 1960 *coup d'etat* in Vientiane. A near-unknown Captain of a battalion of paratroopers, Kong Le led Neutralist forces in an overthrow of the Royal Lao government, the ancient monarchy: corrupt, earlier supportive of the French, and in 1960 supported by the United States. The novel's theme is positive—in itself placing *Land of a Million Elephants* among the few rather than the many—reassuring: Though deplorable, wars are a part of time, of the universal symmetry; and Southeast Asia, and the world, will survive. This paper will isolate the major techniques through which Baber, drawing a veil of humor, credulity, child-fantasy, historicity, cultural mythos, and opium smoke over both the horrors of war and the contest of wills that tore at American during the conflict, distances himself and thus the reader and allows the story to make the least judgmental, least forced, and most organic thematic statement to be found among the early novels.

The immediately obvious technique is the author's choice of narrative point of view. After addressing the reader in what can be read only as his own voice—"This is the story of how the Crew got together and what they did. Credit to you if you stay with it. Once you've read it, you might even decide to come over to Chanda yourself. In which case come" (13)—the author disappears as completely as author or narrator or presence in any sense as a writer can. The point of view becomes dramatic-objective with occasional slips into omniscience, the latter generally limited to passages providing historical background. No narrator, no character-narrator, no single identifiable, authoritative voice appears in the book for the reader to identify with, object to, be guided by. Quite successfully the authorial stance allows the characters and actions in effect to make free, autonomous statements.

A second, and perhaps in relation to theme the most important distancing technique, is the novel's basic narrative formatting. Baber uses neither uninterrupted chronology nor any of the time/consciousness strategies, nor does he divide his novel into conventional chapters or parts marked by shifts in time, locale, or theme-intent. Instead the novel unfolds as a series of 71 marked segments, the shortest but a few lines, the longest just under eight pages, some segments self-contained, others ordered fragments of longer narrative lines. The four longest contained treatments of sustained actions are Russian Ambassador Nadolsky's comically bungled rape attempt upon the beautiful deaf-mute Dawn ("The perfect woman," Nadolsky says, 61); Danny Campo and Harry Mennan's search for an elephant to purchase as Colonel Kelly's Big Gesture, an elephant-symbol to show American appreciation of Chandan culture; General Grider's war games back in Virginia; and the joint Russian-American-Royal Lao attack upon the people on the Plain of Elephants, an attack that like the rape attempt and the elephant search fails: The Russian tanks slip their tracks and America's Big Bomb detonates weakly and showers the Plain with thousands of mushrooms.

Of actions presented in interrupted sequence, the most memorable begins on page 104, is interrupted on page 106, resumes on page 122. The first segment ends with Andreas, the Greek hotel manager-spy-pimp, having enticed Nadolsky's KGB0-trained secretary away from her radio watch, making love to her. She says "You must hurry, Andreas, for my watch ends in two hours;" and he, entering her, responds, "You set the limit...let me set the pace" (106). The scene then resumes on page

122 as the first sentence of the segment describing Kong Le's attack upon the Royal City: "The first round of illumination caught Andreas in mid-stroke. He grunted in surprise and came. Marya screamed in anger and pounded her heels into his kidneys.   'Wait for me,'   she sobbed over and over" (122).

Baber's narrative structure both effects the distancing he seeks for the reader and reinforces the novel's theme. In the first context, the mix of segments—some short, some longer, some in verse, a few in the form of maxims, one a simple description of popular Chandan dishes—and the balance among the longer segments and consequent lack of a dominating action, preclude any of the book's movement's overwhelming the rest. The impression is that Grider's war games in Virginia, for example, are as significant as the attack upon the Plain of Elephants and that attack no more important than the attack upon Dawn; and in fact they all come to the same thing. Buon Kong points the second context when he says, "Time does not move from past to present to future on a line. Rather it swings like the seasons" (131). So it is in *Land of a Million Elephants* as images, characters, and fragments of narratives appear, fade, and then reappear, not in defined chronology but in a broadly patterned, cyclic rhythm consonant with the thematic statement. The rhythm is underscored especially by the two a-new-day-begins segments, one the first segment in the book, the other, an almost verbatim repetition, positioned near the end as The Crew sets up quarters on the Plain, and, in a multiplicity of ways, life begins anew.

Carefully controlled characterization is a third important technique. Just as no voice and no action are allowed to dominate, no character is permitted to claim either the reader's affection or enmity: There are in the book no conventional heroes, no villains. Even major/minor character distinctions are blurry, and throughout the story attractive qualities among the characters are balanced by features less attractive. The Russian Ambassador is neither more nor less objectionable than the American officers, nor they than Tay Vinh, the North Vietnamese cultural Attache who doubles as an Officer in the Artillery, reconciling his disparate roles by writing a poem entitled "Ode to the Breechblock," nor he than Kong Le, the patriot. By far the closest to a dominating character is Buon Kong, formerly keeper of an elephant for the Royal Stable, and now keeper of the *phi* mythos,[2] elder statesman of the opium den, and one of the mellowest characters not only in Vietnam fiction but probably in all fiction. He speaks often in parables and aphorisms, at one point dismaying his audience with a story that seems to illustrate nothing and responding to their queries, "Well...I am sorry, too, but sometimes my stories don't turn out the way I want them to" (101). Buon Kong, however, dismissed from the court for pomposity, cannot easily be disassociated from the nonsense aura of "the Great Panjandrum himself"[3] from the book's epigraph; and he is, further, less man than fantasy figure or spirit, an extension of the mythos.[4] According to rumor, the elephant Babu is a *phi* of one of Buon Kong's ancestors, and elephant and rider frequently converse "in a strange language" (30).

Brief descriptions of several other characters will illustrate Baber's character equipollence. King Six, whose Laotian analogue would have been King Savang Vatthana, sixth in the line of descent from the time of the 1836 Siamese Expansion, is as harmless and as totally mystified by the activity around him as he is short. His mistress Wampoon, a lascivious young lady who entertains herself on idle afternoons by lying naked on a bed, sprinkling grain on her legs and letting a peacock eat the grain, deserts him to march to the Plain, and he joins the Russian and American leaders in their effort to bombard the travellers back into the city. Baber's description of Master Sergeant Danny Campo, especially, illustrates the technique of balancing positive and negative qualities:

Going on thirty years in the organization [the Marine Corps] he was a walking history book. Captured at Wake Island in World War II, prisoner of war who had worked on the Manchurian Railroad, veteran of the Chosin Reservoir in Korea, French interpreter for American Advisers at Dien Bien Phu, he was, on paper, ideal.

And in life he was truly brave, experienced, energetic. He tried hard to do things by the book. Thus his red-faced dress-blued approach down the main street of Royal City.

But Danny Campo was a beefy, human fuckup. There was always something canted and skewed about him; either a medal pinned on improperly or insignia reversed or instructions misunderstood. It was for this reason that he was shunted out of the infantry billets and led into intelligence assignments. There, it was thought, he would do less harm. (31)

And one final example: Kong Le, Chanda's would-be saviour, seen by his mentor Colonel Kelly as a "crotch-scratching, betel-chewing, phlegm-spitting case of Asian retardation" (46-47), is not without appeal. Herewith a partial scene from a morning briefing with Colonel Kelly:

"Captain, today your men won't bring chickens along, OK? No pots, no mangoes, no nothing. We got C rations for noon chow. OK?"

"Maybe some bananas, OK?"

"Not OK. Nothing."

Kong Le smiled as if this was the best news he had heard that morning. "Maybe cut-up chicken and one pot?"

"Nothing! No transistor radios, no goats or monkeys! Nothing! You can't run a defensive perimeter like a country farm, godammit."

"I fix," Kong Le said. "Never happen."

Colonel Kelly breathed deeply. "One last thing, Captain. Attitude. Attitude. I don't understand why you can't get your boys up for this, get them pissed off, you know? Ready to kill! Just like Quantico, remember? That's why we sent you there."

Kong Le tried to click his heels but one trousers leg had become unbloused and covered his boot. "My boys very pissed off today. The Colonel. They going to kill Communists and protect happy homes. My boys good and pissed today. We fight like tigers who smell flood."

"Blood," said the Colonel. Kong Le smiled and saluted, did an About Face and left the room. His canteen was big as a coconut on his hip and the Colonel wondered what kind of wine the Captain was carrying that day. (48-49)

A fourth distancing technique is Babar's use of echoes from other literature, most generating pleasant associations thus distancing the reader from the War. Leaving their weighty prints throughout the novel are of course the elephants, significant in both Buddhism and the *phi* folk religion which together engender Buon Kong's non-narcotic inspirations, and traditional symbols of strength, wisdom, and longevity. Fittingly, then, among the book's literary echoes, and especially apparent in the segments in which Babu appears, are several from the child-fantasy Babar the Elephant books. Noteworthy in the following two passages, the first from *Land of a Million Elephants*, the second from the Haas translation of the de Brunhoff's *The Story of Babar the Little Elephant*, are the similarities not only of situation and "elephant consciousness" but also of sentence rhythm:

So one day Babu was captured and led down from the great Plain where most of the elephants lived.

When he was first exposed to the noise of the Royal City, Babu was terrified and broke from the caravan....

For an hour Babu roamed the back streets. Once he knocked a small hut off its stilts. He stepped through the vegetable gardens. He crushed a mortar and pestle rice mill. Girls screamed and children laughed to see the Royal Keeper running in fat waddling steps through a rice paddy in pursuit of the elephant. (28)

And from de Brunhoff:

Babar is riding happily on his mother's back when a wicked hunter, hidden in some bushes, shoots at them. The hunter has killed Babar's mother! The monkey hides, the birds fly away, Babar cries. The hunter runs up to catch poor Babar.

Babar runs away because he is afraid of the hunter. After several days, very tired indeed, he comes to a town. He hardly knows what to make of it because this is the first time he has seen so many houses.

So many things are new to him! The broad streets! the automobiles and buses. However, he is especially interested in two gentlemen he notices on the street.[5]

Other echoes of children's literature appear in Buon Kong's parables: The story of the smuggler, for example, is in one version or another a hazy recollection from most childhoods. In Baber's version a man carrying two bundles of rags every day rides ponyback past the border guards. Convinced that he is smuggling, the guards each day frantically but futilely search the bundles. Years later one of the guards, now retired, meets the man, obviously living well, in a Hong Kong bar and begs him to reveal what he had been smuggling. "Ponies," the man replies. Functioning similarly are the tales of Buon Kong's last days at Court, Danny Campo's opium dream, and the description of Danny Campo walking down the street like a Pied Piper "with a crowd of children running after him" (30). In itself a distancing device, the book's epigraph while not from children's literature sounds as though it should be with its "Picninnies," "Joblillies," "Garyulies," and "the great Panjandrum himself." The echoes from children's literature distance the War and do much to establish and sustain the attractive—and necessary—air of credulity.

Child-fantasy echoes give way to echoes from adventure fiction in the rape-attempt scene. Harry Mennan crashes through the door and arrives "with wooden splinters in his shoulders" (64) to foil the attempt; and while he is fighting Nadolsky and Andreas, fighting "like a cowpuncher," (65) Charlie Dog, clinging to a vine, appears on the window ledge and *a la* Tarzan swings off into the garden with Dawn.

Echoes from well-known adult fiction also are many. Few readers, for example would miss the parallels between Hemingway's Jake Barnes/ Bill Gorton picnic in the Basque country and the picnic that ends in Glover's death. Warmed by the sun and the wine, Barnes and Gorton talk nonsense for awhile—the let-us-utilize exchange—then fall asleep by the stream. The experience is nearly identical for Glover, Edelman, and Margaret. They discuss southeast Asian diseases: "—You got three, no, four kind worm, Roundeye," said Walter in mock-Oriental manner. "You got Menu A, hookworm and strongyles. You got Menu B, roundworm and tapeworm. You also got in fortune cookie: trachoma, pellagra—"(109-110). Keats's deserted village echoes through the description of the Royal City following Kong Le's attack, and the journal entry written by a 1636 traveller from the Netherlands is noticeably Gulliver-like. The several other tags of folk tales and cross-cultural myths, the description of the Chandan ruling family—these defy reader-age classifications but help establish not only an air of credulity but also a sense of universality, of cultural kinship.

Providing further distance from the War in much the same manner and contributing to the development of and validity of the book's theme are the many segments asserting the permanence of Chanda and its culture: Chanda has been there for thousands of years, has survived other wars, will survive this one. The first of the history segments, the fourth segment overall in the book, contributes both timelessness and the important equipoise between good an bad:

The history of Chanda is happy and sad.

When the great god Khang came out of the sky and chose his living place many thousands of years ago, he settled in what was to become Chanda. He loved the trees and rivers and hills. He mated with a sea serpent and they had four sons. Three of the sons were OK guys. The fourth was a real shit. His name was Yak. He was short and ugly and his mother dressed him funny. (13)

The earlier noted 1636 journal entry provides another example of the way in which historicity is animated in the novel. The seventeenth century was the Laotian Golden age; and what the Dutch traveller observed of the Chandans has changed little. In the journal he remarks their complacent natures, sexuality, love of narcotics, dancing, ceremony. Past and present are fused. Positioned throughout the book, the historical segments and the description of the countryside, the poppy fields, the recipes, the ceremonies—all contribute to the sense of permanence.

In war the bottom line is death, and the final distancing technique to be discussed concerns Baber's handling of death in *Land of a Million Elephants*. Only one war-death occurs in the novel. Their picnic lunch finished, Margaret naked and Glover and Edelman in only their undershorts lie napping near the river in the sun:

The three of them slept.

Until Glover felt the pressure of his bladder building. He pulled himself away so that he would not wake her. He tiptoes, ludicrously as if he was crossing a creaking floor, towards the thicket line to find a place. "I've got to pee," he kept saying to himself, and then he admonished his stiff dick, begging it to droop long enough for comfort. "Come on," he said to it, "where are you when I need you?"

It was probably his last full thought, for as his foot kicked past a vine his toe caught on a rigid catgut fishline that was tied to a treeroot, and the line led up to the rusted ring of a grenade that was wedged in the fork of the tree he stumbled against, and the ring snapped away with a slight ping-sound that could be heard over the water or the air, and as Walter straightened his back and looked down at his feet to see what had tripped him, the grenade passed through its time-delay and blasted off most of the right side of his head. (111)

With such brief transition from idyllic ease to ultimated violence and with the time-arrested effect created by the prose, the death is the more horrible for its abruptness and in this sense is akin to the battle-deaths in the most vivid of realistic treatments; Baber, however, makes certain that the reader's immediate reaction will not be a lasting one.

First, characterization prevents its being a "full-impact" death. Glover is not a reader-identification character; nearly everything about him, in fact, separates him from the more nearly typical victims in war fiction. He is a statesider, a fawning general's aide on an inspection tour, and, as he says of himself, he is suited not even "to battle over conference tables" (89). And, second and more importantly, Baber begins preparing the reader for the death in the early pages of the novel. An early segment discusses Chandan burial customs:

The mountain people of Chanda are called Lo. They bury their dead high on the hills above the rubber plantations. They make tombstones out of katafa wood. The statues are life-sized. A sort of coitus non interruptus, these carvings, catching all ancestors in the act, unified in death in frozen couplings.

"We praise their love of life. Death is merely a last accident." So says the raja who acts as gatekeeper. (18-19)

Minimizing the significance of death, the segment asserts the death-regeneration continuum. In the description of Glover's death, the conspicuous image of regeneration similarly mitigates death's finality.

Subsequent to his death, Walter becomes not an American dead on foreign soil, but simply a part of the Chandan response to death. Like a "bulky sausage," (123) his body is slung over the back of a pony and taken by the marchers to the Plain of Elephants for burial. Buon Kong says, "Here you see the poppy harvest being taken in, a burial prepared, mothers about to give birth. These are the vital things for us" (133). The body is washed in perfumed water, placed in a coffin, that surrounded by pictures of people making love, and amidst a bacchanal of dancing, feasting, loving it is burned.

It is primarily the life-sex-death continuum that allows the novel's theme to be fully articulated. Three incidents are especially germane, the first two largely comic, the third less so and considerably more pointed and poignant. The first is the previously identified scene in which Nadolsky's moment of sexual completion coincides to the instant with the first burst of Kong Le's military assault upon the Royal City, a scene that is to be mirrored later on the Plain. On an evening shortly before The Crew is attacked by the joint forces, Harry Mennan lies asleep with Wampoon. Hearing reconnaissance planes overhead and knowing they are photographing in preparation for the attack, he reacts with an appropriate gesture of defiance:

He rips the blanket off both of them to show their nakedness. Wampoon yelps and tries to pull the covers back. Mennan laughs and rattles his stiff prong at the sky. "Take a look at that when you get back to the labs, boys!" Wampoon throws a blanket over them and mounts him. (139)

The third incident says essentially the same thing, albeit more poetically. The novel's two most elusive characters are Charlie Dog and Dawn. Charlie Dog comes to Chanda for the poppies, not for the war. In California, halfway through a second prison term for bringing dope back across the Mexican border, he escapes, finances a "little-diddle pot franchise" (20) with money stolen from a laundromat change-maker, and buys a one-way ticket to Chanda. Once there, he manages to leave the opium den long enough to fall in love with Dawn. Nobody knows who Dawn is or why she gets on a plane in Los Angeles and comes to Southeast Asia, but everyone is glad she did:

> In the morning her skin seemed basted in butter. It held the color of oranges. Iridian and prismatic she was, the best of many races. Red heavy lips and eyes that would be as hard to photograph as sand. The slightest Mongol slant to her eyelids, a pug nose, the tall body of a child. (36-37)

Woman mysterious, possessing identity only of gender, she is young, strong, fecund, one more reminder of the continuum. Just before Glover's funeral, Charlie Dog tells her that he would like to "make us a baby" (121); and the day after the funeral celebration—"while the tanks are coming and the bombs are dropping" (142)—they consecrate their love in a "love-sun" ceremony. The segment ends as "the music begins again" (143).

There is of course no mistaking Baber's condemnation of the War or his concern for its victims, especially its Southeast Asian victims: As Buon Kong says, "When buffalos fight it is the grass that suffers" (39). But as a fiction, *Land of a Million Elephants* generates an aura of objectivity that lets *all* the characters and *all* the actions speak to and persuade the reader with muted voices. It is a soft-sell novel in a genre characterized by the hard-sell.

Notes

[1] Asa Baber, *Land of a Million Elephants* (New York: Morrow, 1970). The book's publication was preceded by serialized presentation in the 1970 February, March, and April issues of *Playboy*.

[2] The *phi* cult is an animism substantially predating the official Buddist faith of Laos. Featuring an elaborate network of spirits, or *phi*, this folk religion continues to coexist with, often to fuse with, the conventional religion and to influence the lives of most Laotians. The *phi*, good and bad, exist in bewildering numbers: The four elements have their *phi*; moral principles have their *phi*; souls of the departed are reincarnated as *phi*. *Phi* inhabit the forests, the streams, the bodies of animals, etc., protecting the worthy and punishing the unworthy. See Frank M. LeBar and Adrienne Suddard, eds., *Laos: Its People; Its Society; Its Culture* (New Haven: HRAF Press, 1960).

[3] In *Samuel Foote: A Biography* (London, 1910; rpt. New York: Benjamin Bloom, 1972) Percy Fitzgerald attributes the first use of "the Great Panjandrum" to this minor eighteenth-century dramatist who allegedly wrote the now-famous nonsense speech extemporaneously as a challenge to a lecturer claiming great capacity for memorization:

> So she went into the garden to cut a cabbage leaf to make an apple-pie, and, at the same time, a great she-bear, coming up the street, pops its head into the shop. 'What no soap?' So he died, and she very imprudently married the barber; and there were present the Picninnies and the Joblillies and the

Garolillies and the Grand Panjandrum himself with the little round button at top, and they all fell to playing the game of Catch-as-catch-can till the gunpowder ran out of the heels of their boots. (108-109)

[4]A too-literal reading of Buon Kong may in part be responsible for James Wilson's objections to *Land of a Million Elephants*. In *Vietnam in Prose and Film* (Jefferson, North Carolina: McFarland, 1982), he reads Buon Kong as a "drug cult guru...leading his followers into a neverneverland where the spirits always protect and the good guys always win" and concludes, "Baber seems to imply that if everyone would have followed his guru to the 'Plain of Elephants,' the war would have disappeared" (41-42). Except in a limited aggressive/nonaggressive context, distinctions between good guys and bad guys do not obtain in the novel; and certainly there are no winners, only survivors. The effectiveness of Buon Kong as a fictional character lies in his phantasm: As an Asian and an unlikely "hero," he is mysterious and not wholly accessible, remaining on the periphery of the reader's comprehension and acceptance, but representing the qualities of patience and fortitude that ultimately allow the "grass" to survive.

[5]Jan de Brunhoff; trans. by Merle S. Haas (New York: Random House, 1933), pp. 7-10.

"Narrative Distance in Asa Baber's *Land of a Million Elephants*" was presented at the 1986 meeting of the PCA in Atlanta, April 2-4.

David Rabe's
Theater of War and Remembering

N. Bradley Christie

The playwright becomes more important than the historian, for in no other war
of our history was the private word more important than the public
pronouncements...conflicts within [the soldiers'] own memory...are the very stuff
of the stage.

James Reston, Jr.

In a sense, only a single drama is ever staged in this "nonplace," the endlessly repeated
play of dominations.

Michel Foucault,
"Nietzsche, Genealogy, History"

Before any novel by a Vietnam veteran won a National Book Award,
and before any Vietnam film won an Academy Award, David Rabe's
Vietnam dramas were earning nearly every major prize in the American
theater. Joseph Papp closed a show at the New York Shakespeare Festival
Public Theater to make room for *The Basic Training of Pavlo Hummel*
to open in May, 1971; *Pavlo* won Drama Desk, Drama Guild, and Obie
awards that year. Six months later Rabe became the first playwright
other than Shakespeare to have two of his plays running simultaneously
at the Public. *Sticks and Bones*, the second play, was moved to Broadway
in March; it won Dramatists Guild, *Variety* Poll, and Outer Circle awards,
before garnering the 1972 Tony Award for Best Play.[1] Four years and
three plays later, Rabe was to complete his arresting Vietnam trilogy
with *Streamers*, the New York drama critics' choice for Best American
Play of 1976 and Rabe's most powerful play to date.[2]

This brief catalogue of critical honors is telling, for it highlights
an interesting feature of the early history of the war's burgeoning
literature: in respectable numbers, theater-goers were attending Vietnam
plays years before moviegoers and readers of novels would pay to see
the war again. Any useful bibliography of Vietnam War materials will
list dozens of novels, some of them quite good, written well before the
American public was ready to read them. Within months of David Rabe's

discharge from the U.S. Army in 1967, two major literary figures published novels about Vietnam: Norman Mailer's *Why Are We in Vietnam?* and David Halberstam's *One Very Hot Day*. Other significant novels emerged as Rabe worked to get *Pavlo Hummel* seen by a director who would recognize its promise; James Crumley's *One to Count Cadence* and William Eastlake's *The Bamboo Bed* came out in 1969, James Park Sloan's *War Games* in 1970. Despite the merit of such works, they remained relatively unread until recent years when an expanding sector of the artistic community—and the culture at large—has come to engage itself more intensively with the subject.[3] Meanwhile the professional theater was already exposing receptive audiences to Megan Terry's *Viet Rock* and Barbara Garson's *MacBird* as early as 1967. Joe Papp opened the Public Theatre that year with the controversial American Tribal Love-Rock Musical, *Hair,* which went on to run for 1,750 performances. Ron Cowen's *Summertree* and Arthur Kopit's *Indians* opened the following year. John Guare's *Muzeeka* and Michael Weller's *Moonchildren* premiered as *Pavlo Hummel* ran at the Public in 1971. This trend embodied the theater community's opposition to the war, or perhaps the theater merely viewed "the hot war" as a vehicle for rejuvenating a business in decline. Who was producing and patronizing these plays, anyway? Certainly they attracted numbers of people whose affluence and/ or ingenuity had spared them a tour in Vietnam. Whatever the reasons, the theater and its patrons seemed ready, or at least willing, to confront the volatile issues raised by America's involvement in Indochina a full decade before works in more popular media became best sellers or box-office hits.

This country's professional theater establishment, including producers, directors, actors, and his fellow playwrights, quickly recognized in David Rabe an exceptional talent. That his best work happened to evolve out of his military service in Vietnam was more than fortuitous historical coincidence. Rabe has noted that what he experienced in Vietnam "obsessed" him when he was there and when he returned to the States. Awarded a Rockefeller grant in playwrighting, he planned to postpone his "serious" writing on Vietnam which was to take the form of a novel. "But when I sat down to write, regardless of form," he recalls, "I found it impossible to avoid the things most crowding my mind, and because these memories and ideas were of such extreme value to me, I could deal with them with nothing less than my best effort."[4]

Though not a writer (as Rabe was even before he went to Vietnam), *Pavlo Hummel* encounters that same impossibility in Rabe's first attempt to lend formal shape to his Vietnam memories. Pavlo dies at the end of *The Basic Training of Pavlo Hummel,* but not before he has dredged up the rest of the play's events from his waning consciousness. In *Sticks and Bones,* David returns from Vietnam to play out the things most crowding his mind in the theater of Ozzie and Harriet's living room, a "nonplace" familiar to every American who grew up before or during the Vietnam War. Possessed by the horrors he witnessed before being blinded, David also dies at the end of this play, but not before his bitter rage has called into question the cultural assumptions that shape the Nelson family as a banal American archetype. Finally, in *Streamers* Rabe retrospectively considers how during the war years the specter of Vietnam possessed a generation of Americans then approaching adulthood, and how it affected an older generation raised on more salutary wars. *Pavlo Hummel* and *Sticks and Bones* are both fine plays, skillfully constructed and highly theatrical, nearly Brechtian in their most surreal moments. *Sticks and Bones* especially depends upon stylization and a careful blend of various presentational (i.e., non-"realistic") techniques for its most successful effect.[5] *Streamers* is not as technically unconventional as the earlier plays, but it achieves a dramatic intensity and power unmatched in Rabe's work—perhaps in the whole of contemporary American theater. It remains, simply, this war's most penetrating and compassionate drama.

Streamers is perhaps most immediately striking for its distinct focus on a handful of interesting characters. More singularly than either of the earlier plays, *Streamers* derives its power from the sharp delineation of figures forced to interact with each other in a consistent, contained, and rigidly regulated setting.[6] From the initial impact of that large, confining space "thrusting angularly toward the audience."[7] Rabe deftly begins to define the tensions that drive this play to its violent and powerful conclusion.

The drama opens with Martin, a frightened enlisted man who has just (barely) cut his own wrist because he "just can't stand it" anymore and wants out. His feeble suicide attempt is thwarted by Richie, who intuitively understands the situation and quickly acts to alleviate it. His efforts are interrupted first by Carlyle and then by Billy, both of whom are thoroughly confused by Martin's desperate claims that he has slashed his wrists and Richie's controlled assurances that he hasn't. We quickly see that Martin is merely a device, that he is intrinsically less interesting than the responses his action triggers from other characters who enter before the playwright can shuffle him off the stage forever.

Introducing Richie and Billy in Martin's moment of crisis, Rabe clearly posits the fundamental similarities and differences between these central characters. Although Richie instinctively knows things which Billy is slower to apprehend, both are quick to take action. Both share a physical impulsiveness to participate in Martin's pain, though each acts upon a different motivation. Richie sees past the shallow flesh wound to the threatening fear behind it—"You're just scared. It's just fear," he tells Martin (5). He quickly moves to get Martin out of the confining cadre room, "outside" where that fear can be defused and where it cannot spread among the others who must live there. By contrast, Billy wants to see the blood—"Can I see? I mean, did he really do it?" (7).

At this point, the audience is challenged to answer an obvious question. Richie identifies Martin's problem as fear, but what is it that frightens him enough even to attempt suicide? Martin says he hates the army, and most reader/viewers will satisfy themselves with that answer: what does he fear so much? the army—he says so, twice. But the answer is more complex—or at least more specific—than that, and audiences may easily miss it because Rabe does not provide the clues until after Martin has left the stage altogether. Only then, in a casual conversation between Billy and Roger (Richie and Billy's other bunkmate), does Rabe disclose the real fear that threatens every member of this man's army. Kidding each other about being "more regular army than the goddamn sergeants around this place" (9), Roger suddenly asks, "Don't you think L.B.J. want to have some sergeants in that Vietnam, man? In Disneyland, baby? Lord have mercy on the ole sarge. He goin' over there to be Mickey Mouse" (10). The real fear—not only Martin's, but Billy's and Roger's, and everyone else's in this theater—is Vietnam, a war, as Billy remarks, that "didn't even exist...as a war we might be in" (11) when kids like him received their draft notices. "It don't seem possible. I mean, people shootin' at you. Shootin' at you to kill you.... It's somethin' " (12). Roger and Billy are only the first to articulate the pervasive suspicion that the war itself may be theater, a deadly theater of the absurd, or Disneyland.

Though Martin is long gone by the time Carlyle reappears, Rabe presents the volatile young black radical rather as a photographic negative of the white boy wound too tight. Rapping with Roger, whom he has sought out simply because "This outfit look like it a little short on soul" (19), Carlyle suddenly turns angry, *without warning or transition*, according to Rabe's stage directions. His anger suspiciously echoes Martin's fear: "Oh, man, I hate this goddamn army. I hate this bastard army." Like the reverse image of Martin, Carlyle directs his rage outward, toward others:

They don't pull any a that petty shit, now, do they—that goddamn petty basic training bullshit? They do and I'm gonna be bustin' some head—my hand is gonna be upside all kinds a heads, 'cause I ain't gonna be able to endure it, man, not that kinda crap—understand?

He even appeals to Roger's memory of the 'outside.' "Jesus, baby, can't you remember the outside?... It is so sweet out there, nigger; you got it all forgot." Finally, just as in the earlier scene between Billy and Roger, Carlyle arrives at the real object of his rage, "this whole Vietnam THING—I do not dig it." Again, Rabe's stage notes indicate that this is where *[Carlyle's] anger overwhelms him... And then a real fear pulses through him to nearly fill the pose he has taken* (21).

Posing as a suicide, Martin was overwhelmed by the same fear. Unfortunately, Carlyle is wound even tighter than Martin, and when the fear finally breaks him, he will make good on his promise to strike out at "Some-damn-body!" He hasn't exploded yet, but before the play ends, Carlyle too will vent his frustrations with a knife, and with far more bloody and fatal results. Before the first act ends, Carlyle returns again, this time like a photographic negative of the drunken NCO's ostensibly in charge of these novice soldiers. He enters *drunk and playing*, making war noises, doing "The low crawl; like [he] was taught in basic..." Shortly, *the anger explodes out of the grieving*, and Carlyle once more ironically articulates the dread they all share: "They are gonna kill me. They are gonna send me over there to get me killed, goddamnit. WHAT'S A MATTER WITH ALL YOU PEOPLE?" (50).

Between Carlyle's three appearances in Act One, Rabe intersperses scenes developing the ways in which Richie, Billy, and Roger simultaneously reflect and distinguish themselves from each other. With Carlyle out of the room, they reveal themselves in response to him as they did initially in response to Martin. Individually, they relate dreams to their bunkmates, narratives from their innermost selves, presumably shared to explain—to everyone present, including the dreamer and the audience—who each of these young men is. Struggling with his sexuality, Richie taunts Billy, who vehemently professes absolute confidence in his own, only to have Richie irritate him to distraction:

...I know how you think—how you keep lookin' out and seein' yourself, and that's what I'm trying' to tell you because that's all that's happenin', Rich. That's all there is to it when you look out at me and think there's some kind of approval or whatever you see in my eyes—you're just seein' yourself. (27)

And, true to a pattern that by now is clear, when the tension peaks, the man feeling the most pressure targets its definitive source. When he hears that even Roger, the most level-headed man in the room, has a "screamin' goddamn faggot" story to tell, Billy suddenly asks, "How long you think we got.... Till they pack us up, man ship us out?" Even regular army Roger echoes Carlyle, but without the psychotic distortion:

Do you know I cry at the goddamn anthem sometimes? The flag is flyin' at a ball game, the ole Roger gets all wet in the eye. After all the shit been done to his black ass. But I don't know what I think about this war. I do not know. (30)

Readers who know *Streamers* know that I have so far ignored the two remaining figures central to the play, the dipsomaniacal old-timers, Sergeants Cokes and Rooney, who in the first act enlighten their young charges about the machismo rite of jumping out of airplanes and the occasional misfortune of streamers, parachutes—or jumpers attached to 'chutes—that fail to open. Cokes' relation of the streamer story and the sergeants' drunken rendition of "Beautiful Streamer," "what a man sings, he's going' down through the air, his chute don't open" (42), are among the most poignant moments in the play. This sequence in Robert Altman's 1983 film version of *Streamers* is beautifully executed and features a brilliant performance by George Dzundza as Sergeant Cokes, who uses a crumpled handkerchief to show the young men what a streamer is like, "like a tulip, only white, you know. All twisted and never gonna open. Like a big icicle sticking straight up above him" (41).[8] Clearly, Rabe includes Cokes and Rooney in his first act pattern, presenting them as another set of paired characters at once similar and different, and offering them as patently ironic role models for the novice soldiers composing the rest of the cast. But I want now to consider these two, and especially Cokes, as agents of memory; for it strikes me that in addition to being a play about character, *Streamers* (like *Pavlo Hummel* before it) largely concerns various functions of remembering.[9] And memory functions here in signally curious ways.

Recall, first, the young men's apprehensions, the fact that they can only imagine what doesn't even seem possible to Billy early in the play, the notion of shooting at, and being shot at by, other people. Cokes and Rooney are the only ones around who have experiential memory of war; they are the only ones who have real war stories to tell—that is, war stories based on personal experience. As it happens, Rooney is so caught up in macho posturing and living vicariously through his highly decorated hero-buddy that Cokes emerges as the master story-teller. And Cokes enjoys another distinction that elevates him in Rooney's eyes and secures his role as a model for the others: he has "just come back from the war! The goddamn war!," Rooney announces (36). Cokes is the only character in the play who has been in Vietnam.

Cokes tells several wonderful stories in the play. In Act One he tells the story of O'Flannigan, the paradigm of macho recklessness, who attempted to release his chute lever in mid-air, "then reach up, grab the lines and float on down, hanging." O'Flannigan ended up going "into the ground like a knife" (40). Cokes next tells of "This guy with his chute goin' straight up above him in a streamer... He went right by me. We met eyes, sort of. He was lookin' real puzzled. He looks right at me. Then he looks up in the air at the chute, then down at the ground" (41). Finally Cokes remembers trapping "this little guy in his spider hole," dropping a live grenade into the hole, and sitting on the lid until it went off, with the trapped man "bouncin' and yellin'... Bouncin' and yellin' under the lid. I could hear him and feel him. I just sat there" (42). These three war stories preface Cokes and Rooney's singing of the song, "Beautiful Streamer" (sung to the tune of "Beautiful Dreamer"). For O'Flannigan, the guy whose chute won't open, and the man in the spider hole are all streamers, facing certain death like men, with mettle and bravado. By the end of the scene, we see that Cokes himself is a streamer, too, recalled to the States because he has been diagnosed as having leukemia. Like the protagonists of his war stories, Cokes waits for death, but he is having difficulty maintaining the brand of bravado his macho code demands.

In Act Two Cokes relates two more stories. Unaware that Carlyle has finally snapped, that he has killed both Billy and the foolhardy Rooney (who tried to fend off a knife-wielding psychopath with a broken beer bottle), Cokes stumbles into the cadre room searching for Rooney. He tells Richie and Roger the poignantly funny story of the sergeants' day in town, where they were inadvertently involved in four accidents and fights before returning to the area to play a drunken game of hide-and-go-seek. Waiting, he once more recalls the story of the spider-hole: "Oh, how'm I ever gonna forget it? That funny little guy. I'm runnin' along, he pops up outa that hole. I'm never gonna forget him—how'm I ever gonna forget him?" (108). And he sings the streamer song in *a makeshift language imitating Korean*. That last detail from Rabe's stage directions underscores a crucial fact about Cokes' memory. Moving story-teller that he is, Cokes demonstrates a remarkable knack for remembering and for representing his memories in effective story form. It is striking, however, that of all the war stories he tells, none represents a memory of Vietnam.

Audiences nearly always assume that the funny little man in the spider-hole is Vietnamese, but we must remember Cokes' original telling of the story, where Rooney sets it up by relating how "Cokes got the Silver Star for rollin' a barrel a oil down a hill in Korea into forty-seven chinky Chinese gooks who were climbin' up the hill...." "But the one I remember," Cokes says in the very next speech, "is this little guy in his spider hole...." (41). Consider, then, how Cokes' memory operates. It is readily apparent that his story-telling, like his excessive drinking, is a function of his own fear, that he tells stories to fill the gaps while he waits for his fatal disease to kill him. Dreading the future since he knows what it holds for him, Cokes looks to significant moments in his past in an effort to make sense of the present. For whatever reason/s, Cokes cannot or will not remember his most recent past, that moment of such crucial significance to the other characters in this play. Consistently he substitutes memories of earlier wars for his recollections of Vietnam, exhibiting what I call selective short circuit memory. Urged by Rooney to capitalize upon his recent heroics in the war before this captive audience for whom Vietnam represents the threat of a deadly future, Cokes' memory short-circuits, providing images of earlier, related events, pre-events, as it were, which in effect disarm (or prevent) that deadly threat for the moment.

Rather like the way the war happened to thousands of us who lived through it at home, images of Vietnam are always presented through distorting filters in this play. To recall my earlier metaphor of the photographic negative, Cokes with his short circuit memory functions as the reverse image of Billy, Richie, Roger, and even Carlyle, who (like him) dread the future, but because they do not know what it holds for them. Since the war figures as a likely element of a future to be dreaded, the younger men try to disarm its threat by pre-viewing Vietnam in their collective imagination, their substitute for experiential memory of the event. Imagination, aided by recollection of other experiences (from books, movies, television, etc.), is their filter. Memory, aided by broader experience to choose from, is Cokes'.

First-time readers or viewers often ask what this play has to do with Vietnam. As I hope I have made clear, *Streamers* is a Vietnam play, for the real dangers manifested there inform the entire work. From first scene to last, "this whole Vietnam THING," as Carlyle calls it, defines the tensions that drive the internal mechanisms of every character in the play. Inasmuch as *Streamers* is a play about character, this thing then drives the machinery of the play itself. Inasmuch as *Streamers* is also a play about remembering, it remains a fascinating text with which to explore our culture's recollection of Vietnam as it evolved from deadly potential [what may happen] to deadly reality [what did happen] to deadly reminder [what must not happen again].

Rabe's expansion of the remembering consciousness in this play finally depicts a communal mind, one analogous to that of the viewing audience. Watching (or reading) *Streamers,* a postwar construct after all, audiences necessarily participate in a theater of memory, and for countless viewers the preventing strategies employed by Cokes and his young charges mirror our own. This ultimate extension of the memory theme suggests a vast corporate memory mechanism comprising a network of private recollection activities. In short, Rabe seems to dramatize the cultural memory map narratively figured in a book like Michael Herr's *Dispatches*. Foregrounding the men and their fears rather than the war itself, Rabe sharpens our focus on the cultural context in which the war was fought. Indirectly he subscribes to Herr's notion "that Vietnam was where the Trail of Tears was headed all along,"[10] another (a New) frontier on which to rehearse the endless play of dominations so central to the formation and perpetuation of American culture.

And like *Dispatches, Streamers* partly concerns the function/s of myth as another filter which may distort the map of human memory like the veil that lay over Herr's unreal map of Vietnam. These writers finally seem to propose that a national mythic consciousness may function retrospectively to provide predictable explanations for the way certain events turned out. In *Streamers,* for instance, Billy recalls images of heroes returning from battle as he imagines his own homecoming from Vietnam—"Be a great place to come back from, man, you know? I keep thinkin' about that. To have gone there, to have been there, to have seen it and lived" (30). Shooting and being shot at and the other hazards of war do not figure in Billy's imagined future, and of course his real-life exemplar of a returning hero is Sergeant Cokes, himself a disillusioned product of mythic thinking. In the end, it should come as no surprise that Billy and Rooney die before they ever get to prove themselves in the Southeast Asian jungle: neither one would have survived Vietnam. By extension, neither should events in Vietnam have surprised Americans familiar with attitudes and actions—real and mythologized—from our culture's frontier past. As Michael Herr concluded, "There'd been nothing happening there that hadn't already existed here, coiled up and waiting, back in the World" (268). More vividly than any other drama of the period, *Streamers* portrays that volatile situation of pent-up energies finally unleashed, this time upon ourselves.

The broad reach of cultural memory does not supersede the vital workings of individual recall in its various modes. Indeed, communal recovery is only made possible by private acts of remembering. Likewise, as James Reston, Jr. remarks in his introduction to the first anthology of Vietnam plays, "the very stuff of the stage" derives from conflicts played out within the memory of each soldier who lived the war.[11] David Rabe established himself as a young playwright of promise by recasting his own Vietnam experience in dramatic form, creating characters who in turn play out their own wars in a provocative theater of memory. The remembering process comes full circle, of course, when audiences bring their own internal conflicts to the theater where, as Reston notes, they may test their own perceptions against the concept of history presented in the play. Reston closes his remarks with a summary call for the American theater to "recapture its proper confrontational role," to combat once more the dehumanizing representations of professional history and television.[12] Reston's tone is appropriately spirited here, for what he finds absent from more recent American dramas is the abrupt engagement with current social issues so vital to the theater of the Vietnam playwrights.

From *Hair* and *Viet Rock* to the ensemble creation of John DiFusco's recent *Tracers,* the issues raised by our nation's longest and costliest war have engaged American playwrights, most of them Vietnam veterans, for over twenty years. So far, we have managed to avoid "another Vietnam," but that is not the reason these men and women practice their art. The drama of the Vietnam War is not "about" death and the horrors of war, except insofar as death and the horrors of war are integral parts of human actuality. In the best plays about the war, as in the best works in other media, the artists finally elevate certain episodes or figures into emblems, generally positive emblems, of memory, of human diversity and yet of human solidarity, of the truly remarkable capacity of the human being to endure. The drama of (the) war is "about" the life that is the currency of its perpetuation, and the theater obtains its special power from that same life that is the essence of its form. As the body of novels, personal accounts, poetry, and films about the Vietnam War continues to grow, we can surely anticipate more illuminating dramas presenting more of its diverse realities, for such works already have their powerful precedents.

Notes

[1]In 1968 Norman Mailer's *Armies of the Night* won both a Pulitzer Prize and a National Book Award, but no books by Vietnam veterans were so acclaimed until the mid-1970s. National Book Awards went to Robert Stone's *Dog Soldiers* in 1975 and Tim O'Brien's *Going After Cacciato* in 1978. Academy Awards went to *Coming Home* and *The Deer Hunter* in 1978, and to *Apocalypse Now* is 1979.

[2]I should note that another Vietnam play, *The Orphan* (1972), actually preceded *Streamers*, but it bombed so badly that few people ever saw it, and even fewer consider it as a serious part of Rabe's response to the war. When critics and reviewers refer to Rabe's "Vietnam trilogy," they generally mean *Pavlo Hummel, Sticks and Bones*, and *Streamers*.

[3]See John Newman, *Vietnam War Literature* (Metuchen: Scarecrow Press, 1982). Although already outdated, Newman's seminal list remains helpful, especially since it is carefully annotated. See also John Clark Pratt, *Bibliographic Commentary; "From the Fiction, Some Truths,"* in *"Reading the Wind": The Literature of the Vietnam War* by Timothy J. Lomperis (Durham: Duke Univ. Press, 1987).

[4]David Rabe, Introduction, *The Basic Training of Pavlo Hummel* and *Sticks and Bones* (New York: Viking Press, 1973), xiii, xvii.

[5]See Rabe's note following *Sticks and Bones*, 225-26.

[6]In a sense all of Rabe's plays feature this construct, but in *Pavlo Hummel* Pavlo himself is the only character of any lasting interest. Likewise, in *Sticks and Bones* Ozzie, Harriet, and Rick are purposely (maddeningly) less interesting than David. As for settings, the action in *Pavlo* occurs in too many different places—and "the family home" in *Sticks and Bones* is (again purposely) too familiar—to evoke the intensity of the cadre room in *Streamers*.

[7]David Rabe, *Streamers* (New York: Knopf, 1977), 3. All quotations from the play are cited by page number from this edition. As a rule, I have italicized passages quoted from Rabe's stage directions printed in the 1977 text.

[8]Altman came to *Streamers* after making *Come Back to the Five and Dime, Jimmy Dean, Jimmy Dean* (1982), another stage play featuring a restrictive unit set. In both films Altman retains the single set, overcoming the cinematic limitations with striking attention to ensemble acting and meticulous detail. Clearly, the director's faithfulness to the play's original concept convinced Rabe to write the screenplay.

One of Altman and Rabe's most effective changes in the script was to have Martin reappear in the middle of the film. Here he reminds the viewer of his triggering role as Act Two begins to trip the other explosive devices set in the first act, a metaphor also deployed in the film's opening sequence, where Sergeants Cokes and Rooney playfully detonate a string of firecrackers with which they have booby-trapped a frightened young soldier's bunk. Other details effectively link film and play: the contrast between Richie and Billy's motivations in the opening scene is visually underscored in the film by Richie's clear aversion to the sight of blood; Carlyle's fiery anger profits from the versatility of Altman's camera, proving that speech is indeed a physical action; and, again, George Dzundza stirringly renders Cokes' story-telling power.

[9]See Philip D. Beidler, *American Literature and the Experience of Vietnam* (Athens: Univ. of Georgia Press, 1982), 180-82.

[10]Michael Herr, *Dispatches* (New York: Knopf, 1977; Avon Books, 1978), 51.

[11]James Reston, Jr., Introduction, *Coming to Terms: American Plays & the Vietnam War* (New York: Theatre Communications Group, 1985), x.

[12]Reston, xii. He might have added works like *Rambo* or the Saigon Commando series of pulp novels to his catalogue of Reagan-era misrepresentation.

A Selected List of
American Plays about the Vietnam War

Balk, H. Wesley. *The Dramatization of 365 Days*. Minneapolis: Univ. of Minnesota Press, 1972.

Coming To Terms: American Plays & the Vietnam War. New York: Theatre Communications Group, 1985. [Includes *Streamers,* David Rabe; "Boticelli," Terrence McNally; *How I Got that Story,* Amlin Gray; *Medal of Honor Rag,* Tom Cole; *Moonchildren,* Michael Weller; *Still Life,* Emily Mann; and *Strange Snow,* Stephen Metcalfe]

Cowen, Ron. *Summertree*. New York: Random House, 1968.

DiFusco, John, et al. *Tracers*. New York: Hill and Wang, 1986.

Garson, Barbara. *MacBird*. New York: Grove Press, 1967.

Guare, John. *Cop-Out, Muzeeka, Home Fires: Three Plays*. New York: Grove Press, 1971.

Kopit, Arthur. *Indians*. New York: Hill and Wang, 1969.

Rabe, David. *The Basic Training of Pavlo Hummel/Sticks and Bones*. New York: Viking, 1973.

———. *Streamers*. New York: Knopf, 1977.

Terry, Megan. *Viet Rock and Other Plays*. New York: Simon and Schuster, 1967.

The Past and the Possible: Tim O'Brien's Dialectic of Memory and Imagination

Eric James Schroeder

While a work like Michael Herr's *Dispatches* blurs traditional critical distinctions between fiction and nonfiction, more orthodox works such as James Webb's novel *Fields of Fire* or James Jones' only piece of nonfiction, *Viet Journal*, bear witness to their own generic niche. But even these classifications are complicated. Webb's fiction is so strongly aligned with realism that its end often seems journalistic rather than artistic; Jones' account reflects an even odder tendency—he's so self-conscious of following in his *own* footsteps that *Viet Journal's* concluding chapter actually becomes a kind of gloss to *From Here to Eternity*; it doesn't become fiction but actually swings the other direction and becomes a form of hyper-realism: literary criticism.

Several authors, aware not only of Vietnam's inexhaustable potential as subject matter, but also of its various structural problems and pitfalls, attempt to create different versions of Vietnam's "truth" by offering both fictional and nonfictional narratives. The first of these writers was David Halberstam, whose initial piece of nonfiction, *The Making of a Quagmire,* proved to be a prophetic analysis of U.S. involvement in Vietnam and established his national reputation in journalism. His second treatment of Vietnam, the novel *One Very Hot Day,* appeared well before the floodgates of Vietnam fiction opened and has subsequently remained almost unnoticed. Norman Mailer, who never visited Vietnam, nonetheless has written two books in which Vietnam figures prominently: his nonfictional, award-winning account of the peace movement's march on Washington, *The Armies of the Night* and his controversial fictional allegory, *Why Are We in Vietnam?* Tim O'Brien was the first combat veteran to produce both nonfictional and fictional works which deal with the war. His first account, *If I Die in a Combat Zone,* is a carefully crafted, yet ultimately unresolved memoir; as a memoir it is representative of a large group of Vietnam narratives, typified also by Philip Caputo's

A Rumor of War and Ron Kovic's *Born on the Fourth of July*. These books are sometimes memorable but rarely distinguished. O'Brien's novel *Going After Cacciato* is both.

To appreciate O'Brien's achievement in *Going After Cacciato* let us first examine his problems with form in *If I Die*. To hear O'Brien describe it, one imagines *If I Die* as the product of a process that might be labeled spontaneous generation: "it happened while I was there. Partly I began writing little anecdotes, four or five pages. Not stories but vignettes" (Schroeder 148). Upon returning from Vietnam, "I stitched it together into a book and sent it off." In this description, two things are significant: the lexical significance that O'Brien attaches to "vignettes" and the "stitching," the process of *making* a book. This description assumes even greater significance when we examine the book's generic "placement," for though O'Brien regards the book as nonfiction, many reviewers—indeed, at one point his own publisher—have referred to it as fiction. Now this is understandable in many journalistic works, where the author remains detached from the subject, never presuming to intrude upon his own narrative. The matter becomes more complex with works that are (or purport to be) autobiographical. For example, Hunter Thompson's *Fear and Loathing in Las Vegas* contains a bundle of fictional/nonfictional tensions, but the major dialectic is seen in the polarity between content—which because it is often so outrageous prompts us to believe that it must be fictitious—and form—where the strong authorial viewpoint commands us to view the narrative as fact. Thus in this particular instance, despite all of its wild excesses *Fear and Loathing* is proffered (as well as preferred) as nonfiction. *If I Die's* labeling as fiction is rendered all the more paradoxical by the *Fear and Loathing* example, for while O'Brien's authorial stance is not as megalomanic as Thompson's, the narrative nonetheless depends on the author's first person viewpoint for its formal cohesion; furthermore, his content, his participation in the Vietnam War, though of an order that most of his readers have but secondary experience—through books or media, rather than personal involvement—is presented as a shared experience and, more importantly, as a *believable* one. This is the chief distinction between Thompson's and O'Brien's narratives: whereas Thompson's particular style heightens our impression that what we read is a construct, O'Brien's unadorned narrative compliments his purpose—verisimilitude.

But even verisimilitude doesn't adequately describe O'Brien's achievement; he is not concerned that his narrative represent a series of happenings which were *like* his experience, but that it represent his *actual* experience. His word "vignettes" is meant to suggest just this—slices of actual life. And yet there is an obvious complication here, a problem that O'Brien himself acknowledges. Form. He describes the work's form as "straight autobiography or war memoir," but both of these epithets suggest a historical perspective which the book only partially displays. Interwoven with this traditional, "formal" perspective of historical narrative is another sort of formal perspective, one endemic to fiction which O'Brien labels "scene drawing," a practice, he adds, that "creates the illusion of 'happeningness.' "

Therefore his "stitching" hopes to yoke two different types of narratives, "telling" and "showing," or, as Wayne Booth adds, the distinction between "scene" and "summary" (Booth 154-155). In *If I Die* the distinction is apparent enough. In the first chapter, "Days," O'Brien dramatizes the events of an enclosed span of time (approximately sixteen hours) during a particular patrol. Even within this closed period we can mark off individual, distinct scenes; these are generally denoted by clusters of dialogue accompanied by descriptions of setting, physical activity, and corresponding emotions. Short narrative passages which describe the platoon's movement separate particular scenes yet connect them into a longer one. Through this technique O'Brien achieves a synthesis of form with content that suggests the passage of time; not only do the characters' conversations concern the sameness of the day's events, but the chapter's structure reinforces the notion: conversation assume a repetitive pattern as do events themselves. And while O'Brien's technique involves a degree of "telling" (for instance, the narrator's expressed attitudes toward his comrades), the dominant narrative mode is clearly "showing."

The opposite is true in the second chapter, "Pro Patria." O'Brien "tells" us of his origins, his childhood: playing baseball and war games, Fourth of July celebrations, Turkey day, reading in the school library. His purpose here is obviously not to recreate his youth, but to encapsulate it, to represent it. Thus one of the characteristic differences between the two chapters is seen in the treatment of time: whereas "scene drawing" circumscribes temporality, implying the significance of particular events, historical narrative regards events as points on a continuum that derive their significance from their relationship to other points. Tied into this idea is the problem of when various events actually occur. Although the entire book is written in the past tense, the two modes, as evidenced in "Days" and "Pro Patria," resolve themselves into two distinct types of time: what we might call the "present-past" (scene drawing) and the "past-past" (historical narrative). Seen this way, time in Vietnam is present while events prior to Vietnam are past. And even though we can discern a diachronic time-line for events which happen during the war, we simultaneously sense the synchronicity of events—we recognize that they are happening in a time present which is readily discernable from a time past. In this arrangement the present-past assumes precedence over the past-past; we are naturally more interested in the immediate—

events in Vietnam—than we are in the distant—the pre-war experience. Yet we do not discount the past; we value it as a commentary on the present: it enriches our knowledge of the central character's psychology and introduces and illumines many of the moral issues which are acted out as tableaus in the scene drawings.

Precisely this mixture of scene and summary has caused the book to be viewed as something other than conventional "war memoir." For, in fact, this technique isn't at all new; it's a staple of fiction. One of the novel's historical strengths has been its inclusiveness rather than its exclusiveness; it can accommodate under a single roof a wide variety of style and techniques. This contrast between the novel's heterogeneity and nonfiction's traditional homogeneity defines the perceived differences between O'Brien's *If I Die* and Thompson's *Fear and Loathing*. And although he misses its larger significance, Tom Wolfe is correct in claiming that literary realism's very being begins with scenic construction and that this technique grafted onto factual content has been responsible for the recent proliferation and popularity of the nonfictional narrative. But this structural shift has also generated much of the criticism aimed at the new journalism. Scene construction is viewed as an act of creation, and though new journalists claim only to *re*create scenes which they have witnessed, the memory must sometimes be rescued by the imagination. For instance, O'Brien remarks, "I didn't follow the chronology of the events; I switched events around for the purpose of drama" (Schroeder 136). And though this decision does not constitute a violation of the "facts" *per se*, it does significantly reject their positioning in an actual temporal matrix in favor of their arrangement in an artistic one.

But the best example of this conflation between form/content (and the one most often cited by the new journalism's critics) is dialogue. In the same breath that he asserts "It's not fiction," O'Brien acknowledges this imaginative aspect of *If I Die*: "Often I couldn't remember the exact words people said, and yet to give it a dramatic intensity and immediacy I'd make up dialogue that seemed true to the spirit of what was said" (Schroeder 136). This particular practice represents a junction between structure and substance: O'Brien doesn't just employ a formal, fictional device (dialogue) but the content of the device is fictional as well. We might argue O'Brien's intention as a mitigating factor: in representing the "spirit of what was said," O'Brien asserts a mimetic intent. Thus while the dialogue is obviously a product of the memory, of O'Briens' recreation of the event's historicity, it is equally an imaginative construct, and its dual nature pulls us in opposite directions simultaneously. Let me illustrate this point by using an analogy.

Lennard Davis points out that the prefaces of Defoe and his contemporaries consistently stress the *factual* nature of their works, and he introduces the idea of a "prestructure" which incorporates not only such extra-literary devices as the preface, but also such external phenomena as the audience's expectations. Stressing the significance of this prestructure, he concludes: "The term is used to indicate that this presentational context is actually as much a part of the work as the elements of plot, character development and so on" (Davis 12). In his subsequent discussion of prefaces as devices used to shape audience expectation, he distinguishes between a work like Cervantes' *Don Quixote* where we are initially informed that the work is a product of the imagination, and Defoe's *Roxana* where we are told that all the events transpired as told. Davis maintains that this framing device was problematic for eighteenth century readers. Today, however, these devices pose no such problem for the sophisticated reader who apprehends them as merely conventions of fiction.

When a work lacks a discernible prestructure, its audience is all the more dependent on structure itself to clue our reading of the text. When O'Brien therefore states that though the content is nonfictional "the form of the book is fictional," an audience used to the conventions of the novel will read the book accordingly. A perfect example of this is Erik Hansen's letter, which opens Chapter XIX, "Dulce et Decorum." O'Brien presents the letter as a literal document; it not only provides a thematic perspective on his experience and ideas, but also affirms his own narrative's validity by the letter's obtrusive external commentary. Our response, however, is conditioned by the extent to which we recognize it as a device. Epistolary interpolations are common in fiction. Their origins are bound up with the origins of the novel itself. Like Fielding's prefaces, they were originally intended to heighten our experience of realism: the letter's formal nature was welded to its status as "real" document. But again, while the eighteenth century reader of *Pamela* could often be completely drawn in by Richardson's epistolary mode, a reader of Alice Walker's *The Color Purple* will recognize the structure as a literary convention, and following this, may or may not choose to suspend disbelief. Most readers do not discriminate between structure and substance: if a reader perceives *If I Die* as being like fiction, then it won't matter whether details are made up or not.

Having examined *If I Die*'s structural resemblance to fiction, let us consider the tensions which mitigate against this classification. O'Brien's ultimate concern is moral:

I would wish that this book could take the form of a plea for everlasting peace, a plea from one who knows, from one who's been there and come back, an old soldier looking back at a dying war.

That would be good. It would be fine to integrate it all to persuade my younger brother and perhaps some others to say no to wars and other battles.

Or it would be fine to confirm the old beliefs about war: it's horrible, but it's a crucible of men and events and, in the end, it makes more of a man out of you. (*If I Die* 22)

O'Brien's use and repetition of the conditional "would" is significant: the qualification doesn't signal a contradictory or mitigating belief that these intentions aren't the *best* intentions, rather it indicates doubt over his own efficacy:

But, still, none of these notions seems right. Men are killed, dead human beings are heavy and awkward to carry, things smell different in Vietnam, soldiers are afraid and often brave, drill sergeants are boors, some men think the war is proper and just and others don't and most don't care. Is that the stuff for a morality lesson or even for a theme?

Do dreams offer lessons? Do nightmares have themes? Do we awaken and analyze them and live our lives and advise others as a result? Can the foot soldier teach anything important about war, merely for having been there? I think not. He can tell you stories. (22-23)

The series of direct questions which he poses is both pertinent and revealing; their answers, however—both implicit and explicit—are not so simple as they might appear. The subsuming question, the last one, is the most difficult, for it actually implies two questions: "Is the soldier's purpose to teach?" and "Will we learn from him?" Let us presume to answer the first.

While "entertainment" is perhaps too strong a word to describe a war memoir's overt intention, its covert intent—sometimes stated, often merely implied—is polemic: it seems to either justify or condemn the rightness/wrongness of its particular war, often by juxtaposing it to general and theoretical conceptions of past, present and future wars. (Novelists, of course, often attempt the same thing, simply at one further remove.) For example, in discussing the scene in which the squad blows away the water buffalos, O'Brien notes: "There's a lesson there, and it's told in this 'lessony' sort of way: 'here's what happens to men who get frustrated. They blow away a buffalo. Guess what else they blow away'" (Schroeder 142). This example represents an implicit form of didacticism; even more "lessony" are the explicit, authorial intrusions which occur throughout the narrative. Near the book's outset O'Brien proclaims his own political and philosophical allegiances:

And on top of that was the matter of conscience and conviction, uncertain and surface deep but pure nonetheless: I was a confirmed liberal, not a pacifist; but I would have cast my ballot to end the Vietnam War immediately. I would have voted for Eugene McCarthy, hoping he would make peace. (22)

Passages like this make classification difficult. Even if we ignore the generic question and simply regard the passage as fiction, we are still faced with a question: Is this merely story telling, or does our narrator hope to teach us? Serious literature has always had this twin goal, and the novel's origins in particular are inextricably bound up in its authors' professed moral intentions.[1] Thus fiction doesn't cease to be fiction merely because it is didactic. But if it is overly, self-consciously didactic to the extent that it alienates and subverts the reader from the narrative itself, it will accordingly be less successful fiction. No, the real problem in *If I Die* isn't the *presence* of didacticism, but rather its ultimate *thwarting*. This problem is evident at the conclusion of O'Brien's opening biographical sketch: "It was an intellectual and physical stand-off, and I did not have the energy to see it to the end," and, just prior to his wish that the book might be "a plea for everlasting peace," he admits, "And the stand-off is still there" (22). This notion of a "stand-off," of an ultimate sense of irresolution, informs the text. The irresolution even affects the last scene, the airplane flight home. Despite O'Brien's use of the present tense and second person to suggest a sense of immediacy— this moment becomes time present, relegating even the Vietnam experience to time past—his homecoming offers happiness, not answers. Thus even though much of the book is couched in a style which O'Brien himself acknowledges to be "lessony," the *point* of these "morality lessons" remains unclear, even to the narrator himself. Rather than "lessons," then, these particular instances become "dreams" and the worse ones become "nightmares." And while O'Brien obviously would like to waken, analyze them, and advise others how to live, his own continued incertitude paralyze him. As a last resort, he "tells stories."

If we now return to our earlier observations regarding the text's structure, we can see the difficulty which this irresolution poses. Rather than resolve the tension implicit in the various dichotomies—scenic representation/historical narrative, present-past/past-past, external events/interior consciousness—this moral ambivalence exacerbates them by suggesting that whereas a moral order *does* exist, the text itself cannot decode it; the reader must find it for himself. Ironically, however, the possibility of resolution is not completely extinguished; in place of the moral certitude which he so desires, O'Brien substitutes an aesthetic experience. For even though the "morals" of his "war stories" are gnomic and must be assimilated privately by each individual reader, the very act of rendering personal experience into "stories," suggests a process of ordering and shaping. But ultimately even this act is undercut by the sense of suspended judgment. Let me illustrate this point. Robert Scholes argues that ever since Plato first asked, "What good is poetry *as philosophy*?" other theorists have done much the same, substituting their own disciplines in place of philosophy. Placing the question into what he calls its "proper context," Scholes asks, "What good is fiction *as fiction?*" and then offers this gloss: "The Aristotle of *katharsis* is much closer to the mark than the Aristotle of *mimesis*" (Scholes 23-24). While Scholes' point is, I think, very well taken, he seems to miss the implicit connection between the two. Those forms of representation which are patterned most closely on recognizable, credible, human experience have the most potential for evoking a corresponding emotional response. O'Brien's narrative is not undermined by mimetic failure (we have already noted his success on this score) but rather by a moral problem and an artistic one as well: the absence of catharsis. Thus the vacuum in which we are left results from the story's openendedness, and while such an effect might render the narrative more *real* (reminding us of its other "status" as nonfiction), this lack of closure foils our experience of its *realism*.

*   *   *

Over the next six years O'Brien attempted to resolve these moral and aesthetic problems, initially in his first "real" novel, *Northern Lights,* and ultimately in *Going After Cacciato.*[2] In fact, the whole axis of *Going After Cacciato* balances on the same moral questions which he raises in *If I Die.* And while the book is more clearly in the form of fiction, this alone does not account for its success. Rather, O'Brien has shifted the novel's focus away from *resolution* of Paul Berlin's moral ambivalences to the *process* necessary to reach such a resolution: "The central theme of the novel has to do with how we use our imagination to deal with situations around us, not just to cope with them psychologically, but, more importantly, to deal with them philosophically and morally" (Schroeder 139). O'Brien's choice of Paul Berlin as his central character who must deal "philosophically and morally" with his "situation" in Vietnam reveals the complexity of another large issue implicit in the text: the nature of reality. Even O'Brien's relationship with his fictive character illustrates the metaphysics inherent in this question; in contrasting himself with his character, O'Brien suggests that Berlin is "more of a dreamer...more frightened...more sensitive" and then concludes with this curious assertion: "And I think he noticed more. *Cacciato* is filled with more noticings, more odd detail, than I was able to render in *If I Die,* because there I had to stick to exactly what I saw, and I simply didn't see as much as Paul Berlin did" (Schroeder 142-142). O'Brien is again clarifying the distinction between nonfiction and fiction, but he does so in a way that identifies him with his character. This life-giving impulse surfaces particularly in the discussion of what each of them "saw." The notion of "seeing" is complicated by its description, "more noticings, more odd detail." A practical question arises: How can Paul Berlin "see" more than Tim O'Brien? Even its posing posits an order of existence beyond that which we ascribe to fictional characters. We can, of course, resolve all of this quite simply: Paul Berlin's "seeing" is *not* a recording of actual observed phenomena, but is a product of O'Brien's own imagination. And while this is no doubt what O'Brien meant in the first place, the very *manner* in which he talks about his character suggests the blurring of "reality" which occurs throughout the text.

The problem of time clearly illustrates this point. For while not only many of *Cacciato's* themes resemble those of *If I Die*, so, too, do many of its techniques reveal similarities to the earlier work's. In *Cacciato* we also have a distinction between time past and time present and, while initially it seems the distinction is also clearly signposted within the text's structure, this becomes complicated by the introduction of another temporal dimension: time imagined. Furthermore, there are often few clues for determining not only *when* a particular event happened, but *whether* it happened. Even when we are given a specific date, it may or may not refer to an actual event. Thus, we are told both that Cacciato left the war near the end of October, and that the squad spent Christmas in Tehran. The first "fact" we learn at the outset of the narrative, and at this point, once we have already entered the fictional landscape, there is no reason not to believe it. By the time we are told of Christmas festivities, however, we are aware of the fiction within the fiction. We have learned to tell time.

This learning involves more than clocks and calendars. One of the most important means of recording time is alluded to in the book's opening paragraph:

It was a bad time. Billy Boy Watkins was dead and so was Frenchie Tucker.... Bernie Lynn and Lieutenant Sidney Martin had died in tunnels. Pederson was dead and Rudy Chassler was dead. Buff was dead. Ready Mix was dead. They were all among the dead. (13)

This roster of the dead becomes the key to telling time past. It also becomes the chief component of what Doc Perrit keeps referring to as "the facts." Throughout the narrative, then, Paul Berlin's effort to "get the facts straight" is measured by his ability to put his dead in their proper order. As in Michael Herr's *Dispatches*, this learning to tell time is a complex process which is likewise difficult for us to master. Thus at the end of chapter four we are told this anecdote:

'How many days you been at war?' asked Alpha's mail clerk, and Paul Berlin answered that he'd been at the war seven days now.
The clerk cackled. 'Wrong,' he said, 'Tomorrow, man, that's your first day.'

And in the morning PFC Paul Berlin boarded a resupply chopper that took him over charred pocked mangled country...and places he might die, a million possibilities. He couldn't watch....

'How long you been at war?' asked the first man he saw, a wiry soldier with ringworm in his hair. PFC Paul Berlin smiled.

'This is it,' he said. 'My first day.' (64)

The story appears self-contained: Paul Berlin has apparently learned his first lesson about fear. Not until much later do we recognize the irony: it *was* Paul Berlin's first day at the war. We find the first inkling of the day's true significance in chapter thirty, one of the "observation post" chapters. "He concentrated on the order of things, going back to the beginning. His first day at the war. How hot the day had been, and how on his very first day he had witnessed the ultimate war story" (249). By the time we reach this point, we have learned the rudiments of structural time: to borrow from our discussion of *If I Die*, we might term the observation post chapters time present-present. Everything that "happens" in *Cacciato* happens here. Both time remembered and time imagined emanate from Paul Berlin's "observation" post.

Thus in the next chapter, one of time remembered, or past-past, Paul Berlin concentrates, forcing himself to recall the event which he has tried so hard to suppress: the death of Bill Boy Watkins. For that event, which has become something of a joke among the squad ("scared to death"), is an omen to Paul Berlin, who always recalls it with the same ritualistic phrase "Billy Boy Watkins died of fright on the field of battle." The incantation links him with Billy; he realizes his own capacity for fear, and the possibility that he, too, might end like Billy haunts him. Thus as he remembers Billy's death on the night of his "first" day, he is unable to control himself, and as he giggles uncontrollably, hysterically, it is Cacciato who finally subdues him. But Billy's death also represents a beginning; in the next chapter, another "observation" chapter, he separates himself from Billy:

Billy Boy was dead.
Billy Boy Watkins, like the others, was among the dead. It was the simple truth. It was not especially terrible or hard to think about, or even sad. It was a fact. It was the first fact, and leading from it were other facts. Now it was merely a matter of following the facts to where they ended. (263-64)

Of the chapters that deal with time remembered, with the "facts," most of them thus end with death.

In the observation post—the only place where time seems real, where it is measured in minutes and hours—Paul Berlin tries to find some meaning in the facts. Following "Getting Shot" in which he recalls Buff's death (the final fact), Paul Berlin begins to realize that facts are simply facts:

That was all of them. Frenchie, Pederson, Rudy Chassler, Billy Boy Watkins, Bernie Lynn, Ready Mix, Sidney Martin, and Buff. Six months. A few half-remembered faces. That was the curious thing about it. Out of all that time, time aching itself away, his memory sputtered around those scant hours of horror... Odd, because what he remembered was so trivial and embarrassing. War stories. That was what remained: a few stupid war stories, hackneyed and unprofound. Even the lessons were commonplace. It hurts to be shot. Dead men are heavy.... No new messages. No developing drama or tension or direction. No order. (338)

For a moment we think we are hearing O'Brien himself: "War Stories." Like the narrator of *If I Die*, Paul Berlin is unable to find any underlying meaning in events. They are simply random happenings. Once again the only thing left at the end is war stories. Paul Berlin sees "war stories" as being unable to teach him anything but the most obvious "truths." O'Brien, however, recognizes the necessity of *telling* these truths and of other people listening to them. Michael Malone calls the time remembered chapters "realistic" [Malone's quotations] and asserts that these "threnodies on the deaths of fellow squad members" are "the strongest [chapters] in the book"; he concludes, "In fact, they are so remarkably good and so self-contained that the elaborate visionary plot in which they are placed strikes the reader as an afterthought; evocative, intelligent and well-written, but a novelistic bridge with too many of its braces showing" (128). This assessment misses O'Brien's intention completely.

By the time the reader falls through the hole on the road to Paris, s/he realizes that something out of the ordinary is taking place. And although from the very beginning we are struck by the trek's enormity, O'Brien treats it as if it were an ordinary event: "Early on in the book I try to blur the distinctions between what's real and what's imagined, so that the reader thinks that *all* these things are actually happening" (Schroeder 138). This strategy is so successful that we must retrace events all the way back to the first chapter, looking for the beginning of time imagined. The opening chapter, with its mixture of historical narrative and scene drawing, places us in time and supplies us with what is to become the central fact: "In October, near the end of the month, Cacciato left the war" (14). Even this early in the narrative, O'Brien sows the seeds of imagination. A momentary glimpse of Paul Berlin reveals his nature: "Paul Berlin sat alone, playing solitaire in the style of Las Vegas. Pretending ways to spend his earnings. Travel, expensive hotels, tip for everyone.... Pretending was his best trick to forget the war" (24). During the initial pursuit he focuses his "pretending":

Was it really so impossible? Or was there a chance, even one in a million, that it might truly be done? He walked on and considered this, figuring the odds, speculating on how in the end they might reach Paris. He smiled. It was something to think about. (31)

This initial speculation is the germ out of which the trek to Paris grows. For hindsight reveals that all the events of chapter one really happened; it is in chapter two, the first observation post chapter, that the time frame is introduced, and notions of what is real versus what is imagined are clarified. As Paul Berlin stands guard he attempts to ward off the fear which threatens to overwhelm him:

...it wasn't dreaming—it wasn't even pretending, not in the strict sense. It was an idea. It was a working out of the possibilities...It was a way of asking questions. (46)

And though the questions which Paul Berlin initially poses are all concerned with Cacciato's fate, the underlying questions concern himself.

The distinction between simply "pretending" and this systematic pursuit of "an idea" is crucial to O'Brien's purpose, and illustrated in the reference to Las Vegas. This type of "pretending" is simply escapism—not only does Paul Berlin wish to "forget" the war, but he doesn't want to think about any of its attendant problems and issues. On the other hand, Paul Berlin's (and Tim O'Brien's) "working out of the possibilities" represents a mode of not only coping with the war's reality (paradoxically, through the illusion of escaping it) but also of coming to terms with his identity as a soldier. O'Brien emphasizes that the "experience" of the trek is crucial to Paul Berlin's development:

On one level, I think of [the book's mode] as strict realism; that is, even the so-called surreal sections are very real in a way: one's imagination and day-dreams are real. Things actually happen in day-dreams. There's a reality you can't deny. It's not happening in the physical world, but it's certainly happening in the sense data of the brain. There's a reality to imaginative experience that's critical to the book. (Schroeder 138)

Thus the trek after Cacciato really becomes a search for Paul Berlin's own self. Throughout the book there are subtle linkings between Cacciato and Berlin, but it is in the trek that they are firmly related. The fact that Paul Berlin hunts and that Cacciato is literally "the hunted" is but the superficial yoking of the two; they are intrinsically bound up together in the "idea" of the trek: after a while even Cacciato's desertion loses its firmness in the larger construct of Berlin's imagining. And though Paul Berlin initially justifies imagining as a means of coping with both his fear and his boredom, he gradually intuits what O'Brien makes specific:

One of the important themes of the book is how one's memory and one's imagination interpenetrate, interlock... Beyond that, one's imagination is also a way of goal-setting or objective-setting, of figuring out purposes...The imagined journey after Cacciato isn't just a way of escaping from the war in his head—it's that, too, I'm sure—but it's also a way of asking the question, 'Should I go after Cacciato, really?' ...[T]he imagination is a heuristic tool that we can use to help ourselves set goals. We use the outcome of our imaginings. (Schroeder 138)

O'Brien's remark suggests a kind of synthesis between this dialectical opposition of memory and imagination. And although the actual locus where synthesis occurs is the observation post, we see these two "interpenetrate, interlock" in the continuity expressed by certain motifs in successive time remembered and time imagined chapters. Thus as O'Brien points out, while Paul Berlin is at one moment remembering the time when Bernie Lynn and Frenchie Tucker were shot when they were sent into the tunnel (chapter 9), in the next moment he imagines the entire trek falling into a tunnel on a road to Paris (chapter 10).

The connection between these two chapters is not immediately apparent, and this separation emblematizes the levels on which Paul Berlin's mind is working. The time remembered chapter, to use Malone's term, is so "self-contained" that its relationship to the time imagined chapter (in which Paul Berlin's fear of tunnels becomes realized) only emerges in the succession of chapters 12-14: time present, time imagined, and time past. The first of these chapters pinpoints Paul Berlin's current concern: "The issue, of course, was courage" (101). In a curious sort of way, what is *most* real for him are abstractions. Thus seen only as an *event*, the deaths of Bernie Lynn and Frenchie Tucker have no relationship to him, no relevance for him. The tunnel symbolizes what is unknown, and like so many other things in Vietnam, what is ultimately capable of killing you. Thus the subsequent imagined sequence in the tunnel becomes the means for Paul Berlin to discover what is in it. This chapter, "Falling Through a Hole in the Road to Paris," provides us with the first clear-cut example of the type of unreality which one reviewer compared to the "magical realism" of contemporary South American novelists (Freedman 21). But there is an important distinction to be made between these scenes of "magical realism" in *Cacciato* and a work such as Garcia Marquez's *One Hundred Years of Solitude*. In Garcia Marquez's narrative, "magical realism" characterizes the work as a whole. At any point events may occur which defy rational, "realist" explanations and expectations. In *Cacciato*, however, the instances of "magical realism" have their being not in the actual landscape, but only in Paul Berlin's consciousness. In this sense, then, they are neither truly "magical" nor truly "real." And yet O'Brien's insistence that these events are "certainly happening in the sense data of the brain" should be given full weight; for Paul Berlin what happens in the tunnel is just as real as what happens outside it. Therefore, as he begins falling, he reacts in a way which we learn is characteristic of his fear: he pees himself. Even in his imaginative experience Paul Berin cannot escape fear. When he learns the tunnels' "secret," though, he is able to control that fear:

> He had seen the dead. But never had he seen the living enemy. And he had never seen the tunnels. Once he might have: He might have won the Silver Star for Valor, but instead Bernie Lynn went down, and Bernie Lynn won the Silver Star. He had never seen the enemy or the tunnels, or the Silver Star, but he might have.
>
>   Drowsy now, and yet still excited, he felt himself falling. The fear was gone. (106)

Because the unknown—both enemy and tunnels—has been made known, fear is temporarily vanquished.

Having given the enemy a human face and a cozy habitat, Paul Berlin asks a series of questions which reveal his genuine interest in as well as his susceptibility to war stories ("How did they wiggle through wire? Could they fly, could they pass through rock like ghosts?"). But the section's overriding question, muted here, remains the nature of courage. Paul Berlin tries to reconcile the appearance of courage—in this case the winning of the Silver Star—with the essence of courage— the unspoken fact of Bernie Lynn's death. This process is finally complete as Li Van Hgoc instructs Paul to look through his periscope—what he "sees" is the actual past event of Bernie Lynn's death: chapter fourteen. The periscope provides him not only with a detailed view of the event, but also a new perspective, a position from which to weigh the "value"— both merit and cost—of the Silver Star. Thus what Paul Berlin now remembers is the paralysis which afflicts the squad when Frenchie Tucker is shot. No one volunteers to go after him. Finally, "Bernie Lynn swore violently. He dropped his gear...and he entered the tunnel headfirst. 'Fuck it,' he kept saying, 'fuck it.' Bernie had once poured insecticide into Frenchie's canteen" (112). This, then, is the lesson of "courage"— the essence of the squad's collective frustration and an individual's guilt. And it is the memory, sparked by an act of imagination, which separates the mere *appearance* of courage—the Silver Star—and its substance, once again deferred.

Two books after *If I Die* O'Brien has answered his question "Do dreams offer lessons?" For Paul Berlin they certainly do. Rather than being an "afterthought" the time imagined chapters form a set of antithetical responses to Paul Berlin's past experience of the war. His imagination not only kindles his memory but allows him to interpret past experience, to see meaning where before he saw none. In this way the observation post becomes the fulcrum, the point of synthesis.[3] But the dialectic here is dynamic: any resolution we experience is but temporary and becomes the basis for further questioning. Thus while

Paul Berlin sees many examples of what courage is *not*, only very gradually does he become aware of what it *might* be.

Paul Berlin's effort to establish "order" in these chapters acts as a metaphor for O'Brien's activity as author: "Order was the hard part. The facts even when beaded on a chain still did not have real order. Events did not flow" (248). Indeed, this voice—albeit Paul Berlin's— might be O'Brien's discussing his chronological adjustments in *If I Die*. We can also obliquely discern the larger problem which he never overcomes in *If I Die*—that the "facts" offer neither "order" nor moral resolution: "You add things up. You lost a friend to the war, and you gained a friend. You compromised one principle and fulfilled another" (*If I Die* 198). This summing up, this attempt at resolution by arithmetic, is too convenient a method for disposing with the question that still troubles him at the book's end: "Should I have run away?" Thus in *Cacciato* Paul Berlin's realistic (both remembered and imagined) narrative is mirrored in O'Brien's metafictional quest. For both character and author this quest to establish order and meaning is the same: "That was the end of it. The last known fact. what remained were possibilities. With courage it might have been done" (380). But what is the "it" here? Undertaking the pursuit of Cacciato? Capturing him? Or is the "pursuit," after all, merely a justification for their true activity—desertion? Within the larger structural dynamic of memory/imagination many thematic dialectics are proposed, and this one—the sense of a "mission" versus the fact of desertion—is central for illuminating the meaning of courage. For example, Doc Perret and Captain Rhallon debate the issue of "purpose." Rhallon asserts that in war it is moral purpose—the belief that one's side is right—that keeps soldiers fighting. Doc, however, minimizes the individual's sense of allegiance to greater forms of altruism, concluding, "but a bigger part is self-respect. And fear" (240).

Throughout the time-imagined sections this question of mission/ desertion remains suspended in precarious balance with Oscar and the lieutenant at opposite poles and Paul Berlin suspended between them. Whereas Doc's argument appears simply pragmatic, the expanded version of his advocacy for self-respect through a fear of the consequences reveals its own altruism in the Paris peace conference scene. In it Paul Berlin finally confronts his alter ego, Sarkin Aung Wan, who exhorts him, "Having dreamed a marvelous dream, I urge you to step boldly into it, to join your own dream and to live it" (375). She characterizes this step as "the final act of courage." This is the moment of truth for not just the dream persona, but the real Paul Berlin in the observation post. Previously during the "trek" he has more than once experienced failure of the imagination, leaving himself and his comrades temporarily stranded and often in dire straights. But the largest of these "failures," and the one which he is ultimately *unable* to overcome is seen in his

split with Sarkin Aung Wan. Ironically, Paul Berlin defends his decision
to stay with the mission by asserting, "But, look, it's not realistic to
just run off," a claim which tacitly assumes both the plausibility and
motivation for the completed trek (369). The allusion to "reality" also
underlines the difference between them: Paul Berlin's philosophy of
reality might be summed up as Cartesian: "Thinking is being"; Sarkin
Aung Wan, on the other hand, is closer to Sartre's extension of this:
"Being is doing." Unable to forestall his decision any longer, Paul Berlin
must at last accept the challenge of her position. At the conference scene
itself Paul Berlin elaborates on Doc's notions of fear and self-respect;
he describes his own sense of "obligation," his "explicit consents" as
well as his "tacit promises" to family, friends, town, country and fellow
soldiers. His summation stresses the importance of these social bonds:

The real issue is how to find felicity within limits. Within the context of our obligations
to other people...Even in imagination we must obey the logic of what we started.
Even in imagination we must be true to our obligations, for, even in imagination,
obligation cannot be outrun. Imagination, like reality, has its limits. (377-78)

Several critics have argued that Paul Berlin's speech at the "peace
conference" reveals the *real* defeat of imagination in Cacciato.[4] In part,
this failure of imagination is seen in terms of political expediency by
those for whom Paul Berlin's resolution is simply an unacceptable evasion
of personal integrity and responsibility: "At the same time he dreams
of alternatives to reality, his mind abides by the slogans perpetuated
by his government ('a peace we can live with,' 'national honour,'
'democratic idea')—fictions to which Berlin and all American soldiers
in Vietnam owe a prior commitment. The trap is insidious: " 'national
integrity' *feels* more critical than personal desires, even more than personal
safety" (Saltzman 36). It seems to me that in this indictment personal
politics blinkers critical assessment. For Paul Berlin surely recognizes
his government's limitations—"True, the moral climate was imperfect;
there were pressures, constraints"—and stresses the source of his own
"prior commitment:" "My obligation is to people, not to principle or
politics or justice" (376-77). This is hardly an argument for "national
integrity." Rather, what Paul Berlin expresses are his innermost personal
desires, concluding with a litany of his fears:

I am afraid of running away. I am afraid of exile. I fear what might be thought
of me by those I love. I fear the loss of my own reputation...I fear being an outcast.
I fear being thought of as a coward. I fear that even more than cowardice itself.
(377)

Thus he chooses to "obey the logic of what we started," and implicitly elects the mission's implied order and solidarity over the random and solitary condition of desertion. When Oscar rejects his participation in the second Cacciato ambush, Paul Berlin becomes adamant. And though his behavior in the second ambush parallels his actions in the first, there is a difference: the first ambush, at which Paul Berlin was an ambivalent participant, actually occurred; the second one happens in his imagination. Imagination, which originally provides an escape from the war now proves to be the way back in. And even though Paul Berlin still must wrestle with his fear, he need no longer fear being thought of as a coward. In this sense, imagination doesn't fail. It is, as Paul Berlin contends, "a kind of tool to shape the future," (271) and, as O'Brien echoes, "a heuristic tool that we can use to help ourselves set goals" (Schroeder 138).

In assuming his "obligation," in choosing the path which affords him self-respect, Paul Berlin is indeed indistinguishable from Tim O'Brien. Having described his carefully laid plans to go AWOL in *If I Die*, O'Brien is unable to bring himself to do it, and simply concludes: "I was a coward" (65). This conflict, the book's main locus of tension, is therefore apparently resolved one third of the way through the text, and yet an undercurrent of "what if?" persists. We perceive the seeds of *Cacciato* in the unspoken need to arrive at a more satisfactory resolution: "...if we'd had a raft and courage, that ocean could have carried us a thousand miles and more towards home" (*If I Die* 117). But while O'Brien has spent much of the early chapters describing "home" and his obligations to it, we never really get a sense of these obligations; the community he describes is too much like what we imagine small town America to be—a Norman Rockwell illustration. It might best be described as a "failure of the imagination." Not only are Paul Berlin's feelings better articulated, but his sense of obligation has an objective correlative—the squad. We recall his "tacit promises" to family, friends, town, country, and fellow soldiers—an order which seems to suggest a hierarchy. Thus in *Cacciato* the sense of community, of obligations and responsibilities, is not merely asserted, but dramatized in the squad. Although individual soldiers are named in *If I Die*, few are remembered. In *Cacciato* personalities impress us even before we are formally "introduced" to particular characters. The time remembered sections establish a sense of community: the platoon plays together, fights together, and some die together. In the time imagined sequences the bonds become even more pronounced as the platoon is reduced to a squad. Each individual has a particular function and it is in this milieu that Paul Berlin develops his sense of belonging. In this light, his moral resolution, while perhaps displeasing to liberals, is nonetheless credible.

But just what sort of resolution does *Cacciato* achieve? Certainly, in terms of plot we never do learn what becomes of Cacciato either in fact or in imagination any more than we know Paul Berlin's fate, "whose only goal was to live long enough to establish goals worth living for still longer" (43). Rather, resolution is realized morally and aesthetically both within the text and without it. Within the dialectic of mission/ desertion, resolution is achieved partly because Paul Berlin is able to have it both ways: he runs away and he doesn't run away. Like Hemingway's Henry or Heller's Yossarian, Berlin's role in the war itself becomes increasingly meaningless to him. But unlike Hemingway's hero who has allegiance to neither family nor comrades, or Heller's who has no family and whose friends are dead, O'Brien's is unable to conclude a separate peace, since he recognizes his responsibilities to the living. He feels obligated, a position he shares with O'Brien himself. The question which Paul Berlin asks (and answers) at the peace table is the one which O'Brien leaves unresolved in *If I Die*: "If inner peace is the true objective, would I win it in exile?" (*Cacciato* 377).

O'Brien's own "inner peace" is ultimately achieved in the writing of *Cacciato*. Paul Berlin's activity in the tower becomes a metaphor for O'Brien's own creative act: "The very themes of the book are memory and imagination. In that sense [*Cacciato's*] about how one goes about writing fiction, the fictional process" (Schroeder 143-144). The constraint of facts that O'Brien experienced in *If I Die* is not a problem here; more significant, however, is the degree of interpretation that he brings to *Cacciato*: Paul Berlin learns eventually that events do have meaning, but that he himself must impose it. And this is precisely what O'Brien does—in the end, it is impossible to distinguish between the dreamer and the dream, the writer and the written.

Notes

[1]Davis argues this point at some length. See in particular pages 14-15.

[2]Though the novel's themes concern courage and bravery, Vietnam appears only tangentially in *Northern Lights*. In an interview with O'Brien, Larry McCaffery, discussing *Northern Lights*, calls Vietnam a "muted presence" (141).

[3]O'Brien himself makes a similar point in an interview conducted by Larry McCaffery: "*Cacciato* is structured as a teeter-totter, with the 'Observation Post' chapters as the fulcrum—the present of the book. The teeter-totter swings back and forth between reality—the war experience—and fantasy—the imagined trek to Paris" (139).

[4]See Vannetta 244 and Saltzman 36.

Works Cited

Booth, Wayne. *The Rhetoric of Fiction*. The University of Chicago Press, 1961.

Davis, Lennard. *Factual Fictions*. New York: Columbia University Press, 1983.

Freedman, Richard. "A Separate Peace." *The New York Times Book Review*. (February 12, 1978): 1, 31.

Halberstam, David. *The Making of a Quagmire*. New York: Random House, 1965.

———. *One Very Hot Day*. Boston: Houghton Mifflin, 1967.

Herr, Michael. *Dispatches*. New York: Knopf, 1977.

Jones, James. *Viet Journal*. New York: Delacorte, 1974.

Mailer, Norman. *The Armies of the Night*. New York: New American Library, 1969.

———. *Why Are We in Vietnam?* New York: G.P. Putnam's Sons, 1967.

Malone, Michael. *Harper's* 256. (March 1978): 128.

McCaffery, Larry. "Interview with Tim O'Brien." *Chicago Review* vol. 33 no. 2: 129-150.

O'Brien, Tim. *Going After Cacciato*. New York: Dell, 1979.

———. *If I Die in a Combat Zone*. New York: Delacorte, 1973.

Saltzman, Arthur M. "The Betrayal of the Imagination: Paul Bradeur's *The Stunt Man* and Tim O'Brien's *Going After Cacciato*." *Critique* XXII, i (1980): 32-38.

Scholes, Robert. *Fabulation and Metafiction*. University of Illinois Press, 1979.

Schroeder, Eric James. "Two Interviews: Talks with Tim O'Brien and Robert Stone." *Modern Fiction Studies* vol. 30 no. 1 (Spring 1984): 136-163.

Thompson, Hunter S. *Fear and Loathing in Las Vegas*. New York: Random House, 1972.

Vannetta, Dennis. "Theme and Structure in Tim O'Brien's *Going After Cacciato*." *Modern Fiction Studies* vol. 28 no. 2 (Summer 1982): 242-246.

Webb, James. *Fields of Fire*. Englewood Cliffs: Prentice-Hall, 1978.

Wolfe, Tom. *The New Journalism*. New York: Harper & Row, 1973.

Section IV:
Return and Partial Recovery

Soldier's Home:
Images of Alienation in *Sticks and Bones*

James A. Robinson

In February of 1985, the CBS Evening News began "Vietnam Remembered," a series on the human legacy of the Vietnamese War, by offering profiles of several American veterans. The series was the first of many on Vietnam throughout the country, initiating what *The Washington Post* of April 14, 1985, called "a new outpouring of analyses, reminiscences and catechisms of the 'lessons' of the longest and, save the Civil War, most divisive conflict in American history. It included a flood of books by such as former president Richard M. Nixon (*No More Vietnams*), symposiums by intellectuals, retrospective editions of magazines and newspapers, and specially commissioned opinion polls and sociological musing."[1]

In the same issue of the *Post* were the results of a survey headlined "Poll Finds Veterans Are at Home Again," which reported that "Vietnam veterans appear statistically, and perhaps unexpectedly, to have settled down to lives not unlike those of the veterans of World War II."[2] Most, apparently, had come to terms with the resentment they had felt upon their return to a homeland where their sacrifices were not honored because of violent controversy over the war in which they had served; but the poll failed to mention those whom the war radicalized, the embittered veterans who received considerable media attention upon their return in the late 1960s and early 1970s.

David Rabe was one such alienated veteran, who composed a trilogy of plays between 1967 and 1975 about the enlisted man's Vietnam. *The Basic Training of Pavlo Hummel* (1971), set both in Vietnam and a mythical domestic Fort Gordon, concerns the military training, combat activities, and death by grenade—in a Saigon bordello—of Private Hummel. Expressionistic in technique, the play explores the neuroses of its protagonist, whose "street-kid tough guy" image both conceals his pathetic lack of self-knowledge and precipitates his non-heroic death.[3] The realistic *Streamers* (1975) takes place in an army barracks in Virginia, where a small group of soldiers awaits assignment to Vietnam. Again, the outcome is fatal, as the mounting tension between a radical urban black who opposes the war and a young rural white who defends it climaxes in the latter's death. *Sticks and Bones* (1969) shares with its sister plays the radical conviction that self-delusion and racism played major roles in our Vietnamese involvement, but its cast and setting differ considerably. Borrowing his characters' names from the Nelson family popular on television in the 1950s, Rabe depicts the domestic disruption caused to Ozzie, Harriet and Ricky by the return from Vietnam of David, blinded in action and bitterly estranged from his family. That family— shallow, bigoted and materialistic—cannot comprehend the radical vision offered them by their veteran son. As in *Hummel* and *Streamers*, the outcome appears to be another non-combat death for the young soldier: his family gathers together and slits David's wrists just before the final curtain. But when Ozzie reassures Ricky that David is "only gonna nearly die,"[4] Rabe suggests that the veteran's real fate is re-integration with his family—the microcosm of a society whose ignorance and racism represent the very qualities that (so radicals claimed) lay behind our tragic experience in Vietnam in the first place.

The Nelsons' slaying of their son concludes the series of sensational speeches, gestures and events that structure the play.[5] The shocks begin upon David's delivery (complete with shipping receipt) to his home, where his claim not to recognize his parents and brother establishes his alienation immediately. Accompanying him (though unseen by his family) is Zung, a young Vietnamese woman David loves but has left behind due to fear of his family's reaction and his own bigotry. A projection of David's guilt, Zung reappears periodically (finally becoming visible to Ozzie at the end). Ozzie soon discovers David's affair with Zung, which disgusts him because of his conviction that Vietnamese women have "an actual rot alive in them" (148)—one of numerous references to disease in the play. This relationship, plus David's strange, insulting behavior, soon prompts Ozzie to call the police to investigate his own son.

Ozzie's rage at David is also provoked by Ozzie's own identity crisis, articulated in several monologues addressed to the audience. "I lived in a time beyond anything they can ever know," he laments about his family, "a time beyond and separate, and I was nobody's goddamn father and goddamn husband! I was myself!" (150). The father's confusion and alienation both parallel and contrast his son's. Significantly, neither's unhappiness is understood by Ricky and Harriet. When David attempts to objectify his trauma by showing an imageless "film" of a butchered Vietnamese peasant family, Harriet can only respond, "It's so awful the things those yellow people do to one another" (162). When Ozzie reports a disturbing daydream, his poetic pleas that he's looking for "answers...silent and elusive...like fish" also fall on deaf ears.

"Mom...Dad's hungry...I think," Rick responds. "He wants some fish" (173). As the first act ends, Ozzie profanely berates Ricky for his stupidity, attacks Harriet for bearing David, and slaps David for even thinking of fathering "little bitty chinky yellow kids" for his grandchildren (174). In contrast, David closes by quietly recalling his final moments with Zung: " 'She's the thing most possibly of value in my life,' I said. 'She is garbage and filth and I must get her back if I wish to live. Sickness. I must cherish her' " (177).

The second act begins with a visit from Father Donald, the family priest Harriet has summoned to counsel David. First seen briefly at the start of act one, basketball in hand, trying to persuade Ozzie to join the parish team, Father Donald's second appearance is preceded by two slide projections depicting him in boxing poses. When the priest/athlete appears in person, he announces, "I, a priest, am a psychiatrist as well" (179), making clear his symbolic representation of certain social institutions and activities—organized religion, athletics, psychotherapy— which facilitated the returned veteran's reintegration into mainstream American life. His ensuing session with David, however, fails grotesquely. As he initially attempts to bless David, the latter strikes him with his cane; as he later interprets David's relationship with Zung as "the rejection of one's own race" and self—as "sickness"—David renews the attack, driving the cursing Father Donald from his room (188). Meanwhile, David's secular father's crisis intensifies as Ozzie realizes "there's no evidence in the world of me, no sign or trace," and that even in his own home he "can no longer compel recognition" (193, 203). By midway through act two, then, the two male authority figures—one socio-religious, the other familial—have either shown or confessed their impotence. Symbolically, this suggests the declining moral authority of the elders (in church, state and family) who promoted our involvement in a destructive, futile war; and David, perceiving this disarray, announces to Ozzie "I will be your father," in an attempt to establish a new, more enlightened order (195).

After subsequently asserting his power over his mother by afflicting her with a fever, David announces, "I'm home. Little David...Home," as he turns *"to take possession of the house"* (210). With Zung's aid, he soon captures his father as well: accompanied by an *"eerie light,"* Zung's appearance *"makes Ozzie go rigid, as if some current from her has entered into him,"* and a fever soon prostrates him (212). But David's final verbal attempt to win the weakened Ozzie to his radical cause by persuading him to love Zung—"She is sickness. I must cherish her," he repeats—is defeated by Ricky, who knocks David out with his guitar and awakens Ozzie from his feverish trance. Now seeing Zung, Ozzie strangles her, ridding himself of the virus of awareness she represents. At Ricky's suggestion, the family then gathers to help David slit his wrists and "nearly die." The play concludes with Ricky (whose Nelson family counterpart was a popular rock singer) playing his guitar for David: *"the music is alive and fast. It has a rhythm, a drive of happiness that is contagious"* (273). The reassimilation of the alienated veteran is complete.

The summary above highlights the play's allegorical aspects, which point to the political conflicts in the late 1960s between the older "Establishment" and the young radical pacifists, draft-dodgers and disillusioned veterans—with the Establishment emerging triumphant eventually, absorbing the dissidents back into the mainstream. The play's network of image patterns also comments on this central 60s conflict between age and youth. Since that conflict resulted from and reinforced a dangerous lack of communication between the generations, nearly all the significant images are silent ones.

Opening the play is a short series of slide projections arranged chronologically, beginning with Nelson family ancestors from the turn of the century, then moving through portraits of young Ozzie, his dead brother Thomas, Ozzie and Harriet as a young couple, and David and Ricky as children; the sequence concludes with a "color close-up of David from the last moment of the play, a stricken look," and a slide of Ozzie, Harriet and Father Donald which provides transition into the opening scene (119-20). Commenting on the show are the disembodied, conversational voices of Ozzie and Harriet's grandchildren and their parents, who identify the subjects until the close-up of David:

1st CHILD'S VOICE: What's that one?
    MAN'S VOICE: Somebody sick.
1st CHILD'S VOICE: Boy...! (120)

The slide show and commentary serve several purposes. First, they suggest the power of the family unit by picturing it as an envelope in time, with the future generation of Nelson progeny commenting here on David and his ancestors. That David is viewed as "sick," moreover, introduces the play's central metaphor of disease. But more significant is the non-recognition of David's silent "stricken" face from the last moment of the drama. David's anguish is never comprehended by his family, of course; but the incomprehension by the next generation—for whom David's suffering is alien, since the Man's Voice (presumably Ricky's) refuses even to identify their uncle's adult face—points forward to the continuing indifference to the victimized veterans of a war most American citizens would rather forget.

A primary agent of escape from suffering appears in the next soundless image: the malfunctioning television set. Though *"glowing, murmuring"* in the opening scene (120), the television breaks down following David's return, offering (laments the frustrated Ozzie) "a picture but no sound" (137). Comic irony results from Ozzie's frustration, since the characters' names come from a television family, but the soundless T.V. also has more serious implications. Its breakdown, for instance, points up the similar collapse the family suffers from Ozzie's alienation and David's attacks—attacks from which televised entertainment cannot shield them while the set is out of order. Indeed, during David's climactic verbal assault, Ozzie rushes desperately to the set and starts *"wildly turning TV channels,"* muttering "I'll get it fixed. I'll fix it. Who needs to hear it? We'll watch it" (216). But as partial compensation, Ozzie won't have to hear the news programs on Vietnam, our first "living room war," in which television literally brought home the atrocities of the battlefield and the violent domestic protest against them. The soundless set also symbolizes the non-communication between this television family's members. As Rabe points out in his "Author's Note" to the play,

David throws a yelling, screaming tantrum over his feelings of isolation and Harriet confidently, cheerfully offers Ezy Sleep sleeping pills in full faith they will solve his problem.... The point is not that they do not physically see or hear, but that they psychologically ignore. Though they look right at things, though they listen closely, they do not see or hear.[6]

Rabe's note explicates the metaphorical function of this and other silent images. The Nelsons stare at evidence of disturbance (in both David and Ozzie) and "psychologically ignore" it because (Rabe's note continues) they "do not take things seriously until they are forced to, and then they do it for as short a time as they can manage."[7]

Provoking precisely this response is David's "film" of Vietnam, the most eerily disturbing of the soundless images. David's movie not only lacks sound, it even lacks images: nothing shows but *"a flickering of green,"* read the stage directions (160). A gallows-humorous suggestion of the cameraman's blindness, the film (like the earlier slides) has accompanying narration, here provided by David:

They hang in the greenish haze, afflicted by insects: a woman and a man, middle aged...They are all bone and pain, uncontoured and ugly but for the peculiar melon-swelling in her middle which is her pregnancy, which they do not see...he with the back of his head blown off, and she, the rifle jammed exactly and deeply up into her, with a bullet fired directly into the child living there. They ended each buried in a separate place.... (161; my ellipses)

David can picture and relive the suffering vividly, in his mind's eye;[8] but his family cannot fully "imagine" it (hence the lack of image), can only pull the projector's plug and lecture on the barbarity of "yellow people" (Harriet), or complain that David's film defiles their home ("like this house is a meat house," says Ozzie), or literally run away (Rick). The spectacle of suffering produces empathy for neither the yellow victims nor the white witness, who sees that he is only "a young...a blind man in a room...in a house in the dark, raising nothing in a gesture of no meaning toward two voices who are not speaking...of a certain...incredible...*connection!*" (162; Rabe's ellipses and italics).

David's despairing attempt to communicate here represents a plea for familial recognition of his pain and bitterness and its causes; but none of the family understand. Not surprisingly, they prove equally insensitive to the deepest source of David's pain: the soundless image of Zung.[9] Zung's silence is especially intriguing. Like that of David's film, her wordlessness suggests a suffering that lies too deep for language, as well as the voicelessness of the South Vietnamese, impotent pawns in a struggle between larger powers. Her silence also corresponds to David's own voicelessness, his inability to communicate the complexity and intensity of his overseas experience.[10] But the image of Zung also objectifies racism and its causes. While both David and his parents, we recall, equate Zung with sickness, their attitudes toward this differ. "She is garbage and filth and you must get her back if you wish to live," David lectures his stricken father in the play's final scene. "She is sickness, I must cherish her" (216). With the wisdom of love, David realizes that by cherishing the sickness—i.e., by first recognizing that the evil we attribute to other races actually originates within ourselves, and then accepting that evil—we may free ourselves from blind hatred, and become whole. But Ozzie, standing for an unenlightened bigotry that (the play implies) both contributed to and helped perpetuate our involvement in Vietnam, only comprehends what his eyes can see. "I'm sick of the sight of you," he tells Zung, "...your breath sick with rot...You are garbage and filth. You are darkness. I cast you down. Deceit. Animal. Dirty animal" (217; my ellipses). Refusing to make the connection to his own sickness that David demands, Ozzie strangles not only Zung, but the potential for growth within himself. Shortly thereafter, the family "nearly" kills David—making him a true family member once again by stripping him of his growth potential as well.

The soundless images of the slide projections, the broken television, the silent film and Zung all make visible certain crucial failures to connect; but images also operate on another, invisible level in *Sticks and Bones*, presenting Rabe's diagnosis of a national sickness which predates our involvement in Vietnam. Rabe's note to the play refers to the Nelsons'— and America's—

image of how the perfectly happy family should appear. It is this image that the people in the play wish to preserve above all else.... [David] is keeping them from being the happy family they know they must be. He attacks those aspects of their self-image in which reside all their sense of value and sanity. But, curiously, one of the requisites of their self-image is that everything is fine, and, consequently, for a long time they must not even admit that David is attacking.[11]

The happy familial self-image to which Rabe refers corresponds to that of the television Nelsons who provide the characters' names. The Nelsons, it may be recalled, got into numerous "jams" and "scrapes," but never serious trouble; for in the world of the 50s situation comedy, all problems were minor and easily resolvable into happy endings. The popularity of the Nelson show and others like it ("Make Room for Daddy," "Father Knows Best," etc.) derived largely from the appeal of seeing cheerful family members in non-threatening situations, a scenario reflecting the idealized self-image of the bourgeois family that made up the television audience. In a strategy that resembles Albee's *The American Dream*, Rabe employs the Nelsons as a stereotype with broad recognizability and applicability; he then confronts the happy family, in all its cheerful complacency, with the human legacy (David and Zung) of an historical event (Vietnam) that is no mere "jam," won't admit of easy resolution, and threatens the family's benign self-image. This representative family's solution is to pretend the problem doesn't exist and, when that fails, to "kill" the messenger who brings the bad news.

Rabe also chooses a televised image of a family for another reason, connected with a major source of modern imagery: advertising. Network series have sponsors, of course, and the failure to attract a sufficient number of viewers usually results in a series' cancellation by network executives, who are always conscious of the sponsor's desire to vend its products to the largest number. In a very real sense, then, commercial television performers are salespeople, and the play's setting reflects this: the Nelson's bright, modern home conveys the sense *"that this room, these stairs belong in the gloss of an advertisement"* (120). Appropriately, Ozzie and Harriet launch briefly into sales pitches, he for cigarettes ("I light up—I feel like I'm on a ship at sea," 145-46), she for spot remover ("like snow, which brushed away, leaves the fabric clean and fresh like spring" 201). But the immediate context of Ozzie's speech reveals some disturbing truth about advertising's impact on our values and identities. The parents have just learned of David's relationship with Zung and, after sending Harriet off to scramble eggs for David, Ozzie, *"looking about the room like a man in deep water, looking for something to keep him afloat, sees a pack of cigarettes"*; he tells David he has switched brands. But what begins as a conversational escape from an unpleasant subject quickly turns pathological. As he delivers his commercial, *"his voice and manner take on a confidence; he demonstrates; he is self-assured"* (145). A parody of the assurance of commercial spokesmen, Ozzie's behavior also suggests the psychological security we think we receive from the products we purchase. Of course, this is escapist self-deception (note Ozzie's escape to "a ship at sea"), encouraged by Madison Avenue to promote sales. But Ozzie is so convinced of the sense of identity conferred by merchandise that he expands this behavior in act two, immediately after David has begun to assume domestic control. Ozzie enters with *"an absolute confidence, almost smugness,"* and delivers a long speech, *"a kind of commercial on the value of Ozzie."* Confessing the "feeling of being nothing" that has lately haunted him, he bolsters his self-image by compiling and distributing "an inventory of everything I own" (210-11).

Ozzie's speech cannot prevent the virus of Zung from overpowering him; but his advertisement for himself points to a similar promotion of our escalating commitment to South Vietnam by the government's executive branch in the 60s. Confident (like Ozzie) of victory because of our superior "inventory" of weaponry and manpower, President Johnson persuaded the public—and himself—to deepen our involvement in a foreign conflict related (it was repeatedly argued) to our security. Thus, to both the national and family leader, an abundance of *things* conferred confidence. While admitting of this topical interpretation, however, Ozzie's speech functions more significantly to attack the commercialism that shapes our identities in peace as well as war. The spiritual cost is enormous, for beneath Ozzie's itemized list of assets is his "feeling of being nothing," the "sense of hovering over a great pit" (211). This intuition of nothingness is the root cause of Ozzie's crisis; but (as suggested earlier) he chooses not to blame his false material values, but his family, for snatching him from the time when "I was nobody's goddamn father and nobody's goddamn husband. I was myself!" (150). He feels nostalgia for a past of freedom, individualism, energy and glory for the former running champion Ozzie. "I got a scrapbook of victories, a bag of medals and ribbons," he confides to the audience in an act one monologue. "I was the best there was. I'd beaten the finest anybody had to offer.... If there's a prize to be run for, it's me they send for. It's to be the one-sent-for that I run" (150-51, my ellipsis). Ozzie's conception of his personal past corresponds to our national myth of American history as one characterized by glory, vitality, independence—and pride in never losing a war. David, the veteran of a war where victory eluded us, attempts to pull his father into the present: "you're no longer there; you're here...now." But Ozzie stubbornly insists, "that's not the point, Dave. Where I am isn't the point at all" (151). Here, Rabe indicts the mentality that helped prolong our Vietnamese involvement by taking past, European wars as models for the present, neocolonial one; but on a deeper level, he denigrates the nostalgia for a heroic past that prevents us from grappling realistically with problems of alienation and emptiness in the present.

Ironically, the man who deprived Ozzie of his past integrity and freedom is one he considered his best friend, Hank Greenweller. A shadowy figure who is periodically mentioned in the characters' reminiscences, Hank functions like Ben in Miller's *Death of a Salesman* to point up the father's destructive illusions and false values. Ozzie associates this brother figure with happy memories of love, freedom and victory. In act one Ozzie recalls their final time together, with Hank emerging from a woods—note the vital, natural connotations of the name "Greenweller"—and barely losing to Ozzie in a race. Harriet claims Hank lost deliberately because "he didn't want to ruin all the fun"; Ozzie protests that Hank "had to do his very best. Always...No matter what he did or said, it was always meant and true" (125, my ellipsis). Later it is revealed that Hank introduced Ozzie to Harriet, helped them choose their current house, and once encouraged Ozzie to remain with his family when he had considered leaving them. Thus, to Ozzie Hank represents certain unquestioned values of honesty, competitiveness, love, friendship and family coherence, as well as good breeding—"his parents were good, fine people," he solemnly informs David when his son reports a visit from Hank in California shortly before David's departure for Vietnam (140). But David's memories of Hank contradict his father's. David recalls sitting on Hank's lap as a child, noticing that "his hand was gone—the bone showed in his skin" (139); and when Ozzie attributes this to an auto accident, David reveals that it was actually an early symptom of a congenital disease from which Hank was dying at the time of the California visit. "Why did you make me think him perfect?" he asks his father (141)—prompting the confused Ozzie to change the subject.

The figure of Hank thus functions to underscore David's disillusion with the "perfect" American dream his father has passed on to him. Where his father feels indebted to Hank and worships him, David views him as a betrayer who "has hated us always—always sick with rot" (170). For beneath Hank's apparent robust health and wise guidance is the sickness that permeates *Sticks and Bones*. It engenders the racism that all express toward Zung; it fosters the alienation that prompts David to torment his family, and the family to "kill" him; and it symbolizes the national sickness which (radicals argued) actually mired us in Vietnam, whatever the moral reasons offered by our leaders. Hank's symbolic disease also infects Ozzie, for Hank stifled Ozzie's development as a runner in his youth. Riding a train as a hobo during the Depression, Ozzie sees Hank for the first time in the guise of a brakeman who orders Ozzie to jump. But when he sees Ozzie is a runner, "he moves to embrace me," Ozzie recalls, "and with both hands lifts me high above his head—holds me there trembling, then flings me far out and I fall, I roll. All in the air, then slam down breathless, raw from the cinders" (168). Subsequently befriending him, Hank delivers Harriet, selects their home, and urges Ozzie to remain there for the family's sake. Though Ozzie fails to connect his current malise to Hank's ritualistic sacrifice of him, the congenitally sick Hank had redirected Ozzie's dreams of fulfillment

into the familial, material rut that now entraps him. As usual, only
the blind David perceives this: "He threw you off a fast free train, Ozzie"
he tells him; "He told you gold, he gave you shit" (195). Typically,
Ozzie resists the awareness, and ultimately re-integrates with his family
at the end—where he ritualistically sacrifices the next generation, as he
had been sacrificed before.

In his introduction to the Viking edition of *The Basic Training
of Pavlo Hummel and Sticks and Bones*, Rabe wrote, "I have written
them to diagnose, as best I can, certain phenomena that went on in
and around me. It seems presumptuous and pointless to call them
'antiwar' plays...if there is (as I deeply hope there is) more content
in these plays than the thin line of political tract, then to categorize
them as such is to diminish them."[12] Though I believe the "thin line
of political tract" is somewhat thicker than Rabe admits, my reading
of *Sticks and Bones* essentially concurs with his claim. Clearly, the play
points to bigotry and confusion as bearing some blame for our Vietnam
involvement; equally clearly, it laments the inability of Americans to
comprehend the alienation of its returned Vietnamese veterans, and our
refusal to learn from them. But the many soundless images that structure
the play are not, at their deepest levels, about the historical moment
of Vietnam, but about American society—its values, it myths, its initiation
rituals. The generational conflict between Ozzie and David repeats that
found in numerous modern American theatre classics, from *Long Day's
Journey Into Night* through *Death of a Salesman* to *Who's Afraid of
Virginia Woolf?* and *Buried Child*. Here, the resolution of this conflict
is deeply pessimistic, for in Rabe's eyes the power belongs to the fathers,
and to those who follow them into the mainstream of society. The two
elections of Ronald Reagan seem to confirm this, at least for the 80s;
and the fact that both Reagan and Richard Nixon have lately begun
rewriting history by referring to Vietnam as a military victory suggests
we have not lost our capacity for self-deception, either.

Notes

[1]Richard Harwood and Haynes Johnson, "The War's Final Battle," *The
Washington Post*, April 14, 1985: Al.

[2]Barry Sussman and Kenneth E. John, "Poll Finds Veterans Are at Home Again,"
The Washington Post, April 14, 1985: Al.

[3]The "street kid tough guy" phrase is Rabe's, from his "Author's Note" to *Hummel*
in *The Basic Training of Pavlo Hummel; Sticks and Bones: Two Plays by David
Rabe* (Viking, 1973), p. 110.

[4]*Two Plays*, p. 223. All subsequent quotations from the play are documented
parenthetically within the text.

[5]The play was felt to be so controversial that CBS cancelled a showing of a television version of the play in 1973, rescheduling it for later in the same year—when over half the affiliates refused to carry it.

[6]"Author's Note" to *Sticks and Bones*, in *Two Plays*, p. 225 (my ellipses).

[7]*Ibid.*

[8]My allusion to *Hamlet* (I, ii, l.185) is deliberate, since Shakespeare's play clearly lies behind *Sticks and Bones:* David is, like Hamlet, deeply alienated from his elders, unable to execute his revenge plot against them, more philosophical than those around him—and one who sees a ghost where others cannot. For another Shakespearean source, see Thomas P. Adler, " 'The Blind Leading the Blind:' Rabe's *Sticks and Bones* and Shakespeare's *King Lear*," *Papers on Language and Literature*, 15 (1979): 203-206.

[9]Zung's image, it should be noted, also hints at another connection missed by Ozzie and Harriet: that between the domestic racial conflicts in America's cities in the 60s, and our foreign involvement against people of another race. Rabe sees the connection, as *Streamers* (where a black soldier kills a white one) and *Pavlo Hummel* (where Hummel's alter-ego is a streetwise black named Ardell) make clear—but this particular connection is largely peripherial to *Sticks and Bones*.

[10]This frustration embodies that of his creator, who acknowledged that "all I knew in Vietnam were facts, nothing more: all simple facts of such complexity that the job of communicating any part of them accurately seemed impossibly beyond my reach" ("Introduction" to *Two Plays*, p. xxii).

[11]"Author's Note" to *Sticks and Bones*, p. 225 (my ellipses). For an interesting approach to how Rabe's trilogy reflects Vietnam's impact on both national and personal self-images, see Barbara Hurrel, "American Self-Image in David Rabe's Vietnam Trilogy," *Journal of American Culture*, 4 (1981): 95-107.

[12]"Introduction," *Two Plays*, p. xxv (my ellipsis).

Walking Wounded:
Vietnam War Novels of Return

William J. Searle

"His gun has powerful recoil and he fires it combat style—with a two-handed grip, shooting from a slight crouch," (20) assert the writers of *Newsweek*, concerning the notorious Son of Sam in July 1977. Citing a hand writing expert, they mention the "Marine Corps macho" (21) in the strokes of the killer's note to columnist Jimmy Breslin. For many, many weeks the Son of Sam seemed to fit an already available stereotype of the 1970s, that of the psychotic Vietnam combat veteran. The speculation of the murderer's background, however, differed from the reality of David Berkowitz's life, as *Newsweek* admitted on August 22, 1977. "But instead of the Vietnam trauma or street hardened police career some had expected, Berkowitz's past offered only a noncombat tour in Korea and eight months volunteer work inside a Bronx station house" (16). The image of the crazy Nam vet is one that several of the more recent novelists of the Vietnam War, those writing of the returning veteran, contend with and succumb to.

Before an analysis of the "sick vet" image in Charles Coleman's *Sergeant Back Again* (1980), Robert Bausch's *On the Way Home* (1982), and Stephen Wright's *Mediations in Green* (1983), some discussion of the predominant attitudes toward returning veterans in the 1970s, the fictional world of the novels, will provide a context for those works. In their thorough anthology *Strangers At Home: Vietnam Veterans Since the War*, Charles Figley and Seymour Leventman point out that just as "glorious wars produce heroic veterans," so too do "inglorious wars produce anti-heroes, even villains and deviants" ("Introduction: Estrangement and Victimization" xxi). The North Vietnamese Tet Offensive early in 1968, the Chicago police riot against anti-war protesters during that summer, the American invasion of Laos and the consequent Kent State murders in 1970, and especially the revelation of the My Lai massacre in 1969 contributed to make the conflict in Vietnam the least popular war in American history. After exposure of My Lai, news stories were quick to mention that perpetrators of crimes were Vietnam veterans

147

to account for "psychopathic actions" (Figley and Leventman xxvii), a tendency which persists in the 1980s. "For the most part," Myra MacPherson notes, "the public hears only of the 'crazed' veteran stereotype, reinforced every time a headline points out the ex-marine who holds up a liquor store or holds a wife hostage" (218). Television prime time police programs, according to Figley and Leventman, furthered the "negative image of veterans by portraying them as major antagonists—addicts, rapists, mass murderers, and particularly offensive criminals" (xxviii). Norma Wikler in "Hidden Injuries of the War" concurs, "Television, especially, portrayed Vietnam veterans as crazed killers coming back hooked on drugs or disposed toward uncontrollable violence" (104). Motion pictures followed suit with a repertoire of fine actors portraying crazed combat vets—Bruce Dern in *Black Sunday* and *Coming Home*, Christopher Walken in *The Deer Hunter*, Marlon Brando and Dennis Hopper in *Apocalypse Now*. It is Figley and Leventman's contention that "anti-war sentiment of their authors" influenced "many early psychiatric studies" so that "vets were portrayed as pathetic victims of the war, but nevertheless personally disorganized, problem ridden, and potentially dangerous" (xxix). Of course, attention on the faults of veterans reinforced the "sick vet" image. Whatever the origin of the stereotype, mentally healthy Vietnam veterans shared the stigma of those psychologically wounded.

Ambushed at home, returning combat soldiers, reminders of "dishonor and embarrassment" (Figley and Leventman xxvii) feared hostility and blame from their peers who did not fight in an "immoral" war and also suffered from a lack of respect by veterans of earlier wars who blamed them for not winning a war against a military inferior. Norma Wikler notes that "never before had America's men returned home so quietly and so unwelcomed" (103). While many returning soldiers began to fear and even dislike civilians; many civilians in turn feared and disliked them as possible threats to domestic tranquility. "The passions of the Vietnam War," Charles Moskos reminds us, "carried over into the popular imagery of returning service men" (82-83). Apprehensive civilians in the 1970s were concerned that veterans would also import the popularized evils of the Vietnam War—"heroin addiction, incurable strains of venereal disease, a propensity for violence, in addition to their own skills of destruction developed in combat" (Figley and Leventman xxvii). The cultural milieu supported these fears, for in the print media, "television, movies, novels, and scholarly studies, veterans were stereotyped variously as crazy, guilt-ridden, drug addicted, violence prone, alienated, and bitter" (Moskos 83). Given American disgust with the war, it is understandable that the "sick vet" image found a receptive audience, even among some returning veterans. In a unique switch from earlier American wars, during the Vietnam conflict, several anti-war veteran's groups formed, organizations which often received considerable media attention. Perhaps guilt-ridden, perhaps seeking in an oblique way, respect and deference, otherwise denied them, many of these anti-war vets substituted stories of atrocity for the usual heroic tales told by veterans of more noble conflicts (Moskos 84). "By speaking out against the war," Guenter Lewy writes, "they could hope to improve their rapport with the dominant currents of opinion in the society they were re-entering" (319). While not denying that atrocities were committed, Myra MacPherson points out the possibility of embellishment, even pure invention, in some of the veterans' stories, "Some were, no doubt, fabricated for the benefit of the media, overly willing to portray them as lost souls" (215). In any case, suspicions of the cruelties of Vietnam, embodied in the vets themselves, were reaffirmed.

There were, however, other realities for the returning veterans in the 1970s, but these realities are not dealt with by Coleman, Bausch, and Wright—the novelists under discussion. The American economy in the 1970s was not prosperous enough to absorb all veterans into its labor force. While draftees sacrificed time, limb, or psyche, or any combination of the three to a war of dubious value, many of those not selected for military service forged ahead occupationally or professionally in a competitive society. For those veterans wishing to further their education, Uncle Sam did not really pick up the tab. Educational benefits contained in constant dollars less than half of the benefits of the GI Bill of World War II. To underline the common sense of avoiding military service, the federal government's "postwar amnesty program was less generous to soldiers who received bad discharges than to draft evaders" (Moskos 83). In the 1970s "it expanded grants and loans to students who had not served in the military," and "in 1978 the administration sought to curtail veteran's preferences in the civil service" (Moskos 83). Though the media made much of drug addiction in Vietnam, "the vast majority who had become addicted to narcotics in Vietnam, a small portion to begin with, had abandoned their drug habits upon their return to the states" (Moskos 83), a fact which has received little attention in the media or in the fiction.

Instead of concentrating on a harsh economic reality or drug reform, Coleman, Bausch, and Wright return to the stereotype of the "sick vet," but use it to comment on the nature of the war and to depict the major struggle of the returning servicemen—the attempt to regain a sense of dignity, a sense of self-respect, in an alien environment. The journey home of all three protagonists—Coleman's Andrew Collins, Bausch's Michael Sumner, and Wright's James Griffin—has been disrupted, for all have been broken in some way. Stateside for all three returnees is the America of the 1970s, a time of disillusionment with the war on the part of many civilians and soldiers. Charles Coleman's urge to reveal in *Sergeant Back Again,* Robert Bausch's emphasis on compassion in *On the Way Home,* and Stephen Wright's focus on a partial homecoming in *Meditations in Green* explain that disillusionment and its consequences upon those returning from Vietnam.

Coleman's desire to reveal the impact of the horrible absurdities of Vietnam upon American survivors is clearly implied in his didactic Foreword to *Sergeant Back Again:*

I did not *make* this story; it came that way, ready-made, defined by historical circumstances, generated by the soldiers who have had to fight the most insidious and intimate battle: the one with yourself. That battle, which has become part of a new consciousness in the American mind, has one hopes—just commenced. Indeed, the lessons for us to learn are not in the vacant battle-fields of South Vietnam or Cambodia.... The lessons are within us the living...if we would only look.... In writing this book, I am mainly a chronicler who has [sic] left no choice but to try to speak for the inarticulate, the psychically scarred, and the wasted....

As the Foreword suggests, the setting of the novel is a psychiatric ward, Chambers Pavilion, Fort Sam Houston, in San Antonio, Texas. The patients, though traumatized, are conscious of their scars. "We all brought home an infection. It'll be around for a long time" (119), says one during a group therapy session. Another veteran delineates a basic assumption of the novel, that no one returned from Vietnam uninjured: "You come back, maybe, but you sure as shit don't come back right. You're maimed, one way or the other" (141). Given this situation, the focus of the novel is on the internal struggle of veterans, particularly the turmoil of its protagonist, Andrew Collins, to regain the sanity to return to normal civilian life.

But Coleman encloses Collins' story within a larger purpose—to reveal how so many soldiers became psychically injured. Essential to Coleman's purpose is Captain Pollard, "a thirty-year-old Asian-history prof who left Berkeley and enlisted, only to end up supervising the torture of the very people whose culture" (64) he most revered. Pollard inspires Collins, a medical school dropout and Wright, a college graduate in chemistry, "to turn an utterly destructive experience into a constructive product" (63). Just as when one has "an urgent dispatch that must get through," he sends out more than one man, so the three inmates form a pact, one which they hope will give "purpose and strength," a reason to escape from Chambers Pavilion. Pollard suggests that the inmate to attain freedom promise to reveal to the entire world an important tale, why and how soldiers became demented as well as why Americans were failing in Vietnam, a tale similar to the one Coleman himself attempts to write. Though Collins doubts that the indifferent American public would listen, by the novel's end, Coleman notes, "Forty-eight hours after his boarding,''...Collins "began to write about himself and Pollard and Captain Nieland" (237).

Obsessed with repairing broken men, Collins steps over the edge when one of his ex-patients returns with a fatal wound. His psychiatrist, Dr. Nieland, explains Collins' disease: " 'They're all compensating for losses.... They do that in a variety of ways. Only in his case, he developed an anthropomorphic obsession by trying to compensate in behalf of other soldiers in the most tangible terms.... He compensated for others' losses by substituting his own fictionalized anatomy until there was nothing left of his own identity" (90). The situation for Collins and those like him is a serious one, for if they do not recover within 90 days, they become permanent residents of a V.A. asylum. Collins' situation is further complicated by his past anti-war activities while in the service and his possible future court martial for treason.

During the late 1960s and early 1970s, disenchantment with the war caused many soldiers to confront the implications of their own acts. Coleman's Dr. Nieland is aware of this internal stress on veterans returning from Vietnam, " 'Never in the history of this country has the American fighting man ever felt that he had to justify his presence in a foreign country to *himself*, as well as to his peers when he came home" (92). Perhaps to avoid this stress and to feel justified, Collins became an active participant in an underground anti-war group, the ESR, Every Soldier's Responsibility. His duties included disclosing classified information to the media, namely CBS. In particular, Collins revealed the discrepancies between the official field reports of enemy fatalities and actual eyewitness accounts, exposing incidents of fraud, torture, and murder. But truth-telling, in Coleman's novel, has its consequences, as Collins learns during an interrogation: " 'The ESR was directly responsible for at least eighteen to twenty-two-hundred American casualties' " (208) during the time Collins served that underground group. In short, the ESR created casualties that surgical specialists like Collins treated. Captain Pollard, the former intelligence officer, summarizes the circle of absurdity for Collins:

I helped to create the casualties that you later tried to bring back to life while you were out gathering evidence against men like me while other jokers were running around trying to find evidence against you. The circle jerk. All of which creates more dissension, more casualties, more psychosis, more atrocities, more trials, more insanity,—which brings us back to Chambers Pavilion.... (62)

Dr. Nieland views the inmates as "victims of a moral catastrophe" (91). Brought up in an atmosphere of idealism, Americans were later forced to witness and in some cases participate in the annihilation of both Vietnamese and Americans. According to Nieland, the conflict between an idealistic upbringing and the reality of jungle warfare would result in "lethal disintegration of person," a sure passport to Chambers Pavilion. Coleman illustrates, however, that the conflict caused stress for older veterans as well, as one thirty-nine year old career soldier asserts: " 'What I thought was right and what the Army said was right were the same for the past twenty years. Then I go to Nam and wake up one morning and I knew one of us was wrong' " (167).

Much of the novel is composed of scenes in which doctors and aides attempt to expose inmates to "normal" activities—watching television, attending group therapy sessions, dances, religious services, or taking a field trip. While most of these episodes illuminate, the group therapy sessions are the most informative. In one session, Wright, a chemist responsible for defoliating swaths of jungle with Agent Orange, expresses the impact of the war on himself and those men like him, " 'If you go doing things like killing people and you're not sure what you're doing is right, then you're playing Russian roulette with your sanity' " (119). Yet while in Vietnam it was difficult for soldiers not to be antagonistic toward South Vietnamese, since many of those in uniform were either cowardly or ineffective and so many civilians were apparently in sympathy with the enemy. When Dr. Goldfarb in one therapy session uses the phrase " 'bad attitude toward Asians,' " "half the patients slid off their chairs and fell to the floor in fits of laughter" (168). One veteran amidst tears of laughter, manages to say of a fellow inmate: " 'Prout loves the fuckin' gooks. We all do!' " after which "another round of hysteria swept over the group" (168). Coleman suggests a parallel between racism in Vietnam and a type of unconventional warfare in the United States. " 'Can you imagine,' " asks Major Clifford Olsen, an officer relieved of his command, " 'guardsmen wasting our own kids on a campus in Ohio in the 1970s and the politicians saying, basically, that the kids got what they deserved' " (172). From this perspective, protesting students became enemies, "gooks." "Supported by much of public opinion," write Seymour Leventman and Paul Comacho, law enforcement "units conceived of their foes as inferior beings and therefore expendable. One result was official killing of both students and blacks at Kent State, Watts, Jackson State...." (68n). Attendance at these group therapy sessions where racism and murder are discussed fill the sensitive Collins with self-loathing.

War for Collins is one of "reflection, not action" (157). Imagining a phone call to his father, Collins catalogues deception, corruption, meaningless sacrifice, which broke American spirit, pride, will to win, and ultimately will to live. He concludes, "We destroyed ourselves over there. Not the V.C." (155). As American soldiers died one way or another, as Collins believes, for nothing, so did Collins' efforts to restore them to health also amount to nothing; as his patients became dismembered, so too did Collins disintegrate. The reintegration of Collins is a gradual one, climaxed by his symbolic construction of a universal soldier made from the clay of a stream bed. Coleman would have his audience believe that in assembling this clay effigy of all Americans killed and wounded, Collins was putting himself back together. Similarly, dressing the clay soldier in his own shirt, Collins was returning to civilian life by removing his military identity. Once removed from Chambers Pavilion, he realizes that making sense out of nonsense is "not the futile plea of a madman" (236).

As Coleman's *Sergeant Back Again* is the story of a veteran's release from a mental institution, Robert Bausch's *On the Way Home* deals in part with a soldier's eventual return to it. Bausch's novel complicates the basic situation of the returning veteran—that both home and homecomer have changed. As sociologist Alfred Schuetz notes:

> The home to which he returns is by no means the home he left or the home which he recalled and longed for during his absence. And, for the same reason, the homecomer is not the same man who left. He is neither the same for himself nor for those who await his return. (119)

But Bausch creates a story which develops this change of home and veteran to its logical extreme. His protagonist Michael Sumner was first reported dead, then released from the Army as an escaped P.O.W. " 'troubled' and even 'slightly unstable' " (15). Reacting to their son's reported death, his father, Dale, retires early and both he and his wife, Anne, leave Chicago to start a new life in Florida. Given this new situation, "Michael's first day home was like a play in which everyone forgot the lines" (21), any promise of peaceful retirement shattered.

While the novel explores the pain parents and son experience as strangers to each other, other residents of sunny Florida have also been touched by the Vietnam War. The brother-in-law of Michael's sympathetic employer was killed in Vietnam and his mutilated body left in the jungle. Eddie, Dale's best friend, lost two sons in that same war. Of greater importance to the novel, Lucy, the young wife of a retired neighbor was first married to a marine, who, as she says, " 'came back so fucked up he didn't know who I was' " (40). Even more significant to the plot is Dale's casual meeting with a one-armed combat veteran who tells war stories in exchange for free beers. One story that Michael's father cannot forget deals with a combat vet that " 'went into a supermarket and grabbed a can of grapefruit juice and a bag of pistachios and walked up to his hotel room and started firing a pistol down the street' " (74).

Even before encountering the talkative one-armed soldier, Dale, hurt by and fearful of the stranger his son has become, perceives Michael as in some way criminal, "Michael comes in too slowly—as if he is on some solitary voyage of crime" (13). Later pondering his conversation in the bar, Dale tells Anne, " 'He's going to do one of those things loners do.... Assassinate a president. Axe-murder somebody...' " (68). The image of his son on the brink of violent crime becomes an obsession with Dale, "Michael would explode and assassinate somebody, he was sure, but he didn't know what he or anyone else could do about it" (77). Dale's fears are echoed by Lucy's husband, Ben, " 'Well, Ben says sometimes men who are unstable do crazy things' " (105). Even Anne, Michael's understanding and patient mother, briefly envisions Michael slashing bodies. Such apprehensions make homecoming for Michael Sumner a truly difficult adjustment.

Whether unable or unwilling to communicate, Michael himself does very little to alleviate their fears. According to Norma Wikler, "the capacity for intimacy was often damaged by the experiences of war" for many a Vietnam veteran (105). This burden of "re-establishing close personal ties" (93) is particularly acute in Bausch's novel, for Michael Sumner has been severely traumatized by his experience as a prisoner of war. Having lost his capacity for affection, Michael takes long walks, stares at the ocean, occasionally refuses his mother's compassion, and reveals his innermost thoughts to a tape recorder, which he frequently and significantly misplaces. Afraid *for* his parents, Michael also explains his incapacity to articulate his trauma to his psychiatrist, " 'I'm afraid I'm going to be afraid' " (61). Events in the novel support his fears: Fourth of July fireworks cause him to jump into a nearby ditch, wartime memories force him to immerse himself in the ocean like a fish, innocent questions concerning his experiences stimulate shaking and moaning. At one point, Michael admits, "I shouldn't have lived. I shouldn't have come here" (196), a wish occasionally shared by both his parents. Leaving the psychiatrist's office, Michael reveals his alienation in a strange land, "I want to go back home. Instead, I go to the door and cross the street into the park and head for my father's house" (62).

The potentially healing powers of love and intimacy are further obstructed by veterans of earlier wars. Full of self-pity Dale is repulsed by and impatient with his son's apparent lack of willpower. When Michael breaks down in front of Eddie, Dale's fishing buddy, Dale is embarrassed enough to listen to Eddie's hasty generalizations. According to Eddie, a tough World War II combat veteran, soldiers in Vietnam are too sensitive, too easily influenced by the trauma of combat because " 'they've had it too easy' " (48). His loss of two sons in a no-win war requires scapegoats. " 'There's no manhood anymore,' " Eddie says and then reflects, " 'I guess it'd be pretty hard to be a man when everybody else is acting like a sissy' " (47). Eddie's analysis of the homefront is as limited, as he points out that anti-war congressmen are acting like communists. Though Dale, who spent World War II stateside in Georgia, is less harsh, he sees an essential contrast between his generation and that of his son:

They are more conscious of how they feel, or perhaps they are better at showing it, and they value life as if it were a sacrament, an ecstacy full of noise and pleasure which older people cannot understand. They don't believe in or understand struggle. They don't build for anything. Life is a movie. (48)

Michael, at times, does see himself as a character in a movie (129), but chooses to walk out of the picture, becoming a "forgotten piece in a chess game." To Eddie's condescending wish that Michael " 'doesn't lose it again' " (113), the returned prisoner of war implies an experience that Eddie, a victorious survivor of a war with clearly defined goals, did not have to endure, "What have I lost that Eddie can possibly know?" (113).

There are, however, characters who try to nudge Michael toward a psychic reconciliation: his psychiatrist, Kessler, a kind businessman, Mr. Baldwin, Lucy, a young wife, and his mother, Anne. But their efforts are frustrated by Lucy's disappearance and the assumption that the mentally disturbed Vietnam veteran, Michael Sumner, must be responsible for it, an assumption which undermines his sanity. To Lucy's husband, Ben, and Dale Sumner, Lucy's disappearance is a fulfillment of their fears concerning Michael. Outraged at her husband's accusations concerning her son, Anne snaps on the television, perhaps hoping to find a crazed Vietnam vet on one of those police programs so popular in the 1970s. " 'Here,' " she says, " 'maybe you can find a plot to fit what's going on in your head' " (184). Later, after Lucy returns and after another of Michael's breakdowns, Anne cannot resist mocking her husband's inquiries concerning Lucy's whereabouts, " 'Michael dragged her off and cut her pretty little throat' " (218). As Lucy returns, so Michael asks to go in. Indeed, a mental institution may be a kinder environment for a disturbed young vet than stateside civilian life in the 1970s. Although Michael does receive a small amount of love, patience, and understanding, he is also psychically overwhelmed by the negative stigmata surrounding Vietnam veterans, images enriched by the novel. While Michael Sumner is innocent of any wrongdoing, Robert Bausch preserves the stereotype, for Lucy was abducted by another disturbed veteran—her first husband. " 'He came and got her.... He was violent. Took her to Georgia. Apparently it was an ordeal' " (222).

Stephen Wright's *Meditations in Green* is in part another novel of a Vietnam veteran only half-way home. Its protagonist, James Griffin, is haunted by his past, so much so that the mention of "a children's breakfast cereal, Crispy Critters," reminiscent of a slang term for bodies charred to a crisp by napalm, reference to the perfume, Charlie, also the nickname for Viet Cong, and even the radio sound of "We Gotta Get Out of This Place," a tune popular in Vietnam, fill him with melancholy. Once Griffin returns, as he says, "to the colony" (19), crouching amidst the Tropical Rain Forest in an urban Botanical Garden.

His wartime buddy, Trips, a veteran even more disturbed than Griffin, points out, " 'You're out in the boonies...I think the war's got you bent out of shape. You're all twisted up' " (143). On another occasion, Griffin borrows a friend's car for a frantic all night search. "I could drive like this forever," he reveals, "swift and loose, senses drowned in a shriek, headlights boring holes in the void, because somewhere out here there must be a way home" (185).

Less fortunate than Griffin is his good friend, Trips, a character perhaps created to illustrate government neglect of wartime casualties. Trips describes his release from a mental hospital: " 'Gave me a comb, bottle of Thorazine, showed me the gate. They let a bunch of us go every year on the anniversary of Freud's birth' " (37). Griffin's girlfriend, Huette Mirandella, cannot understand why Trips is released, as she notes his aberrant behavior: " 'This is the guy who masturbated on the television. Right on the warm screen.' " With his flair for sensationalism, Wright has Trips explain that this is not an isolated case:

We had one poor guy raping grandmother's with a bayonet, rolling hand grenades into orphanages, all the time he's screaming and bawling and tossing the chairs, kicking the Ping-Pong tables to pieces, chewing padding off the walls, a jazz solo, man and he finishes up by wetting his pants and collapsing against the Coke machine. He was back on the street in a week (39).

Reminiscent of Heller's *Catch-22*, in Wright's novel federal bureaucracy solves the problem by denying that there is a problem.

Wright's *Meditations in Green* is indebted to *Catch-22* in its use of absurd briefings, a war zone section structured around the deaths of the protagonist's buddies, and satire of monomaniacal enlisted men, outrageously incompetent staff officers, and military corruption. But Wright's novel differs from Heller's masterpiece in its inclusion of the stereotypes of the Vietnam War. While such media favorites as racism, troop insubordination, and atrocity are revealed in *Meditations in Green*, drug abuse and fragging, particularly good copy in the 1970s, receive special emphasis. Motivation for drug use is succinctly expressed in Griffin's reflection on the war, "incredible boredom punctuated by exclamation marks of orgiastic horror" (96). For Griffin there is escape, "Marijuana, happily, elevated tolerance levels and seemed to produce a beneficial air-conditioning effect on the body" (210). In this novel, as cliche suggests, Griffin gradually turns to harder stuff, LSD, opium, heroin. With Dexedrine handy "in case of an emergency," Griffin becomes a heavy opium user, a stoned soldier, who withdrawn and introverted, is viewed by his commanding officer as a " 'model troop,' " " 'one of my best people.' " Of course, Griffin becomes less efficient as his drug abuse increases. After he "passed out at work," "...frames of film had melted against his face." As one might expect, "he didn't feel a thing" (296). Whether he volunteered or was assigned, he performs guard duty on the perimeter, where the easy availability of drugs is represented by a Vietnamese "milkman" on a motorcycle yelling, " 'Acid, speed, grass, and scag. Acid, speed, grass, and scag' " (297). From Griffin's stoned perspective, heaven becomes a "Doors concert on acid" (300). His adjustment to life stateside is complicated by his re-introduction to opium. Seeking guidance, he confides to an advocate of holistic medicine, Dr. Arden, " 'My problem is I don't know whether I'm addicted to the 0, the war, or that stupid sweet kid who once was me' " (89).

Like so many returning veterans, Griffin cleaves to his own kind, his old army buddy, Trips, who is obsessed with taking revenge on his former First Sergeant, a theme abundantly prepared for in the novel's Vietnam sections, where fraggings or attempted fraggings are routine. A plane crash causing the death of the commanding officer is a result of sabotage by disgruntled enlisted men. Assassination attempts are directed at both the new Commanding Officer, Major Holly, a proponent of spit and polish, and his Executive Officer. Later Major Holly finds an obvious warning, a severed oriental head in his tulip patch. Even creative acts echo the theme. Wendell's attempted Vietnam movie includes a simulated murder of an officer, while Griffin and Trips suggest writing volumes one and two of "Famous Drill Sergeants We'd Like to Off." Although Griffin merely speaks hyperbolically out of frustration, Trips sincerely wants revenge, for Sergeant Anstin, acting on orders, was responsible for the death of Trips' pet dog. Griffin's attempts to dissuade Trips from a stateside fragging are futile:

I'm not mad, I'm cool, I'm Frosty the Snowman. No heat, no sweat. Cool me. Cool Trips. I can't get a job, my family doesn't speak to me, the VA wouldn't give me a Band-Aid if I slit my wrists in their lobby. That's okay, I'm cool. I learned this in the army. (116)

It does not matter to Trips that his dog was killed seven years earlier; from his warped perspective he can only see revenge as an answer to his anguish. " 'I'll tell you a joke,' " he says to Griffin. " 'You're gonna help me kill the bastard' " (116). Griffin does accompany trips on his assassination attempt but only to prevent it.

In a parody of a search and destroy mission, the two wounded veterans reconnoiter Anstin's apartment and follow their prey to a downtown disco. While Trips tries to trigger the ambush, Griffin, after knocking away his friend's revolver, is stabbed, and inspired by anger, stabs Trips in return during hand-to-hand combat. Griffin applies half-forgotten emergency first-aid techniques, first learned in basic training, to save Trips' life. Looking around, Griffin notices he is "at the center of an arena of shocked eyes." Soon after Griffin responds in a less programmed manner: "The chills started...and I didn't care, all control gone, slumped on the sidewalk, warm blood washing over my hand, and under the flashing lights, the gaze of the crowd, I cried and couldn't stop" (319).

Perhaps the scene of the two veterans wounded once again because of their war experiences, in pain before an uncomprehending audience, is an appropriate tableau for many a returning Vietnam War veteran. Sergeant Anstin's response concerning Trips, " 'Who is this guy?' " . . . " 'I never saw him before in my life,' " underlines the point. So, too, do the words of the protagonist. To the bewildered police, who ask, " 'You the hero?' " Griffin responds, " 'I hope not' " (319). To their request for information concerning the attempted murder, Griffin, perhaps realizing the answer is at least a novel long says, " 'I don't know. . . Somebody killed his dog' " (319).

Coleman, Bausch, and Wright contend with and succumb to the "sick vet" image. The protagonists of their novels are sensitive, fundamentally decent, vulnerable young men who were reluctant soldiers while in Southeast Asia. For Andrew Collins, Michael Sumner, and James Griffin, the war still continues within while they are stateside. All three young men attain a measure of dignity, despite their Vietnam experiences. Andrew Collins escapes the limbo of a V.A. asylum; Michael Sumner is innocent of violent crime; and James Griffin saves two lives, though he hopes he is not a hero. Victories in these novels, however, are only partial. Collins cannot save Pollard who helped cure him; Sumner is institutionalized once again; and Griffin remains addicted. While the protagonists win reader sympathy, the "sick vet" image is alive and well, for all three novels contain other crazed vets, who, far less admirable, fulfill the stereotype—Trips, Lucy's first husband, the psychos wandering around Chambers Pavilion. Yes, Coleman, Bausch, and Wright also succumb to the stigma surrounding Vietnam veterans.

Works Cited

Axthelm, Pete with Michael Reese, Susan Agrest, Stuart Seidel, William D. Marbach, Eric Gelman. "The Sick World of 'Son of Sam'." *Newsweek*. 22 August 1977: 16-23.

Bausch, Robert. *On The Way Home*. New York: Avon, 1983.

Coleman, Charles. *Sergeant Back Again*. New York: Harper & Row, 1980.

Figley, Charles and Seymour Leventman. "Introduction: Estrangement and Victimization." *Strangers At Home: Vietnam Veterans Since the War*. Ed. Charles R. Figley and Seymour Leventman. New York: Praeger, 1980. xxi-xxxi.

Heller, Joseph. *Catch-22*. New York: Dell, 1961.

Leventman, Seymour and Paul Camacho. "The 'Gook' Syndrome: The Vietnam War as a Racial Encounter." *Strangers At Home: Vietnam Veterans Since the War*.

Ed. Charles R. Figley and Seymour Leventman. New York: Praeger, 1980. 55-70.

Lewy, Guenter. *America in Vietnam*. New York: Oxford University Press, 1978.

MacPherson, Myra. *Long Time Passing: Vietnam & The Haunted Generation*. New York: New American Library, 1984.

Mathews, Tom, Tony Fuller, Susan Agrest, Betsy Carter, Michael Reese, Dan Shapiro. "Hunting the 'Son of Sam'." *Newsweek*. 11 July 1977: 18-21.

Moskos, Charles. "Surviving the War in Vietnam." *Strangers At Home: Vietnam Veterans Since the War*. Ed. Charles R. Figley and Seymour Leventman. New York: Praeger, 1980. 71-85.

Schuetz, Alfred. "The Homecomer." *Strangers At Home: Vietnam Veterans Since the War*. Ed. Charles R. Figley and Seymour Leventman. New York: Preager, 1980. 115-122.

Wikler, Norma. "Hidden Injuries of War." *Strangers At Home: Vietnam Veterans Since the War*. Ed. Charles R. Figley and Seymour Leventman. New York: Praeger, 1980. 87-106.

Wright, Stephen. *Meditations in Green*. New York: Charles Scribner's Sons, 1983.

"Walking Wounded: Vietnam War Novels" was presented at the 1984 meeting of the PCA in Toronto, March 29-April 1.

Bringing Vietnam Home:
Bruce Weigl's *The Monkey Wars*

Vicente F. Gotera

Wars have always had poetic respondents, and the role of the warrior-poet is a familiar posture. Two typical examples are Peter Bowman's *Beach Red* (from World War II) and Michael Casey's *Obscenities* (from Vietnam). Literature about war is often radically experimental (note, for example, *The Enormous Room* or *Catch-22*), and neither Bowman nor Casey is an exception: *Beach Red* is a second-person narrative in Whitmanesque verse, and *Obscenities* is conceived as a verse-novel, "not as a random collection of poems" (x), according to Stanley Kunitz's introduction to this Yale prize-winner. While such experiments may be significant, they are not always successful: Casey's enigmatic syntax and anti-epic language become merely gimmicky, and Bowman's device of the hero "you" depicted in elevated language finally calls undue attention to itself. And this is all too often the case in literature about war. In *The Monkey Wars*, however, Bruce Weigl hits his target square in the bull's eye, because he does not self-consciously reach for avant-garde modes.

Weigl succeeds where Bowman and Casey fail because he uses the short lyric, a familiar staple, and keeps his language simple—almost brutally so. Jeffrey Walsh has pointed out that the "apprehension of war constitutes a distinctive and central element in the modern literary consciousness. Military terrain and situations have become familiar, often assuming mythic connotations" (1). Weigl uses this familiarity to "raise the consciousness." of the complacent American, as 1970s argot would term it. Lorrie Smith is absolutely correct in pointing out that poetry by Vietnam veterans dismantles the popular myth that we have regained our national innocence [by confessing] that U.S. involvement in Vietnam was a mistake (14). In *The Monkey Wars*, Weigl forces us to re-view Vietnam through his persona's obsessive review of and sequent inability to revise the Vietnam experience.

What *is* innovative about Weigl's re-view in *The Monkey Wars*, given the context of other poets revisioning Vietnam, is Weigl's assumption of responsibility. Casey and other Vietnam-veteran poets have implied that perhaps the American soldier was a sort of victim, certainly active in the violence but absolved to some extent by emotional anesthesia. Weigl's poems in *The Monkey Wars* include the speaker among the guilty, if only through the penance of memory. The opening poem, "Amnesia," illustrates this:

> If there was a world more disturbing than this
> Where black clouds bowed down and swallowed you whole

> * * *

> * * *

> You don't remember it.

> You tell yourself no and cry a thousand days.

> * * *

> * * *

Weigl's title here is ironic as well as wishful: a desire to forget about Vietnam and a concomitant drive to remember, once again to fly in innocence, "to be...useful." Smith claims that in this poem, "Vietnam has obliterated the memory of a world before war" (15); this reading requires that the referent for the pronoun "this" in line 1 be Vietnam. If this were so, lines 2-7 should be in present tense to clarify the dramatic setting. Occam's razor demands a simpler reading. I propose that "this" in line 1 refers to America in the 1980s and that the "world more disturbing" is Vietnam. But the presence of the comparative adverb implies that the present is disturbing, and it is disturbing precisely *because* of the Vietnam War having happened (in general and to the speaker). Hence in this initial octave of an anti-sonnet, the speaker claims, "You don't remember it"; he is protesting that he has forgotten Vietnam. But the concrete force of the description of this inwardly re-created Vietnam belies such "amnesia": the speaker *cannot* forget. The interesting strategy here is Weigl's use of "You," an accusing finger pointing out that *we* "don't remember it" either (Smith's notion of our "regained...national innocence.")

The acceptance of memory and hence guilt is the pivot into the closing sestet, which highlights the poet's (and our own) responsibility. The ultimate usefulness here is the poet's sacrifice, a determination to face once more the unfaceable "world more disturbing," to wrest from it some boon. The grim yet necessary responsibility: social and personal therapy. As introduction to *The Monkey Wars*, this poem emphasizes Weigl's project: to reintegrate himself into reality, into nature, "crows," "autumn," "wind." The last, as a metaphor for language, is his connection with us, his medium to remind us of what we must never forget.

"[T]he task of the Vietnam writer [is] to create a landscape that never was," asserts Philip Beidler, "a landscape of consciousness where it might be possible to accommodate experience remembered within a new kind of imaginative cartography" (16). Michael Stephens describes Weigl's "cartography" as a "mythical and violent Midwest [and] a disruptive, war-gutted Vietnamese landscape" (149). Weigl's landscape is hard and elemental, a masculine landscape, not in the narrow sense of patriarchal or anti-feminist, but in terms of a primal confrontation with a violent, indifferent world.

Of course, Weigl's landscape is literally a "wordscape," and its salient features are those words he uses most, accreting into figurative escarpments, bluffs, skyscrapers and, for Weigl, mill stacks. Such an accounting of a poet's obsessive words can often be instructive, and so it especially is in *The Monkey Wars*.

The colors Weigl uses are restricted to basic colors; *red, yellow, green, blue, gray, brown*. No indigo here, and certainly no cyan or magenta, much less ochre or obsidian. His fancier colors are relatively plebeian: *olive drab, silver, scarlet, gold*. Of most note, however, is that *white* occurs 17 times, *black* 12 (as compared to the highest count for the colors named above: 7 for *blue*). Weigl's world is essentially monochromatic, with occasional brushstrokes of color.

Interestingly enough, although these strokes may describe "red sun" or "blue water," the sudden splashes of color in this drab landscape are not most often jungle blossoms or Midwestern cornflowers, as one might expect, but birds: 7 references to the generic word *bird*, with a myriad types mentioned: *gulls, crows, starlings, chickens, sparrows, herons, egrets, hawks,* and *doves* (and not the *homo sapiens* variety of the last two). Even *monkey*, so conspicuous in the book's title, only appears 5 times, and 3 of these occurrences of the word are in a single poem.

It should come as no surprise, therefore, that of the four classical elements, *air* scores 17 while the *combined* total for *earth, water* and *fire* only comes to 13. And *wing* occurs a whopping 19 times. Of other anatomical words, the most numerous pertain to the upper body: *face* 13, *head* 12, *eye* 11, *arm* 10, *hand* 10. And the words which describe upper-body functions are also numerous: *think* 16, *watch* 13, *see* 13, *sing* 13, *remember/recall* 13. An interesting phenomenon here is the ratio of incidental to deliberate actions: *see* 13 and *look* 2, *hear* 7 and *listen* 1. One inference may be that the poet, in Weigl's cosmos, is to some extent without choice, rather like Alex who is forced to watch horrific films in *Clockwork Orange*; yet the poet must observe, he must record and contemplate, for he will be asked to remember, ultimately to sing.

That this landscape is masculine is also demonstrable. *Man* occurs 11 times compared to 7 for *woman, boy* 10 to *girl* 8; the most telling, however, as 11 for *father* compared to 2 times for *mother*. The contrasts among Vietnam, America and Europe are stark: men in the latter two are farmers or industrial workers, while in Vietnam men are represented by a monk with a "charge / Wired between his teeth and the floor" (23); in Zagreb or Texas, "women thrash wheat" (9) or a "woman finish[es] her song" (27), but in Vietnam, they are "a bar girl [with] terrible scars" (14), a "mama san . . . slam[med] to her knees" (26), and a "girl / Running from her village, napalm / Stuck to her dress" (46).

This last image is not an exception; the inanimate verb that occurs most often is *burn* (17 times). And of course references to *flares, fire, blaze, smoke, flame* "crackling signs" (5) and "crackling / Muscles" (47). Despite this negative aura, however, there is *hope* and *mercy* and *beauty* and *laughter* here; most important, the word *love* appears 17 times compared to 7 for *hate*.

Daniel Guillory faults Weigl for "not offer[ing] many startling turns of phrase" (64); this reviewer has missed the point. Weigl has deliberately used a plain style so that the "penetrating images of death and suffering," which Guillory himself notes, will speak eloquently, without recourse to ornate language. Weigl limits his diction to a small vocabulary of "hard" Anglo-Saxon words as, I propose, an active resistance to what writers on Vietnam have called the "jargon stream," with its "incongruity [to] hide the reality of moral outrage," as Walsh puts it (206). John Felstiner proposes that "Washington's need was to sanitize reality and quarantine the fact from the word—precisely what much poetry avoids" (10). Weigl wants to reunite "fact" and "word," insisting on the most basic of vocabulary, as common a denominator as possible—at what risk to his art, some critics may argue—in order to deflate terms like "kill ratio," "defoliant," and "pacification," exposing their real connotations.

The effective result of Weigl's limited diction is that the obsessive repetitions of the words themselves telegraph, as do terminal words in a sestina or refrains in a villanelle, the author's own obsessive relationship with the subject and thus the reader's necessity for attention. In this respect, Weigl resembles a poet such as Louise Glück, who works within an obsessively pared-down vocabulary—a mixture of Anglo-Saxon and Greco-Roman.

Weigl's recourse to a plain style, however, does not mean that he cannot "turn a startling phrase." As does Glück, Weigl mixes etymologies: "pyramids of pipe" (Latin and Anglo-Saxon), "calligraphy of wings" (Greek and Anglo-Saxon), and "jungle of our indulgences" (Sanskrit and Latin). These three examples illustrate sophisticated sound effects, especially the last: assonance (j*UnglE* and ind*UlgE*nces) interwoven with consonance (the play of J, L, N, D and G sounds).

Of course, the final judgment of this book must rest on the poems. The overall ambience of *The Monkey Wars* is an insoluble reagent of loss and hope, concocted in reaction to overwhelming despair. The titles themselves show this: "Song for a Lost First Cousin," "Song of the Lost Private," and "Small Song for Andrew." This last poem describes Weigl's son as "more beautiful/Than the light / Before the light has touched anything"—lines which are indeed hopeful. But this is the high point; this is only a "Small Song," the title claims. More typical is "Song for a Lost First Cousin" which mourns the loss of childhood, the impossibility of continuing an innocent boys' relationship with a gay cousin:

> I couldn't tell you I remembered how we'd stripped:
> Beautiful boys in the shower at the public beach,
>
> * * *
>
> The minutes break open as eggs
> And when I try to speak
> I only stutter, only lie. (7)

Loss in the present is foreshadowed by loss in the past: In "Flight," Weigl describes his grandmother's first sight of an airplane in 1919 Zagreb; her father takes the frightened girl

> Into his arms to listen
> To the huge bird, the flight, the shadow
> Burned into wheat. (9)

The harbinger of technology, perhaps a World War I dogfighter, is seen as almost a natural phenomenon, but one which is a "dark shape eating air," and it *burns*. An elegy for his grandfather, "Killing Chickens," is set in a pastoral Midwest which is already on its way to wasteland: "Red sun...burning out / Past slag heaps of the mill" (15) is the backdrop against which we see the grandfather's farm. In fact, the grandfather is himself a symbol of the oncoming desolation of the American landscape:

> In August he didn't feel the fly
> Come into his cancerous ear and lay its eggs.

He didn't feel the maggots hatch
As he sat dazed with pills in the sun. (16)

Middle America in *The Monkey Wars* has fulfilled this prophecy in our own present: an inferno of "the slag air[,] the flaming steel and the shitty bars / And the steady grind of a mile of industry" is the setting for the poem ironically titled "Hope" (19). In "Noise," we see that even suburbia—that isolationistic refuge of the twentieth century—has been affected:

Next door the newlyweds
Scream at each other, three A.M.
I hate your fucking guts he says. (33)

And finally we find that the wasteland extends even to the country—the rural bailiwick of Jefferson's chosen people, the yoeman farmers. Hunting is no longer the countryman's heritage to his son; the "good boy" now must "steal away" from his father to hunt an egret,

Wiping out from the blue face of the pond
What he hadn't even known he loved, blasting
Such beauty into nothing. (45)

Little hope for the future, it would seem: when even Andrew, Weigl's "son [who] / Is strong and sure of himself" may grow up to be such a boy—a hunter who doesn't understand the intimate connection to quarry.

The point is that, for Weigl, there is ultimately no separation between the landscape of Vietnam and that of America; in fact, the equation extends even to the ancestral landscapes of Europe. This fusion is not merely occurring within tortured memory; the landscapes are joined by violence. As Smith rightly argues, "The dark underside of Vietnam is finally...a monstrous exaggeration and a logical extension of the more banal forms of violence and moral depletion of home" (16). Hence, even though many poems in this collection do not expressly mention Vietnam as such, they are all illuminated by a spectrum of violence—a spectrum of minute gradations in which Vietnam is not a different, separate violence but only the most visible.

These gradations are highlighted by imagistic associations: the "biplane" in Zagreb is a precursor to the Huey helicopter in Vietnam. The "fly / Come into [Grandfather's] cancerous ear" is cognate to a variety of Vietnam commonplaces: the intrusion of the war into our living room TVs, the "cancer" of dissension eating even into the bastions of the middle class, the decay of discipline in the enlisted ranks (e.g., the many incidents of "fragging"—the removal of inept officers via fragmentation grenade). The "good boy" hunting the egret, Smith has noted, "re-enacts a soldier's naive killing" (17).

These subtle connections among Vietnam, American and Europe allow Weigl to evoke the incredible violence of Vietnam without the surrealistic bloodshed or dadaistic nihilism to which earlier Vietnam-veteran poets have resorted. Don Receveur's "night fear" is a typical example:

> i heard my meatless bones
> clunk together

> * * *

> and the worms in my belly
> moved sluggishly
> delighted.
>
> > (Rottman *et al*, 15)

In order to avoid such triteness and overstatement, and yet keep Receveur's driving sincerity, Weigl roots his poems in realism and subtlety so that they speak softly as well as forcefully for themselves. For example, "Temple Near Quang Tri, Not on the Map" tells its muted but harrowing account in a realistic setting:

> * * *

> Birds move on the walls of the temple
> Shaping their calligraphy of wings. (22)

Mentioning "calligraphy" and "carved faces for incense" prepares us for the monk who "Sits legs askew in the shadow" and is "bent over." Where another poet may have resorted to gratuitous violence, in the climactic scene Weigl writes:

> We bend him to sit straight
> And when he's nearly peaked
> At the top of his slow uncurling
> His face becomes visible, (23)

> * * *

> * * *

What is significant here is what is left out. We don't literally *know* if the booby trap explodes; the narration's immediacy implies that the speaker is physically present and close to the bomb. And Weigl makes no direct statement about either the deviousness of the Viet Cong in changing a priest into a bomb or the callousness of the officer who "wants to ignore" the monk who is in obvious difficulty. But the poem is eminently satisfying because of its emotional completeness, its simple fluency, and the way in which the opening image of "sparrows / Squawking" is brought full-circle into that soundless explosion of sparrows at the end.

Smith has proposed that *The Monkey Wars* is "a darker view of the limitations of transcendent and redemptive imagination" (16) and that "the lyric imagination utterly fails to ameliorate or transform the memory of Vietnam" (17). The seeming tragedy is that of the speaker of "Burning Shit at An Khe," who regrets:

> Only now I can't fly,
>   I lay down in it
>
> * * *
>
> Until I'm covered and there's only one smell,
>   One word. (11)

We are reminded of the earthbound speaker of "Amnesia." In "Noise," it is not only the speaker who is caged in by the "triangle" of the dramatic scene ("me," "newlyweds," and "trainmen"), but Weigl himself who seems trapped by the triple conspiracies of history, of time, of place— Vietnam, America, Europe—the entire human world of which the third world is only one part:

> A triangle of nervous noise
> Because the noise is in my head too,
> The noise is always in my head. (33)

And the "noise" is not limited *within* the confines of the book. Stephens argues that the "violent moments" of *The Monkey Wars* "are used to unmask and to articulate our troubled emotions" (150), eventually pointing to our own complicity in the violence.

I propose, however, that Weigl *does* offer us hope. Smith is too ready to attest to "the limitations of a lyric response to Vietnam" (14). She closes her argument by citing the poem "Song of Napalm," in which Weigl, sharing a pastoral moment with his wife, remembers a running girl smeared with flaming napalm. The speaker attempts to transform the image:

I try to imagine she runs down the road and wings
Beat inside her until she rises
Above the stinking jungle and her pain
Eases, and your pain, and mine.

But the poet finds that "the lie swings back again" because "The lie
works only as long as it takes to speak." The girl, forever ablaze, falls

Into that final position
Burning bodies so perfectly assume. (47)

* * *

The important aspects to remember here of Weigl's method in *The
Monkey Wars* are the sense-laden vibration of air and breath at the end
of each poem, as in the exploding sparrows of "Temple Near Quang
Tri," and the subtle way connections among Vietnam, America, and
Europe are drawn, strings of silence which pierce the white space
surrounding each poem. So we must listen to echoes, trust to inference,
catch the resonations.

What is unsaid, but doubly important, is that the horrible image
that dominates "Song of Napalm" does not itself *deny* the "good love"
of wives and husbands and children; "good love" nevertheless exists and
flourishes. The upshot of the lines "So I can keep on living,/So I can
stay here beside you" and "But the lie swings back again" seems to
be that lyric imagination fails; but Weigl nonetheless *does* "stay here
beside" his wife. And *does* continue to write poems, failure of lyricism
or no.

Smith has assumed that in over a decade of writing and publishing
poems on Vietnam—*The Executioner* in 1976, *A Romance* in 1979, *The
Monkey Wars* in 1985—"Weigl cannot finally shake his monkey" (17).
I propose that the failed lyric impulse Smith has observed is merely
part of the artful surface of *The Monkey Wars*, but that the vigorous
subtext here is an ongoing war with the "monkey"—and with no
surrender in sight. Although the soldier who "Burns[s] Shit at An Khe"
can only see his own self as "one smell,/One word," Weigl fights this
nihilism with his basic, obsessive words. This grounding in the hardy
roots of language will still rescue lyricism; in *The Monkey Wars*, Weigl
comes very close indeed to learning once more to fly with crows, "to
be black" and therefore human. Weigl is not merely, as Smith argues,
"guard[ing] against the peculiarly American habit of denying history"
(18), he is fighting a battle to save the enterprise of poetry as something
redemptory and "once more useful to the wind."

Works Cited

Beidler, Philip D. *American Literature and the Experience of Vietnam*. Athens: U. of Georgia P., 1982.

Bowman, Peter. *Beach Red*. New York: Random, 1945.

Casey, Michael. *Obscenities*. Yale Series of Younger Poets, v. 67. New Haven: Yale UP, 1972.

Felstiner, John. "American Poetry and the War in Vietnam." *Stand* 19.2 (1978): 4-11.

Guillory, Daniel L. Rev. of *The Monkey Wars*, by Bruce Weigl. *Library Journal* 15 June 1985: 64.

Rottmann, Larry, Jan Barry, and Basil T. Paquet, eds. *Winning Hearts & Minds: War Poems by Vietnam Veterans*. New York: McGraw-Hill, 1972.

Smith, Lorrie. "A Sense-Making Perspective in Recent Poetry by Vietnam Veterans." *American Poetry Review* 15.6 (Nov./Dec. 1986): 13-18.

Stephens, Michael. "Combat Zones." Rev. of *The Monkey Wars*. *The Nation* 8 Feb. 1986: 149-50.

Walsh, Jeffrey. *American War Literature: 1914 to Vietnam*. New York: St. Martin's, 1982.

Weigl, Bruce. *The Monkey Wars*. Athens: U of Georgia Press, 1985.

Section V:
Wider Perspectives

Women in Vietnam War Novels

Kathleen M. Puhr

A subject as broad as "Women in Vietnam War Novels" invites a number of approaches. Certainly one could talk about the portrayals of American women at home. Numerous accounts describe soldiers receiving a "Dear John" letter and charging to their deaths that very day. Particularly when women were involved in the anti-war movement did they incur the wrath of the men in Vietnam. The comments of an Army Ranger named Mopar in Kenn Miller's *Tiger the Lurp Dog* are typical of this sentiment. Mopar thinks angrily about his "peace creep" girlfriend, Sybill Street: "She was smart, but she wasn't smart enough to understand about the war. She didn't understand anything that wasn't part of her comfortable civilian world" (203). One could also mention the involvement of mothers of soldiers in the war, especially when their sons returned as psychological casualties, as in Robert Bausch's *On the Way Home*. Recently even daughters of veterans have appeared in fiction, notably in Bobbi Ann Mason's *In Country*.

In marked contrast to the depiction of American women in the fiction, Vietnamese women play a much more vital role in novels about the war both in their involvement with the Viet Cong and North Vietnamese Army forces and with American soldiers. As prostitutes, hootch maids and bar girls, they are mentioned in almost every Vietnam War novel. Perhaps the most fully developed portrayal of a Vietnamese woman appears in Robert Olen Butler's *The Alleys of Eden*. The novel is set in Saigon in the last days of the war and in the United States in 1975-76. Butler explores cultural differences through two characters: Cliff, an Army deserter hiding in Saigon, and Lahn, his Vietnamese girlfriend. After fleeing to America, Cliff and Lahn fail to reconcile their differences, their failure symbolic of the entire war. Lahn is not given the chance to be completely Vietnamese since she must assimilate into American culture. Undoubtedly she embodies an important type: the Vietnamese woman whose destiny became inextricably linked to a specific American's.

Even with all of these approaches to the subject of women in Vietnam War novels available, another important area remains: the role of American nurses in Vietnam as presented both in selected memoirs and in three novels: Leonard B. Scott's *Charlie Mike* (1985), Evelyn Hawkins' *Vietnam Nurse* (1984), and Patricia Walsh's *Forever Sad the Hearts* (1982).

I was not even aware of the participation of American women, particularly nurses, in the Vietnam War until I read Lynda Van Devanter's *Home Before Morning* in 1983. My ignorance is indicative of the ignorance of most Americans about the role of women in this war. What accounts for this ignorance? Obviously, American women, unlike their male counterparts, did not need to flee to Canada or Sweden, burn draft cards, or carry weapons through the jungles of Southeast Asia, tracking an elusive enemy. Women could make their moral choices about the war in the comfort of their homes or dormitories rather than at the local draft board or on the battlefield. Yet as the media during the past few years have reminded us, women did go to Vietnam, all of them as volunteers and most of them older than the males who were fighting there. The women served as missionaries, Red Cross volunteers, nurses, and journalists (among whom number such luminaries as Gloria Emerson, Frances Fitzgerald, Marguerite Higgins, and Mary McCarthy), but also as doctors, aerial reconnaissance engineers, entertainers, clerks, secretaries, photographers, and business/support personnel (Austin 8).

It might be helpful to compare facts about the role of women in Vietnam with that of women in the "good war," World War II. In World War II, 350,000 women served; they drove trucks, repaired planes, rigged parachutes, were gunnery instructors, air traffic controllers, naval air navigators, and nurses. These nurses, actively recruited by the Red Cross, were paid well, had status, and enjoyed popular support. According to D'Ann Campbell in *Women at War with America*, "Nurses were seen as heroines, achieving distinction while maintaining a feminine image" (61). In the "not-so-good war," Vietnam, approximately 7400 women served as nurses although Pentagon officials admit they are not sure about the exact number. They are more certain about the number of women who died and whose names are inscribed on the Vietnam Memorial: eight. The 1.2 million women veterans account for 4.1 percent of all living veterans, (Grimes 3) but it was not until 1978 that the VFW allowed women veterans to join. As Vietnam veteran Lynda Van Devanter reports, when she tried to march with the Vietnam Veterans Against the War, in 1971 one member told her: " 'You don't look like a vet...If we have women marching Nixon and the network news reporters might think we're swelling the ranks with nonvets' " (231). The movement to recognize women veterans, popularized by writers such as Lynda Van Devanter, is exemplified by the efforts of U.S. representative Mary Rose Dakar of Ohio who has written a bill to authorize the construction in Washington of a memorial to "women under fire," but her efforts are opposed by Department of the Interior officials who argue that too many military monuments exist already (Grimes 3).

Writing in *The Women's Review of Books*, Jacqueline Austin points out that in spite of a strong women's movement in America during the Vietnam era, the war "remained a situation for, by, and about men" (8). She adds that three facts apply for every American woman who went to Vietnam: nobody forced her to go; she was protected from combat; and she recorded little history at the time (8). Austin states that the majority of women did not publicize their participation and that "unless she was the mother or wife of a soldier, the media tended to ignore or ridicule her" (8).

Because of their small numbers, and because of the unpopularity of the war in which they participated, American women appear in few of the war's novels. The novels in which they are featured seem to be little more than Harlequin romances set in Vietnam, e.g. Evelyn Hawkins' *Vietnam Nurse* and Leonard B. Scott's *Charlie Mike*. The women in these works volunteered to serve in Vietnam for various reasons, but their priority seems to be forming alliances with strikingly handsome American soldiers. The women are not interested in the politics of the war, in military tactics, or even in the war's moral implications. Someone reading these works would have all biases against American women in war confirmed. In the memoirs and oral histories, however, and in Patricia Walsh's *Forever Sad the Hearts*, the most credible novel about American women, we are reminded that American nurses, particularly by virtue of their contribution to the war, have something to share with all of us even though they have had difficulty motivating us to listen to them. As Van Devanter notes in her memoir for years she tried to talk about Vietnam, but no one listened:

Who would have wanted to listen? Mine were not nice neat stories. There was love, but no cute little love stories; heroes, but no grand, heroic war stories; winners, but you had to look hard to tell them from the losers.... The stories, even the funny ones, were all dirty. They were rotten and they stank. The moments, good and bad, were permeated with the stench of death and napalm. (13)

Guided by the example of Van Devanter, however, American nurses are beginning to speak out both in their memoirs and in oral histories such as Al Santoli's *Everything We Had* and Myra MacPherson's history of the Vietnam generation, *Long Time Passing*.

According to Myra MacPherson, who has recorded the comments of several Vietnam nurses, these women like some male veterans experienced post traumatic stress disorder although they often did not recognize their problems as being war-related. One former nurse was diagnosed as schizophrenic, spent nine years in mental institutions and endured forty-five shock treatments before her stress disorder was acknowledged. Another interviewee, Saralee McGoran, served in the 12th Evacuation Hospital at Cu Chi. She was twenty-six when she went to

Vietnam, volunteering because she " 'was single, there was a war and American boys were in it, and they needed American nurses' " (506). As did other American women, she suffered severe "emotional mauling" through her experiences, more so than many grunts who enjoyed respites from combat. McGoran treated wounded who never would have been taken from the battlefield in other wars (511). When she returned to the United States in January, 1968, McGoran felt alienated and alone, and when attending college she felt as if she were the enemy: "I didn't tell *anyone* I was a Vietnam veteran" (504).

In *Everything We Had*, the comments of Gayle Smith, a nurse at the 3rd Surgical Hospital at Binh Thuy from 1970-71 echo those of McGoran. One of twenty American nurses at the hospital, Smith felt herself become enraged at the Vietnamese: "I did not consider the Vietnamese to be people.... They weren't like us, so it was okay to kill them" (142). This woman, like American men in combat, had to dehumanize the Vietnamese in order to survive.

The most vocal female veteran, Lynda Van Devanter, served in Pleiku and Qui Nhon in 1969. Since 1980 she has been the national Veteran's Administration spokesman for Vietnam women veterans and in May, 1982 she was one of nine persons allowed to return to Vietnam. She dedicates her memoir, *Home Before Morning*, to "all of the unknown women who served forgotten in their wars."

Sounding much like other nurses and like Phillip Caputo in *A Rumor of War*, Van Devanter in *Home Before Morning* writes of her reason for joining the Army in 1968:

I saw the United States pursuing a course that President Kennedy had talked about in his inaugural address: we were saving a country from communism. There were brave boys fighting and dying for democracy, I thought. And if our boys were being blown apart, then somebody better be over there putting them back together again. I started to think that maybe that somebody should be me. (49)

Her arrival in Vietnam was inauspicious: her plane was shelled while attempting to land at Tan San Nhut in June 1969. She writes of her long hours at work in the hospital, standing in mud and blood and serving seventy-two hour shifts, experiencing rocket barrages, treating casualties from combat in Cambodia a year before the official U.S. invasion of that country, and escaping from the horrors by getting drunk or stoned at parties at "the Bastille." She also grew close to many people with whom she served, especially the doctors: "When you work under the intense conditions of a combat zone, you find yourself forming stronger bonds than you might have imagined in a peacetime world....[to] remind you that, after it's finished, you're still human" (105-6). Upon arrival in America Van Devanter experienced the re-entry ritual of being spat upon by a couple of hippies in a VW bus: she wondered why they were angry at her: "...didn't they understand that I didn't want this war any more than the most vocal of peace marchers? Didn't they realize that those of us who had seen the war firsthand were probably more antiwar than they were? That we had seen friends suffer and die?" (211) Her coming to terms with the war has been as difficult a battle as that waged by many male veterans.

An interesting sidelight to the Van Devanter memoir is the reaction it elicited from other women who served in Vietnam. Many challenged the book, saying that Van Devanter had treated the war too lightly, while others called her a "foul-mouthed slut" who "slept around while in Vietnam and exaggerated the horrors of her experience" (Austin 9). Colonel Mary Grace, a nurse supervisor in evacuation hospitals where Van Devanter worked, states that she did not recognize the conditions Van Devanter describes, adding: " 'I'd say she's been watching too much *MASH*' " (MacPherson 508). Retired colonel Edith Knox, former head nurse of the 67th Evacuation Hospital, Qui Nhon, says: " 'This book makes us look like a bunch of bed-hopping, foul-mouthed things' " (MacPherson 508). Jo Ann Webb, former Army nurse and wife of novelist James Webb, accused Van Devanter of being motivated by greed: " 'She talks about this endless flow of casualties, and official Army figures show the hospital was 50 percent full. I'm incensed that she's become a professional veteran and now she's making money off it' " (MacPherson 508). Van Devanter defends her memoir and emphasizes the neglect that women veterans have experienced: " 'What haunts me...is that nobody knows of the contribution of these women. The major legacy study of Vietnam veterans does not include *one* woman' " (MacPherson 509-510). Keith Walker has attempted to acknowledge the contributions of women to the Vietnam War through his recently published oral history, *A Piece of My Heart*, which contains the comments of twenty-six women who served in Vietnam in various capacities. Numerous women mention their gratitude to Lynda Van Devanter for being the first woman to step forward to tell her story about her service in Vietnam.

For the most part the dedication and the pain of these American women has not found its way into the war's fiction; instead, as noted earlier, the works in which American women are featured depict them as interested in little more than finding a good man and as possessing embarrassingly little knowledge of the politics of the war. Perhaps these novels are geared toward a predominantly female audience whom the authors assume prefer love stories to war stories; certainly Evelyn Hawkins' *Vietnam Nurse* fits such a category.

One wonders just how close to Vietnam Evelyn Hawkins came. Her novel is little more than a poorly crafted romance set in Vietnam in 1966: a romance which, like the war itself, ends unhappily but which, for the reader, at least ends. The novel's cover, with its bold assertion,

"She was a woman in a man's war," alerts one quite early to expect no literary masterpiece, as does the publisher: Zebra Books, known for such other models of stylistic excellence as *Sweet Vietnam*. The generic title of Hawkins' novel reminds one of the adolescent series, *Cherry Ames: Student Nurse*, only this time an x-rated Cherry Ames is patching up patients in Vietnam instead of in an American hospital.

The novel's protagonist is twenty-three-year-old Oklahoma native Sybil Watkins, a volunteer at Saigon's 555th Field Hospital who lets us know on page 224, after the love plot has been developed, why she volunteered to serve in Vietnam. The placement of this explanation of course indicates the priorities of the novelist: no moral treatises, initiation stories, or insights about wartime casualties here but a love story written in cliches and wooden prose. The passage in which Sybil reviews her reasons for volunteering for duty in Vietnam exemplifies the novel's style:

She knew what blood was. Injuries, maimings, and even death were no strangers to her. But there was still a sense of romantic adventure involved in her dedication to volunteer for the service.... She had a deeply patriotic love of country. Communism, with its totalitarian system and smothering of civil liberties and capitalist enterprises, was certainly a menace to freedom-loving people everywhere...and it was not unpleasant to realize she could be of some comfort and succor to the young men who were wounded while fighting that evil. (224)

Sybil is especially excited about succoring Brian Mallory, Green Beret. When he first walks in to the hospital, Sybil feels "primitive, undeniable lust" (83). In diction characteristic of the novel, we learn more about her feelings for Brian:

The man moved with a fluid grace, his slim hips sensuous in his tight-fitting fatigue uniform as he strode silently on the rubber soles of his jungle boots. This was the warrior incarnate.... She could imagine him in a plumed helmet with a shining breastplate of armor, his muscular calves showing above the high-top sandals. (83)

During their big date at the Officers' Club, Brian and she share a toast before dinner; after the toast, Sybil "looked into his eyes and felt a thrill at what she perceived there. Deep, deep in her heart, Sybil knew a relationship was developing" (164). Figuring out this fact causes "ripples of excitement to travel through [her] female soul" (167). The dialogue on their first date should indicate to the reader just how much Sybil and Brian have to offer one another. As they enter the cafeteria, Sybil points out to Brian, " 'There's a table over in the corner,' " and Brian says, " 'Okay. You're on the point.' " Of course Sybil is unfamiliar with the term, having only been in Vietnam for several months, so Brian explains: " 'The first man in a column or patrol is called the point man.... He leads the way.' " Sybil's response is " 'Oooh!...Sounds dangerous' " (89). After a few minutes of conversation in the cafeteria, Sybil thinks about "how very much she would like to go to bed with him if the right circumstances ever presented themselves" (89). They do, several times, and a substantial portion of the novel is devoted to recounting Sybil's sexual activities both through flashbacks to Oklahoma and through scenes in Vietnam.

Perhaps the most telling passages in this novel present Sybil's profound insight about the war: "Sybil looked around the garrison area and sighed. Except for Brian—and her friendship with Connie and Ernie—this whole Vietnam episode was growing intolerable. This was definitely not the way she had pictured her life in the army to be" (224). When Brian returns to the field, Sybil is truly depressed: "He was her man—kind, considerate, caring, loving—and he was out somewhere in that terrible war. Maybe deep behind enemy lines [apparently no one reminded Sybil that she was in Vietnam and not in Europe in the 1940s] involved in that awful guerilla fighting the Green Berets participated in" (305).

One of the novel's few redeeming features is Sybil's hispanic coworker, Connie Montaldo, who brings a bit more intelligence to the story through her arguments with the nursing supervisor, "Mother" Moorehead, regarding the double standard in the military's attitude about sexual conduct. When Moorehead reminds the nurses not to " 'provide sexual relief to the troops,' " (317), Connie replies: " 'To hell with the male sex drive. What about the female sex drive...at least we don't go out banging hell out of half the population and spreading VD around like a common cold' " (318). Lynda Van Devanter mentions this same problem of the military's double standard:

If the guys wanted to go carousing to all hours of the night and screw ninety-seven prostitutes in a day it was to be expected.... Every PX stocked plenty of GI-issue condoms...However, if we wanted to have a relationship, or to occasionally be with a man we cared deeply about, we were not conducting ourselves as 'ladies' should. And if we might be unladylike enough to want birth control pills, which were kept in a safe and rarely dispensed, we could expect the wrath of God, or our commander, to descend upon us. (122)

With its unintentional humor, ludicrous plot, and simplistic style, this novel ranks as one of the worst to emanate from the Vietnam War.

American nurses and Red Cross volunteers fare no better in Leonard B. Scott's *Charlie Mike*, a novel set in 1969-70 and dealing with Army Rangers in the An Khe area, but one could expect such treatment in a work by a male career officer. Interestingly, however, Scott presents not only American nurses and Red Cross volunteers but also Vietnamese women, and while the American women are mere accessories to the men, Scott highlights the integral role of Vietnamese women in the war effort as nurses, soldiers, and even as entertainers. For example, he describes a group of three women entertainers, a "happiness group," who accompany various NVA units on their march through the jungle. These women have arrived from the north to lift the spirits of the soldiers, and for their efforts they are honored by the units they visit.

In contrast, as portrayed in Scott's novel, American women have a minimal impact on the activities of the war. His two main female characters are an Army nurse, Capt. Jean O'Neal, and a Red Cross volunteer, Sarah Boyce. Unlike Vietnam nurse, Sybil, Jean is reluctant to become romantically involved with the soldiers, notably the pilots: "The pilots did very well dating nurses. The helicopter pilots especially could provide the benefits of their profession. Free helicopter rides to almost anywhere in Vietnam and, of course, lots of money, which they spent freely. But they were a high-risk group" (151). In spite of her resolutions, Jean falls in love with a pilot. The Red Cross volunteer, Sarah Boyce, is a spoiled rich girl who joins the Red Cross to escape her old way of life. A two-week orientation course fails to enhance her interest in the war: "Soldiers, insignia, rank, rules, uniforms, Red Cross history and traditions, Vietnam history and customs—all of it meant nothing except that she was leaving, escaping" (206). Escaping to Vietnam, however, proves disastrous; she detests the place and her work: "The job itself was stupid—fixing Kool-Aid in the too-heavy jugs that had to be lugged around and cleaned, and playing dumb games with the soldiers" (207). But after falling in love with Ranger Sgt. David Grady, her whole attitude about the war changes; as the blurb on the novel's front page states: "For all her life, *she'd* been her whole world. She thought she knew it well. Then, in Vietnam, she was overwhelmed by something that completely confused her. People called it love." As she tells her roommate Mary Ann: " 'I guess I'm beginning to feel that I'm really doing something worthwhile. I can talk to these young men and find what they're proud of or what they like and...it makes me feel good when they smile and talk to me about things' " (324). Even so, she realizes that "she was in the midst of a man's world of camaraderie that was understood by the men alone" (424). Maybe what Scott is suggesting is precisely this: women have a place in war, but a secondary one.

Taking a secondary place in war is an attitude which novelist Patricia Walsh rejects in her novel, *Forever Sad the Hearts*. The novel conveys the experiences of a civilian nurse in Vietnam and reminds one of Van Devanter's memoir. Walsh's story was published in 1982 as part of Avon's series of Vietnam War novels. Walsh's narrative is credible due to her actual participation in the war: at age twenty-four Walsh volunteered to serve as a nurse-anesthetist in a civilian hospital established by the U.S. Agency for International Development, and she spent fourteen months in DaNang and two years in a U.S. hospital recovering from injuries suffered in the war.

In *Forever Sad the Hearts*, the first-person narrator is Kate Shea, a DaNang nurse-anesthetist serving in 1967 with other American volunteers and an ever-changing cast of surgeons and administrators. Kate volunteered for an eighteen-month tour of Vietnam after seeing an ad in the Los Angeles *Times* asking for volunteers. Like Van Devanter, Kate's "ask what you can do for your country" spirit is undermined by the horrors that she witnesses. In the novel's first fifteen pages, she treats the reader to descriptions of Vietnamese civilians vomiting during the flight from Saigon to DaNang, her attempt to revive herself by drinking a beer and finding a worm at the bottom of the bottle, and her encounters with flies, beetle nut juice, human feces as vegetable garden fertilizer, and enema tubes reused as endotracheal tubes.

Throughout the novel, Kate spends time treating an endless stream of civilian casualties, trying to locate supplies that are always inadequate and often diverted to the Viet Cong, arguing with new surgeons about her decisions in triage, dealing with hostile American reporters, enduring the animosity of military nurses who viewed the civilian nurses as "riff raff," and trying to help the Vietnamese nursing students overcome their superstitions about such tactics as resuscitating patients. She also holds the hands of dying Vietnamese civilians and dying American soldiers, feeling guilty for being sadder about American casualties than Vietnamese ones. She shows her concern for the Vietnamese by aiding villagers and by donating time and money to the French nuns running a nearby orphanage.

The contrast in tone between this novel and *Vietnam Nurse* is readily apparent. In Kate, we have a protagonist who is concerned about the war itself. Quite early in the novel, Kate notes the absurdity of her actions in relation to those of American soldiers: "American military were shooting people whom they'd later pick up and bring to an ill-equipped hospital staffed by American government workers, to be cared for with supplies [begged] from the military" (26). This point is brought home numerous times in the novel, notably in Kate's conversation with an American soldier on a beach near DaNang when, learning of her job, he remarks: " 'You mean we shoot 'em and you fix 'em up?...Crazy...war. You're over here risking your life to save people I'm risking my life to shoot' " (109). She later tells her Marine boyfriend, Dan: " 'We aren't teaching the people anything about basic hygiene and health care. We just patch them up and send them out to get shot again' " (265). This vantagepoint is one that few if any other Vietnam war novels give us: the healer versus the injurer.

Although the novel contains a love plot, Kate's relationship with Dan transcends the one-dimensional portrayals in many war novels; unfortunately, the relationship ends when Dan is killed. After Dan's death, Kate pursues an "eat, drink and be merry" philosophy: a philosophy which "seemed more like an inevitable side effect of being in a situation where life really was taken one day at a time. None of us actually believed we would be killed, but we lived as though we did" (249). She begins to have nightmares of trying to hide charred bodies in her apartment back in the U.S. and although desperate to return to America, feels guilty: " 'How could I go home and work in a modern antiseptic institution with the cries of napalm victims interrupting my every thought' " (376). She loses her Catholic faith and at one point contemplates suicide.

Her release from the prison of the war occurs when she sustains a back injury during the Tet Offensive. In preparation for her return to the U.S. she takes some medicine to flush the parasites from her intestines, adding: " 'I thought it unfortunate they couldn't give me something to flush my mind as well' " (381). Her co-worker, Jean, advises her about how to deal with her re-entry: " 'Don't expect people back home to understand what you're going through or you'll never make it' " (391). Describing her return flight, Kate dwells on her conspicuousness as one of the few females on the jet; as she studies the landscape she notes that it was "no longer the lush green it had been the day I'd first flown into DaNang. It had all been cruelly defoliated: stripped as naked as I had" (384). The passenger seated next to her, an American businessman, asks: " 'What was a little girl like you doing over here for a year?' " Kate replies: " 'Working' " (385). Although a typical Vietnam novel of lost innocence, in this case the innocence is lost not through the rigors of combat but through treating the products of combat.

Besides its female protagonist, one of the refreshing elements of this book is the passages giving an American female perspective on sexual activities: both R and R and prostitution. One episode describing Vietnamese prostitutes would, in novels by males, include at least rude remarks but in this female novel it features only objective analysis. The American women walk by the local whorehouse, nicknamed the Cabbage Patch, and observe a number of women flapping their dresses in the air and yelling "boom-boom." One of the women, old, toothless, and sagging, competes for business as well although her "boom-boom" is a spiritless monotone. Turning to her companions, Kate asks: " 'Who'd be desperate enough to screw that old broad?' " to which fellow nurse Shelly replies, " 'That's Sophie...Viet Nam's version of a billboard.' " Another nurse, Jean, explains: " 'The commanding general has tried to shut the place down, but the guys keep sneaking back...Several of them have been killed by V.C. grenades while they were in there screwing.' '' Shelly's comment: " 'Talk about the earth moving...' " (72). In spite of the generally serious tone of the novel, Walsh also includes other humorous passages. For example, the nurses' Vietnamese maid, Tien, knowing that Kate is Catholic, wants to give her a special treat: a meat dish. When Kate inquires about the nature of the mystery meat, Tien replies: " 'Woof-woof' " (297). Tien also helps to spread hepatitis to the nurses by serving them the local water in the form of ice cubes, believing that *freezing* water has the same effect as boiling it. We are also treated to the amusing escapades of Gertie Clapsaddle, an old Montana nurse-anesthetist who spends her first night in DaNang picking up young American soldiers. Despite the antics of such characters as Gertie, Walsh's focus on the protagonist, Kate, results in a novel which gives us an idea of the thoughts and actions of a dedicated American woman in Vietnam, a woman drawn from Walsh's first-hand experiences.

What insights can a woman offer about the crucible of manhood, war? What contributions can an American woman in particular make to our knowledge of the Vietnam War? Where do we go to find portrayals of women in this conflict? Our options at this point are fairly limited: a few memoirs and excerpts in oral histories, a couple of novels offering stereotypical portrayals of women who are more interested in men than in their careers or the war itself, and one worthwhile novel in which a nurse emerges as a credible and admirable character. Nevertheless, we *should* be aware of the contributions of American women both to the Vietnam War itself and to the literary canon it has inspired. Our perceptions of the war are incomplete if we confine them to male experiences only. Although no one would argue that war has been a male domain and that the best literature has dealt with males in combat, some noteworthy female characters and chroniclers exist as well.

Works Cited

Austin, Jacqueline. "Women Watching War." *The Women's Review of Books.* Sept. 1984: 8-9.

Butler, Robert Olen. *The Alleys of Eden.* New York: Horizon Press, 1981.

Campbell, D'Ann. *Women at War With America: Private Lives in a Patriotic Era.* Cambridge: Harvard University Press, 1984.

Grimes, Charlotte. " 'Invisible Veterans' Still Struggling for Recognition." St. Louis *Post-Dispatch* 11 Nov. 1985, E3.

Hawkins, Evelyn. *Vietnam Nurse.* New York: Zebra Books, 1984.

MacPherson, Myra. *Long Time Passing: Vietnam and the Haunted Generation.* New York: Doubleday, 1984.

Miller, Kenn. *Tiger the Lurp Dog.* New York: Ballantine Books, 1983.

Santoli, Al. *Everything We Had.* New York: Random House, 1983.

Scott, Leonard B. *Charlie Mike*. New York: Ballantine Books, 1985.
Van Devanter, Lynda. *Home Before Morning*. New York: Beaufort Books, 1983.
Walker, Keith, ed. *A Piece of My Heart*. New York: Ballantine Books, 1987.
Walsh, Patricia L. *Forever Sad the Hearts*. New York: Avon Books, 1982.

"Women in Vietnam War Novels" was presented at the 1986 meeting of the PCA in Atlanta, April 2-4.

Born of Two Fathers:
Gender and Misunderstanding
in *Platoon*

Susan Jeffords

Oliver Stone's record-setting *Platoon* (1986) is often touted as a break
from earlier Vietnam films, giving us, as *Time* magazine proclaims, "Viet
Nam, the way it really was" (Corliss 54). In particular, as John Wheeler,
Vietnam veteran and writer and president of the Center for the Study
of the Viet Nam Generation, describes: " '*Platoon* is a new statement
about Viet Nam veterans. Before, we were either objects of pity or objects
that had to be defused to keep us at a distance. *Platoon* makes us real'
" (quoted in Corliss 57). Showing "a grunt-level view of the war" (Hartl),
Platoon is celebrated as showing what no other Vietnam film dared:
"the brutality, anger, and desire for revenge felt by those in combat"
(Moore). David Halberstam, himself an author of the Vietnam era, declares
with infallible certainty that "*Platoon* is the first real Viet Nam film."
Because, he adds,

Platoon is historically and politically accurate. It understands something that the
architects of the war never did: how the foliage, the thickness of the jungle, negated
U.S. technological superiority. You can see how the forest sucks in American soldiers;
they just disappear.... Thirty years from now, people will think of Viet Nam as
Platoon. (Corliss 57)

What these comments ignore, and what this essay will concentrate
on, is the way in which *Platoon* is instead very much like the Vietnam
representation that preceded it. Specifically, this film promotes and
represents a gendered reading of the war that works not only toward
the exclusion of women from its battleground, but toward the resolution
of gender tensions through the appropriation by the masculine of the
qualities, characteristics, and values of the feminine. As a general
movement in contemporary American culture and its criticism, this
appropriation functions to negate any production of a different reading

184

of gender and reinscribes it as and through the masculine. This is "Viet Nam, the way it really was."

Richard Corliss, in writing of what Vietnam did to American society, recalls that "we were a nation split between left and right, black and white, hip and square, mothers and fathers, parents and children.... Americans were fighting themselves, and both sides lost" (55). But while these divisions may have characterized American society "at home," for the narrators of Vietnam, such differences, especially those of race and class, were eradicated by combat. As John Del Vecchio's Daniel Egan reports, " 'We got a separate culture out here. And in some respects it's better. Fuck Man, an AK round don't care what color your paint job is' " (444). William Broyles, Jr., veteran and past editor of *Newsweek*, concludes about his experiences in Vietnam that

war is the only utopian experience most of us ever have. Individual possessions count for nothing; the group is everything. What you have is shared with your friends. It isn't a particularly selective process, but a love that needs no reasons, that transcends race and personality and education.... It is, simply, brotherly love. (58)

Richard Halloran reported, in his analysis of the American military since the Korean War, that in Vietnam "Relations between whites and blacks were often tense, openly antagonistic, and sometimes violent. The exception was blacks and whites under fire—the fight for survival wiped out color lines in the foxhole and rice paddies" (87). The narrator of John Del Vecchio's classic Vietnam novel, *The 13th Valley*, describes this bonding in its broadest sweep:

The restless infantrymen in the trenches and their clustered sergeants and lieutenants and captains on the landing strip represented the collective consciousness of America. These men...were products of the Great American Experiment, black brown yellow white and red, children of the Melting Pot.... What they had in common was the denominator of American society in the '50s and '60s, a television culture, the army experience—basic, AIT, RVN training, SERTS, the Oh-deuce and now the sitting, waiting in the trench at LZ Sally, I Corps, in the Republic of Vietnam. (145)

It is a bonding that cuts across boundaries that exist in the "World," boundaries that separate men by color, income, accent, and education. Narrative after narrative—from *The 13th Valley* to *The Boys in Company C*, from *The Bamboo Bed* to *Dispatches*—tells the story of the destruction of barriers set up in American society and their replacement by the bonds of war, what Broyles calls "comradeship" (58).

In *Platoon* these bonds are repeated. Chris Taylor (Martin Sheen), the movie's 21-year old hero, dances with blacks, torments a Vietnamese villager to the encouraging "Do him!" of a red-neck Southerner, cleans latrines with California surfers, and smokes dope with lower class men from the Bronx. But his bonding is not immediate. It occurs, following the pattern of Vietnam narration, only after he has been in combat, been wounded, and survived his first patrol. As a "new guy," a "cherry," Taylor is initially separated from the experienced men, looking at them from a distance as he deplanes in Saigon only with confusion and alienation. He tells us, "Nobody cares about the new guys. They don't even want to know your name." And Taylor's college education sets him even further apart from his buddies, most of whom are draftees, as compared to Taylor's "crusading" enlistment. Highlighting the distances that separate them, King early says to Taylor, "You got to be rich to think like that. The poor always get fucked over...Always have, always will." But after he returns from the hospital and is combat-seasoned, Taylor joins King in the "Underworld" and smokes dope with the men there, and these barriers disappear. He is, as King says, no longer Taylor but now Chris: "This ain't Taylor. He been shot. This here's Chris. He been resurrected." While "Taylor" was still separate from the other soldiers, still reeking of the "World," "Chris" is now bonded, a member of the platoon.

But while *Platoon* disrupts barriers between blacks and whites, lower and upper classes, Southerners, New Yorkers, and Californians, this film establishes other groupings, ones that do not depend upon social structures from the "World" but upon a new set of values belonging to the "Nam," Daniel Egan's "separate culture." Chris' introduction to the Underworld of the bunker is crosscut with scenes of the "outerworld" populated by other soldiers. Those in the Underworld smoke dope, laugh, dance together, and seem to share a common vision of the war and its significance. With no tensions about race, these men put their arms around each other and sing together Smoky Robinson's "Tracks of My Tears."

Their closeness and shared activity make their bond not only indiscriminate but erotic as well, with the men's bodies framed by the small bunker that surrounds them. The leader of this world is Sergeant Elias, soon to become the representative of good in the battle for Chris' soul that structures the thematics of the film. His approach to Chris in the Underworld is laden with erotic connotations. After Chris takes his first toke, Elias appears out of the haze and asks, "First time?" He then holds a rifle up to Chris, saying "Put your mouth on this," after which Elias blows smoke through the rifle barrel into Chris' mouth. The oral eroticism here is clearly homosexual (in spite of *Time* magazine's phrasing it a "fraternal toke") and signals Chris' virgin initiation into an underworld defined by homoerotic masculine bonds. Fondled, caressed, and seduced, Chris discards the bonds of the outerworld and joins with these men in a utopian world of "brotherly love."

In contrast to the Underworld, the film cuts first to Bunny and Junior, a Southerner and a city black, arguing over music. Junior calls Bunny's music, "Okie From Muskogee," "honky shit," and wishes he could hear some Motown. With Motown playing in the Underworld, we see the distances between Junior and other blacks in his platoon. More to the point, Junior doesn't smoke dope, believing it is "the white man's way of keeping blacks down." Emphasizing rather than ignoring racial differences, Junior clearly does not belong to the bonds of the Underworld.

The erotic as well is handled differently in the under and outer worlds. Bunny is drinking beer, not smoking dope, biting pieces out of beer cans to offer his lieutenant, while he delivers comments on the relative desirability of women: "Ain't nothing like a piece of pussy, 'cept maybe the Indy 500." And when the lieutenant is invited to join a poker game including sergeants Barnes and O'Neill, he declines, saying "I wouldn't want to get raped by you guys." O'Neill's reply: "Why's that LT? What are you saving up to be? Jewish?" When the lieutenant leaves, O'Neill immediately seeks Barnes' opinion on the lieutenant, concluding he "won't make it," he'll not survive Vietnam.

In this outer world, eroticism is clearly heterosexual, speaking about "pussy" and rape. As with Junior, bonds that separate men are emphasized rather than broken: Bunny thinks of the women who aren't there and O'Neill chides the lieutenant's reluctance with jokes that raise questions of religious difference through sexual terms; finally, O'Neill marks the categories of those who will and those who won't "make it," a difference never raised in the Underworld, where men literally support each other. Significantly, in the outer world, there is no body contact, no touching, no signs of intimacy; there, there is only rape. The voice of authority in this world is not the seductive Elias but the death-decreeing Barnes, the alternate figure in the battle for Chris' soul.

These are the two worlds displayed by the film: not the worlds of black and white, of rich and poor, or of North and South, but the worlds of dope-smoking and beer-drinking, of homoerotic bonding and heterosexual frustration, of comradery and difference. And with Elias and Barnes at their heads, each of these worlds comes in the film to represent a pole in the battle of good and evil that shapes Chris' moral destiny, a battle epitomized by the My Lai scene in which Barnes kills one Vietnamese woman and threatens to kill her daughter in order to get information about the Viet Cong, an act stopped only by Elias' intervention. What seemed initially to be tamer dividing lines—dope, card-playing, and music—become fixed as ways of fighting the war itself.

After the village incident, Elias tells Chris that he no longer believes in war, that "what happened today is just the beginning. We're gonna lose this war." Barnes, on the other hand, is out to win, to keep the "machine" of the military from breaking down. His belief in the war is epitomized in his treatment of the Vietnamese villagers; even though the translator relayed and clearly believed the prisoner's stories about the VC, Barnes insisted they were lying, that he knew the truth of the war from his side. As he tells Chris, "I am reality. There's the way it oughta be, and there's the way it is." With Elias the way things "oughta be," Barnes is clearly "the way it is." After Barnes kills Elias in the jungle, Chris reflects with confusion and frustration: "It's the way the whole thing works. People like Elias get wasted and people like Barnes make up the rules as they go along. And we sit in the middle."

So the lines set up between the Under and outer worlds in the seemingly harmless arena of the base become the boundaries between the right and the wrong way to fight the war, between justice and murder, between understanding and terror, between, as so many of the film's commentators have stated, good and evil itself. But in the terms established for difference by the Under and outer worlds in *Platoon*, this battle must be read through a frame of gender. The erotic, utopian, bonded world of Elias is depicted as more feminine than the more competitive, divided, and stereotypically masculine world of Barnes, characterized by beer-drinking, poker, pin-ups, and violent images of sexuality. The only one to help the "new guys," offering to carry Taylor's excess material on his first patrol and breaking in when the other soldiers try to blame him for falling asleep on watch, Elias takes on a more nurturing and supportive role in contrast to Barnes' masculine machismo. On that same patrol, when one soldier is injured and screaming with pain, Barnes commands, "Shut up and take the pain!" Barnes yells at Taylor about the watch before Elias intervenes. And in the village scene, Elias and Barnes fulfill John Wheeler's dichotomy of feminine and masculine:

I consider my commitment [to the military] as a statement that there are things worth dying for. It is a masculine statement. I think it is *the* masculine statement...Woman expresses the idea that there are things worth living for. (140-1)

While Barnes holds information above life, Elias insists on the reverse, saving life without questioning Barnes' motives or goals. And when Barnes confronts Elias in the jungle, rifle in hand, Elias drops his rifle and smiles, not believing that Barnes will kill him, while Barnes raises his gun and fires.

The difference that seemed at first to be eradicated by the bonding of Vietnam, a difference that is early reformulated in the simplistic terms of dope-smoking and beer-drinking—"honky shit" and Motown—and is thematized as good and evil as the film goes on, must finally be read as a difference of masculine and feminine in which the feminine characteristic "that there are things worth living for" is pitted against the masculine evil of death. Reinserting this construction into the action of the film forces a reinterpretation of the battle that Chris records between Elias and Barnes, "fighting for the possession of my soul," as more than a struggle between good and evil but as a staging of a battle of gender.

Time magazine tries to analyze the key moment of the film, Chris' killing of Barnes, in the frame of good and evil and comes up empty:

[C]an Chris or the audience take moral satisfaction in this deed? Which "father" has he followed? Has Chris become like Elias...? "You have to fight evil if you are going to be a good man," Stone says. "That's why Chris killed Barnes. Because Barnes deserved killing." Or has he emulated the enemy? Has he become Barnes in order to kill him? Stone has another answer: "I also wanted to show that Chris came out of the war stained and soiled—all of us, every vet.... Chris pays a big price. He becomes a murderer." A good man, and a murderer? It is a tribute to *Platoon*'s cunning that it can sell this dilemma both ways, and a mark of Stone's complexity that he can argue either side and believe both. (59)

Stone and his film seem to maintain *both* good and evil in Chris' character, making it unclear who really "wins" the battle for his soul. And surrounding this confusion over the central tension of the film is its overall meaning, whether it should be interpreted as pro- or anti-war, for or against violence, as justifying or supporting American involvement in Vietnam. As Richard Corliss maintains, *"Platoon* could very well be misunderstood into superhit status." Why? He goes on:

The army of Rambo-maniacs will love the picture because it delivers more bang for the buck.... Aging lefties can see the film as a demonstration of war's inhuman futility. Graybeards on the right may call it a tribute to our fighting men.... The intelligentsia can credit *Platoon* with expressing...comradeship and betrayal. (57)

If neither the stated moral theme of the film—good vs. evil—nor political, social, or ethical frames work to produce anything but ambivalent and contradictory interpretations of this film, then what are we to make of it? There is, of course, the possibility that Stone simply made a confusing or confused film, or that he intended the film to have no determinate meaning, perhaps as a comment on the complexities of war itself. Or, perhaps, the frame of interpretation lies elsewhere than in the film's foregrounded issues of politics, morality, and human nature. Reading *Platoon* through a gendered frame produces an interpretation of the film that seems to cut through these confusions to a more systematic and coherent thematics shared by this film and other Vietnam representation. A look at the murder scene will clarify this reading.

If, as the film's early schemes of difference suggest, the battle between Elias and Barnes—between what is called good and evil in the film— is a confrontation of the feminine and the masculine, then Barnes' murder of Elias is a direct attempt to eliminate these feminine qualities from the arena of Vietnam: valuing life over death, nurturing, bonding, and feelings that the war is no longer justifiable. Chris' subsequent murder of Barnes as vengeance for Elias' death would seem then to be a clear reinstatement of the feminine over and against the masculine, with Chris assuming Elias' role in this struggle. But Chris' final soliloquy denies such a simplistic reading, as he says, "Elias is in me and so is Barnes.... I felt like a child born of two fathers." He ends the film, not in the position of the masculine *or* the feminine, but in both.

Several recent critical analyses of American literature focus on just this scenario—the male bond as source for a challenge to traditional gender constructions of man/woman. Joseph A. Boone's reading of 19th century American quest narratives examines texts by Melville, Twain, and London to conclude that they offer "visions of individuality and mutual relationship that attempt to break down conventional sexual categorization by breaking through the limiting forms of culture and the conventions of love-literature" (191). In particular, they perform this by presenting communities of men that allow for "the psychological connection between self-sufficient male identity and an acknowledgement of the 'feminine' within man" (195). In language that could easily be transferred to *Platoon's* Underworld, Boone explains that "American comrades often present a more multifaceted model of loving relationship [than their British counterparts]: their bonds simultaneously partake of brotherly, paternal, filial, even maternal qualities, without being restricted to one definition alone" (193). He labels Ishmael's character "androgynous" (198) and celebrates Huck for being able to "cross boundaries of class, race, and sex with startling ease" (200), qualities they seem to share with *Platoon*'s young hero. And though Boone suggests that "twentieth-century versions of the male quest...have become increasingly ambiguous and self-deceiving as the possibility for escaping into a womanless world has become only a symbolic reality" (210), *Platoon* and its companion Vietnam representations suggest that this genre at least has managed to return to the narrative forms Boone identifies in 19th century America.

Robin Wood's reading of Hollywood films of the 60s through the 80s speaks as well of male-bonding films but insightfully sees them, not as expressions of camaraderie so much as of anxieties about the loss of home. Throughout this period, he identifies the general theme of the dissolution of patriarchy, chiefly seen as the loss of home, the nuclear family, and gender security. Consequently, Wood suggests that "the Restoration of the Father...constitutes...the dominant project...of contemporary Hollywood cinema" (172), one of the consequences of which is to show that "men, if need arises, can fill the woman's role just as well if not better" (172-3). While Wood's analysis correctly pinpoints the restoration of the father as Hollywood's primary interest in recent decades, he then goes on, through a reading of *The Deerhunter*, to offer possibilities for alternatives to such authoritative gender formations in the open exploration of bisexuality and homosexuality in film. Wood concludes that "the problem [of the repression of bisexuality and the oppression of women]...can only be resolved when the boundaries of gender constructions become so blurred that men can move with ease, and without inhibition, into identification with a female position" (291). Thus, while he critiques films that show "that men...can fill a woman's role just as well if not better," Wood valorizes those that enable men to move across gender boundaries "with ease, and without inhibition, into identification with a female position." Much like Huck's ability to "cross boundaries of class, race, and sex with startling ease," Wood's male heroes can move "with ease" across boundaries of gender as well.

Both Boone and Wood highlight a movement in current American criticism that celebrates these "androgynous" tendencies in male characters, encouraging and valorizing their possession of both masculine and feminine qualities, and praising their facility to incorporate both into their character moving across gender boundaries with "startling ease." And as Wood's argument makes clear, this is not a worship of men who can do what women do only "better," but instead a promotion of men who can carry *both* men's and women's characteristics, who can incorporate the two simultaneously and "with ease." What is most significant to both arguments is that neither puts forth a model for women doing the same. This is, in the terms of contemporary American criticism, only a man's game.

With this critical trend in mind, we can now return to *Platoon* and recognize it as a representational scheme of the kinds of gender formations critics like Wood and Boone are putting forth. When Sergeant Barnes murders Elias, he *is* killing the feminine in this film, eliminating it from the film's interpretive structures as a single force. Elias, in the terms set forth by *Platoon*, cannot win this battle. Yet when Chris in turn kills Barnes, he murders the solely masculine as well, suggesting that its frame cannot survive alone either. What does survive is Chris, the "child born of these two fathers." His survival, like that of the heroes Boone cites in 19th century American literature, depends upon his combination of these two positions within himself, of the masculine and the feminine within one character.

Why then is this not a truly androgynous "solution" like that proposed by many feminists,[1] one that takes equally of the masculine and the feminine and produces a third, perhaps better, gender formation? While Chris incorporates Elias' femininity and attitude toward the war into his final character, he uses Barnes' methods in order to do so. Where Elias stood passively while Barnes held the rifle to kill him, Chris acts as Barnes did to murder Barnes himself. He must become Barnes—the masculine—in order to successfully create a space in which he can be "born" as the masculine/feminine child. But more significantly, Chris' character is not "androgynous" because Stone presents in *Platoon* the same kind of structure offered by Wood, one that enables men to occupy "with ease and without inhibition," the position of the feminine. This movement is seen in *Platoon*, as in Wood and Boone, only from a masculine point-of-view, one that allows the masculine to incorporate the feminine into itself, not to become the feminine, but to ingest it, as a means of producing its own character.

Chris' confession that he "felt like a child born of these two fathers" stands metaphorically in *Platoon*'s dialogue, but its literal meaning is equally accurate and indicative of the gendered frame promoted in this film. He has no mother in this film, but only two fathers, is (re)produced by two men. As he first tells us, he goes to war to be "like grandpa in World War I and dad in World War II," initially setting his identity within the frame of these two fathers. In addition, it should not be overlooked that Chris writes, not to his mother or father, but to his grandmother, eliminating his immediate parents from the film's dialogue so that these positions are free to be taken over by Elias and Barnes as Chris' "new" parents. That these parents are both male fulfills what Gena Corea designates as "the patriarchal urge to give birth to oneself, to be one's own mother, and to live forever" (262). While Corea sees this urge literally at operation in reproductive technologies like surrogate mothering, cloning, gestation in artificial wombs, etc. through which "fathers can be, or appear to be, the sole parent" (292-3), this urge is worked out representationally in films like *Platoon*, in which men can be the "child of two fathers," and women and the feminine are entirely eliminated or absorbed into the masculine/father.

To return to the foregrounded thematics of the film—the battle between good and evil—and re-read them through this frame of gender is to reveal this struggle as framed by the masculine bond. Because both Elias and Barnes are incorporated into Chris' character through the masculine point-of-view—"the child of two fathers"—the good and evil they represent are finally not challenges to masculinity itself but reaffirmations of its powers of appropriation. In such terms, the possibility for a "good" that is defined outside the frame of the masculine being presented as an alternative in this film is very remote. At the same time, because of its expansive plot structure—including scenes of bonding, a potential massacre, ambush, battle, death—and its far-reaching themes—addressing aggression, violence, racism, self-meaning, good/evil, identity, class, the value of human life—*Platoon* presents itself as addressing issues not only of war but of life itself. What this film suggests is that these issues can finally be resolved only through a masculine frame, a resolution born, like Chris Taylor, "of two fathers."

The "misunderstanding" that Corliss sees as the interpretive product of *Platoon*, so that antithetical meanings seem to be simultaneously and appropriately produced, is then not so much a misunderstanding as a misdirection. Put into the position of the individual soldier in this film through insistent close-ups and a withholding of establishing shots that offer the viewer perspective on the events of the film, the audience feels, in one of Stone's most effective directorial strategies, the ambivalence, disorientation, and confusion of the soldier in Vietnam. We do not feel finally that Stone is providing for us a clear position from which to interpret this film. Stone's final long-shot of the battlefield from the helicopter taking Chris out of Vietnam (as twice wounded, he doesn't have to return to combat) gives only a false sense of closure to this scene and not a final interpretive stance.

But while *Platoon*'s themes seem unresolvable—"A good man, and a murderer?"—the masculine frame within which these themes are presented is clear. By appropriating to itself the feminine, the masculine point-of-view constructed in this film suggests that all possible solutions to the issues raised in *Platoon* are to be resolved within that frame. In such a construction, that the issues are not clearly resolved here shows, not the insufficiency of the frame, but the difficulty and complexity of the issues, issues that can only begin to seem clear from the view of a helicopter after battle, not before.

Out of this sea of "misunderstanding," Stone sends forth the veterans of this war, who "have an obligation to teach others what we know." What a gendered reading of *Platoon* shows is that what Stone's veterans are teaching is not truth, not justice, not good, not even how to win a war, but that "meaning to this life," Chris' final desire, is to be found only within the frame of men, inside the "platoon."

Notes

[1]Critics like Carolyn Heilbrun celebrate androgyny as the "perfect" combination of the masculine and feminine in one character.

Works Cited

Boone, Joseph A. "Male Independence and the American Quest Genre: Hidden Sexual Politics in the All-Male Worlds of Melville, Twain and London." In *Gender Studies: New Developments in Feminist Criticism*. Ed. Judith Spector. Bowling Green: Bowling Green State University Popular Press, 1986: 187-218.

Broyles, William, Jr. "Why Men Love War." *Esquire* November, 1984: 55.

Corea, Gena. *The Mother Machine: Reproductive Technologies from Artificial Insemination to Artificial Wombs*. New York: Harper and Row, 1985.

Corliss, Richard."*Platoon*: Viet Nam, The Way it Really Was, On Film." *Time* 129.4 (January 26, 1987): 54.

Del Vecchio, John M. *The 13th Valley*. New York: Bantam, 1982.

Halloran, Richard. *To Arm A Nation: Rebuilding America's Endangered Defenses.* New York: MacMillan, 1986.

Hartl, John. "*Platoon*: Vietnam's Shellshocked Reality Hits the Screen." *Seattle Times* January 16, 1987: 16.

Heilbrun, Carolyn. *Toward a Recognition of Androgyny*. New York: Harper, 1973.

Moore, Acel. "Vietnam Film Deserves Another 'Award': For Racism." *Seattle Times* February 18, 1987: A8.

Wheeler, John. *Touched With Fire: The Future of the Vietnam Generation*. New York: Avon, 1984.

Wood, Robin. *Hollywood From Vietnam to Reagan*. New York: Columbia UP, 1986.

Platoon and the Mythology of Realism

Thomas Prasch

When the film *Platoon* made the cover of *Time*, the headline that cut across the movie still on the magazine's cover declared: "VIETNAM AS IT REALLY WAS" (26 January 1987). This sort of response has been typical. *Platoon* has not only received unusually broad press coverage (in addition to the *Time* cover, for instance, it received coverage in ten feature articles in the *New York Times* between mid-December and its sweep of the Oscar awards at the end of March). It has also been almost universally acclaimed as a triumph of "realism" (usually in explicit contrast to such "fantasy" or "fictional" attempts to understand the war as *Apocalypse Now* and *The Deer Hunter*), and declared to be the first film that can be called "a true Vietnam War movie" (Halberstam II: 21; Halberstam is quoted to similar effect in Corliss 57). This label of "realism" has been cemented by the semi-autobiographical character of the film (emphasized in most of the reviews), and by writer/director Oliver Stone's own declaration of intent from the time the film was released to his acceptance speech for the Oscar for best picture.

Yet *Platoon* is, at its most central levels, a fictional film. Its plot consists of an overtly allegorical battle between forces of good and evil, the personifications of those forces blatantly idealized and mythologized. The *Bildungsroman* framework for this battle depends heavily on conventions of the war movie genre. Stone's film techniques serve to accentuate the allegorical and conventional dimensions of the film, merely layering over it a realism of surface detail and incident.

The problem posed by such a divergence between the character of a film and its reception is one of explanation: what purposes does mythification of his experience serve Stone, and what purposes does the misreading of *Platoon* as "realism" serve Stone's audiences? To answer such questions, however, we must begin with a more detailed survey of the reception of *Platoon*, and with a careful analysis of the movie's allegorical elements and the film techniques which reinforce them.

The trumpeted *Time* cover claims for the realism of *Platoon* are reiterated in the cover story itself, not only by film reviewer Richard Corliss (*"Platoon* gives the sense—all five senses—of fighting in Viet Nam"), but also by Corliss' quotations from other commentators ranging from fantasy film director Steven Spielberg ("It's just like being in Viet Nam"—though one has to wonder how Spielberg would know) to Vietnam War correspondent David Halberstam (*"Platoon* is historically and politically accurate...a drama of palpable realism") (56-57). Such claims are echoed in much of the popular press. *Newsweek* subtitled its review of the movie: "Oliver Stone Brings It Brutally Back Home." The review itself followed the general lines of *Time*'s analysis: that "most previous Hollywood movies about Vietnam weren't really about Vietnam" while Stone's realism amounts to a "ruthless...deglamorization of war." The review quotes Stone himself to underscore the claim of realism: "I was under an obligation to show it as it was" (Ansen 57). William Shawcross, commenting on the film for the *Times Literary Supplement*, declared *Platoon* to be "the first American film to try and tell the story like it was for the ordinary American grunt." "There is," he concluded, "nothing allegorical about *Platoon"* (438). Pat McGillan, in an introductory note to an interview with Stone in *Film Comment*, finds his film-trained eye amazed by *"Platoon*'s verisimilitude" (12). An unusual *New York Times* editorial page accolade declares *Platoon* "ultra-realistic" (*"Platoon* Meets Rambo"), and the first review of it to appear in the paper's pages, by Vincent Canby, similarly asserts that the film "deals with the immediate experience of the fighting" ("The Vietnam War" III:12). The *Times* also calls on David Halberstam to legitimate the film's claim of realism, and he amply provides it: *"Platoon* is about Vietnam. It exists, as they say, in the country"; "It is painfully realistic"; "What Mr. Stone has captured and put together is the special reality of Vietnam";"Real it is. This is the ultimate work of witness, something that has the authenticity of documentary" (II:21, 38).

Halberstam's assertions are paired with an analysis by a combat veteran, ex-Marine officer Bernard E. Trainor, whose interpretation is significantly more cautious. Trainor thinks the film "fails to get across" the reality of war, but concedes that to make the war real for an audience in an air-conditioned theater is "a hopeless task" (II:38). Such dissents from the mainstream view are, however, rare. Pauline Kael, reviewing *Platoon* for the *New Yorker*, and Richard A. Blake, criticizing it in the liberal-left Jesuit journal *America*, both undercut the film's realist credentials by emphasizing genre conventions the plot depends upon. Michael Norman, in another of the *New York Times* features on the film, makes a bow to its "graphic realism," but more generally emphasizes its mythic and conventional aspects (II:17).

The most strident public protests against *Platoon* have come from voices on the neoconservative right. Thus Norman Podhoretz has blasted the film for its unpatriotic attitude (qtd. in Corliss 57), and John Simon summarizes his negative assessment for the *National Review* by suggesting that, despite his combat experience, Oliver Stone "managed to make a film scarcely different from the soap operas written by hacks who never got closer to the VC than their VCRs" (54). In contrast, the mainstay magazines of mass media liberalism have, whatever their reservations about the "moral" of the film, largely accepted its realism. The *New Republic*'s reviewer, Stanley Kaufmann, follows the standard line, and the same journal's "TRB" column cites no less an authority on realism than Chuck Norris: "I mean, jeez, if you want all that realism...you can watch the news at night" (4). Tom O'Brien, in *Commonweal*, praises *Platoon*'s "frankness and non-ideological approach" ("Reel Politics" 17), and in a later column goes farther to claim that Stone "simply tells us what happened" ("Oscars step Out" 148). Stone "place[s] the viewer squarely in the center of jungle fighting," the reviewer for the liberal Catholic journal *Crisis* asserts; the "visceral" impact of *Platoon* makes it "the most immediate of war movies" (Allen 43). Combined with the claims of Halberstam, Shawcross, Canby, and others, these arguments amount to a broad liberal consensus about the character of the film.

This consensus is supported by Stone's own statements about his intentions as writer/director, which echo Von Ranke's dictum for writing "objective" history *"wie es eigentlich ist"* to a degree unusual in the maker of a fictional film. He was compelled "to tell the truth as I knew it before it was forgotten" (qtd. in McGilligan 16); his intention was to "make a document of a time and a place" (qtd. in Norman II: 17); his message is simply "Remember. Just remember what the war was" (qtd. in Corliss 61). Reviewers have consistently anchored their claims for the truth value of *Platoon* in Stone's Vietnam combat experience, and in the clear autobiographical parallels between what is known of Stone's tour of duty and that of the film's hero, Chris Taylor (both college dropouts and volunteers for Vietnam service, both wounded twice, etc.). Early film industry promotional material for *Platoon* reinforced this identification by reproducing in ads for the film Polaroid snapshots of Stone in uniform. As an Orion advertising executive put it, "The ads legitimized the picture" (Harmetz III:13).

Stone paves the way as well as for comparisons between *Platoon* and earlier Vietnam films, characterizing *Apocalypse Now* and *The Deer Hunter* as "big, mythic movies, not really authentic" (qtd. in McGilligan 21). Vincent Canby echoes him almost verbatim: "Both *Apocalypse Now* and *The Deer Hunter*...saw the war in terms of mythology" ("The Vietnam War" III:12). Elsewhere, Canby writes that *Apocalypse Now* was "a romantic meditation on a mythical war," and *The Deer Hunter* "more about the mind of America . . . than about the Vietnam War itself" *("Platoon* Finds New Life" II:31).

The other film with which Canby favorably compares *Platoon* is, of course, *Rambo,* a "revisionist comic strip" ("The Vietnam War" III:12). Halberstam's assertion that *Platoon* "passed the test of being a true Vietnam war movie" as no previous film had is similarly grounded in comparison to Stallone's super-warrior: "One cannot truly appreciate his achievement, I think, without comparing it to the work of Sylvester Stallone. If this is not the age of Rambo politically . . . then it most assuredly has been—until *Platoon*—cinematically" (38). Similarly, Michael Norman, writing in the *New York Times,* finds in *Platoon* "a welcome counterpoint to the comic and grotesque character" presented by Stallone (II:17). The *New Republic*'s "TRB" columnist insists that *"Platoon* is clearly *Rambo*'s opposite because it is full of left-wing signifiers" (94). Janet Maslin, in another *New York Times* article, though noting that "the *Rambo* influence can even be seen as playing some role in the box-office success of *Platoon,*" agrees that "Oliver Stone's view of events in Vietnam could not be more different from Mr. Stallone's" (II:21).

The assertion of such a clear difference, however, itself depends on reading into *Platoon*'s presumed realism a level of truth (and the political concomitants of that "truth") which any close study of the film itself belies. Fundamentally, *Platoon* is a fictional film, firmly rooted in allegory and genre conventions; it is once again the play of myth upon the staged "reality" of Vietnam. The implications of its fiction contradict those of its realism; more troubling, however, are the implications of its fiction being taken as "document."

Insofar as *Platoon* does in fact operate as a realistic film, its realism is strictly confined to two levels: that of surface texture, and that of incidental event. The realism of surface texture is established in the platoon's opening march. As we hear the soldiers' obscenity-laced talk over the background noise of the jungle for the first time, the narrator-hero, in rapid succession, looks down at his hands to see how the jungle foliage has cut into them; sees a jungle-rotted corpse which sends him vomiting to the nearest bush; leans back against a tree only to find his neck acrawl moments later with biting jungle ants; and receives warnings about realistic details of the Vietnam soldiers' craft (not to carry too much weight in his pack; not to drink too much water to avoid cramps). This level of realism established in the opening minutes, Stone relaxes the pace for the remainder of the film, throwing in an occasional reminder for his audience: more biting insects wake the hero in the first night's ambush, and a leech clings to his cheek on a later march.

By incidental event I mean that wide range of occurrences, mostly of the dark side of the war, which audiences simply expect a "true" account of Vietnam to take account of. These include such major events as the murder of civilians, the torching of a village, and the near-rape of some Vietnamese girls, all of which Stone at least integrates into his plot. Among these, too, are stereotypes of behavior about the enemy (above all his "invisibility"), the leadership (embodied in the spineless lieutenant), and the grunts themselves (their drug use, for instance). Incidental events also include smaller details scattered throughout the film: the collecting of ears; self-mutilation as a means of escaping combat; the slogans scrawled on the helmets; the cigarettes tucked beneath the helmet bands.

All such events undoubtedly reflect truths about the Vietnam experience (although not truths particularly absent from films such as *Apocalypse Now* and *The Deer Hunter*, the fictionality of which have been derided by *Platoon*'s praisers). They are included by Stone precisely to underscore the realism of his enterprise; they answer to a set of audience expectations shaped first by the television news "reality" of the war, and further honed by the revisionary stream of personal narratives and oral histories of the last few years (Berg 105-106). The proof of this is in Stone's conscious imitation of documentary styles in details of *Platoon*'s camerawork. As in the case of surface detail, the connection is established early in the film, on the platoon's first march: when two men lose their footing on a hill, they roll down *into*, not past, the camera. The documentary style most regularly figures in the fairly consistent use of jungle foliage as *mise en scene*, the leaves flapping back across the lens as the camera moves through the jungle and more or less constantly partially blocking the camera's view of its subjects. In the real jungle, the message reads, there are no clear camera shots. The same style also shows strongly in combat footage, where handheld cameras jarringly follow their rapidly moving subjects and every explosion makes the camera shake. One major point distinguishes Stone's imitative touches from actual documentary footage: in *Platoon* the style is a deliberate choice.

For all Stone's efforts to reinforce them, however, the incidental events remain incidental for the simple reason that they do not determine the course of the film in any significant way. Other events could easily be substituted, the placement of events easily rearranged. Both incidental events and surface details amount to nothing more than audience cues for the "realism" of the movie's storyline, a background of realistic detail to support the fictions that are in fact more central to the film. They are precisely geared to audience expectations because they tell us absolutely nothing that we do not already know—about the jungle, about life in the army, about the war. For the playing out of *Platoon*'s central fictions, even the technical support of camera and soundtrack veers away from the imitation documentary mode.

The overarching framework of the film as fiction is in its presentation as a form of *Bildungsroman*. Chris Taylor comes to the war to learn, as he tells us himself in a voice-over narration early in the film: "Maybe I've finally found it, down here in the mud. Maybe from down here I can start up again, be something to be proud of, without having to fake it, be a fake human being. Maybe I can see something I don't now see or learn something I don't yet know." Through the course of the film he makes the expectable transition from greenhorn to veteran to sage, his progress marked by rituals of transition: his first sighting of the enemy leads to his first wound; his entry to the "underworld" community of grunts is sealed by the sacrament of the marijuana pipe; his eyes are opened to the insanity of the war as a spurt of blood from a crushed skull spatters his face; when he confronts the evil Sergeant Barnes he is again marked, Barnes' knife slashing a scar into his cheek; his final battle and final wound coincide. In his closing narration the hero reminds us he has fought to learn, and projects the process into the future: "Those of us who did make it have an obligation to build again, to teach others what we know and to try with what's left of our lives to find a goodness and meaning to this life."

By employing the *Bildungsroman* narrative as his framework, Stone falls back on perhaps the most familiar conventions in the war movie genre, and one particularly familiar to movies about Vietnam. The prevalence of the device had been noted several years ago by Jay Hyam, who points out that "The combat films of the Vietnam War resemble the films made during the 1920s about World War I: they are about innocent Americans thrust into a war they do not understand" (199). In his recent (but not recent enough to include *Platoon*) survey of the Vietnam War film genre, Rick Berg suggests: "After Wayne's folly *[The Green Berets]*, the films become epistemological dramas. Each attempts to find a means for knowing and understanding the war . . . . . [A]ll turn, each in its own way, on the notion of war as an arena of maturation and education, a place where boys become men, and a realm where lessons are learned" (111). Stone reinforces the *Bildungsroman* framework at the technical level by two obvious devices: narrative envelope and voice-over narration.

The successful education must be marked by closure. Narrative enveloping provides closure by literally enclosing; it creates an encapsulation of the narrative by echoing the beginning in the end. In *Platoon* the narrative envelope is provided by air transport: the movie opens as Taylor is flown into Vietnam (to the tune of Barber's *Adagio for Strings*) and ends as he is flown out (to the tune of Barber's *Adagio for Strings*). The cinematography underlines the enveloping. As the fresh troops march out of the open jaws of the transport plane, the color scheme is of washed-out sepia tones that dissolve into full color when the soldiers confront the spectacle of body bags on the landing strip; the color fades back to sepia at the end of the film as the evacuation helicopter carries Taylor away from the site of his final battle, over the spectacle of a mass grave for the enemy dead. The shifts in color tone not only frame the film as a whole, but suggest as well the faded colors of old photographs, reasserting the character of the enclosed narrative as document.

Even more clearly, the use of voice-over narration serves the *Bildungsroman* framework by privileging the hero's voice, both giving the theater audience an "inside" view of the hero's intellectual development and separating the hero from the other characters in the film, whose voices are only heard when they speak. Not surprisingly, the voice-over narrative is also a standard convention of the war movie in general and the Vietnam War film in particular, a central feature of "fictional" films such as *Apocalypse Now* and "documentary" features such as *The Ten Thousand Day War*. The actual form Taylor's voice-overs take is that most conventional of forms, the letter home; his words presumably are part (although he never holds pen in hand) of letters to his grandmother. The effect of the privileging of the narrator in such voice-over narration closely corresponds to the similar function of the narrator in recent oral histories of the war, the effect of which John Carlos Rowe analyzes:

In the oral histories that attempt to capture the veteran's actual experience in the War...special privilege is claimed for the author-function.... [T]he author's credibility is generally established both by his direct experience of the War *and* his criticism of American conduct in the War. These credentials are generally supported by the popular American mythology of the "author" as a "free-agent," who assumes full responsibility for his statements and intentions. (135)

As in the case of these oral histories, Stone's narrator draws his privilege from the pretense of realism in the film "reality" on which he comments.

In combination with the narrative enveloping, the use of voice-over reinforces closure by closing off the Vietnam experience from the film audience. The envelope holds the "document" that is the narrative. It is "explained" in the voice-overs by a privileged narrator whose voice takes precedence on the one hand over the film audience who cannot share the experience because the enveloping closes it away from them, and on the other hand over the others who shared the Vietnam experience because their voices are not privileged. Between film and audience a further privileging takes place, rooted in the close analogy between Taylor as the narrator of the film and Stone as the writer-director upon whose experiences Taylor's narration is based; press coverage emphasizing the autobiographical character of Stone's film underlines this analogy between the maker of the narrative and the character who narrates it. The multiple closure thus achieved reinforces the film's claim to realism by asserting the narrative's self-enclosed character and by denying to any potential critic grounds from which to comment on it. Like any closed text, *Platoon* resists criticism and insists that it be taken on its own terms (for a discussion of the closed text see Eco 8-9, and more generally 107-172).

The privileging of the narrator has a more literal, biographical grounding as well. The average grunts, Taylor tells us "come from the end of the line, most of 'em. From small towns you never heard of.... Two years' high school's about it. Maybe if they're lucky a job waiting for them back at the factory. But most of 'em got nothing. They're poor, they're the unwanted.... From the bottom of the barrel, and they know it." Taylor (and Stone), in contrast, chose to be there. As he tells a black soldier he shares latrine duty with, "I volunteered. I dropped out of college, told 'em I wanted the infantry, combat, Vietnam." (The grunt's response is telling: "Shit. Ya gotta be rich in the first place to think like that.") Taylor's mission is thus a double one: to learn whatever it is you are supposed to learn from a war, and to convey the truths of that experience not only for himself but for those real grunts who cannot articulate their experience. Stone again asserts the parallel between his narrator's role and his own by dedicating his film to those (presumably voiceless) who served in Vietnam.

A look at the voice-over narrations themselves reinforces the connection between the device and the *Bildungsroman* framework of the film. In the opening narration Taylor admits his ignorance of the basic needs for survival in Vietnam: "I don't even know what I'm doing. A gook could be standing three feet in front of me and I wouldn't even know it." In case we doubt the narrator's voice, Stone offers proof for Taylor's assertion shortly thereafter, when Taylor fails to see a Viet Cong bunker directly in front of him. If his perception is not yet adequate for Vietnam, his mental faculties serve him no better: "Somebody once wrote, hell is the impossibility of reason. That's what this place feels like: hell." In his opening monologue, Taylor reveals himself as utterly unknowing.

In the second voice-over Taylor outlines his reason for coming to Vietnam (rebellion against parents who "wanted me to be just like them: respectable, hard-working, a little house, a family") and sings the praises of the bottom-of-the-barrel grunts, "because a grunt can take it, can take anything." It is shortly thereafter that he decides that "Maybe I've found it, down here in the mud." It takes him some time to finish finding it, however. Several monologues later he can still see "only six inches in front of my face, not much else." He already knows the central truth he will leave Vietnam with, that "we're fighting each other, when we should be fighting them." But he seems not to know he knows it, since in the same speech he confesses that "I don't know what's right and what's wrong anymore." Only as he is helicopered away from the battlefield can he provide the moral of the story. "We did not fight the enemy, we fought ourselves and the enemy was in us," he begins the narration that serves as coda to the film.

The *Bildungsroman* framework developed through the course of the voice-over narration dovetails neatly with the plot device that is the centerpiece of *Platoon*—a battle between good and evil personified in two sergeants, Elias and Barnes. The enveloping device serves to set up the allegorical battle by closing off Vietnam as a separate, sacred space. The naming of that space defines it early in the film: during the initial march through the jungle Barnes sends a new man up to point by telling him to "Get your ass up to hell," and Taylor opens his first narration by calling Vietnam "hell." Within this sacred space, Taylor's "education" is, as noted above, ritually marked, and his progression corresponds closely to the ritual testing of the classic hero.

As any classic hero has both guide and tempter, Taylor has Elias and Barnes. Stone himself says of the models for the characters, "To me...they were gods.... [S]uddenly everything I had read in Homer was coming true" (qtd. in McGilligan 21). Both characters, as Pauline Kael has pointed out, are shot throughout the film from below, giving them a larger-than-life appearance (95). Again stating the obvious in his final monologue, Taylor tells us the two fought for "possession of my soul," and he declares himself the "child born by those two fathers," The Manichean opposition of good and evil forces within the American military is again a standard device of the Vietnam genre, most characteristic of the barely fictional novels that most transparently show their authors' need to rework their personal experience as fiction. It is typical of the Vietnam film as well, and of the subgenre of films prevalent in the 1970s depicting the problems Vietnam veterans faced readjusting to civilian life (Berg 117-118; Paris 23-25).

The battle lines for the allegorical struggle are drawn early in the film, when Taylor is vomiting at the sight of the rotting corpse on the platoon's first march. Barnes passes him by with the contemptuous remark that "You are one sorry-ass son of a bitch"; Elias stops to give fatherly advice and offers to carry himself some of the contents of Taylor's overloaded backpack. The make-up department takes care of any doubts the viewer may have: Barnes' face is a stitch-work of scars, a mapping of his close ties with death, while Elias has the face of the wise man, most creased when touched by mysterious smiles.

Barnes is that classic stock figure of the war film genre, the gung-ho sergeant. It is he who tells the soldier screaming in pain after being wounded in the film's first firefight, "Shut up and take the pain." It is he who begins an object lesson in the realities of Vietnam by saying of a freshly killed soldier, "You all look at this lump of shit," and callously concludes his lecture by calling out, "Doc, tag him and bag him." It is he who commits the film's most blatant atrocity, the cold-blooded murder of an elderly Vietnamese woman, and is only prevented by Elias' intervention from gunning down a child as well. All-knowing Elias explains him to Taylor in simple terms: "Barnes believes in what he's doing."

On a metaphorical level, Barnes is closely associated with death. Of his scars, one grunt tells Taylor: "Barnes been shot seven times and he ain't dead. Barnes isn't meant to die. The only thing that can kill Barnes is Barnes." His role as master of death is made clear by his deliberate shooting of Elias, and at the end by his near-murder of Taylor. When he asks a group of soldiers, "Death?" What do you all know about death?" he asserts his own authority and knowledge, as he does again when he tells a fearful underling, "Everybody gotta die sometime." Even in his last words he asserts his authority over death, saying as Taylor points a gun at his chest, "Do it." The domination of death in the arena of war guarantees Barnes' place in Stone's pantheon. In the context of Vietnam, Barnes makes sense when he declares, "I am reality." As war is hell he is its master, so that he can tell Elias when the latter tries to prevent the murder of the child, "Stay out of this, Elias, it ain't your show."

The logic of the movie depends on his being only half-right. The Elias who helps the overweighted Taylor on his first march, who supervises his initiation into the mysteries of the drug world, who waxes poetic about the stars of the Vietnam sky, and who wrestles with Barnes to prevent another atrocity, may not seem a fit model for a fighter. Certainly Elias tells Taylor that he no longer believes in the war, and Barnes, after Elias' death, labels him a "crusader," the sort of person who clogs the machinery of war.

At the same time, however, at a more mysterious level, Elias is a consummate warrior. No one else among the American troops comes closer to the Viet Cong ideal of invisibility and silence in motion. In his final engagement he shows himself master both of war experience (explaining to the addled lieutenant what the enemy's likely plan of attack will be) and of a more extrasensory jungle awareness ("They're coming," he tells his small patrol, having paused a moment to listen to the jungle's silence). When, just before his death, he runs his solo mission against the incoming NVA swarms, camera and soundtrack both work to enhance the mystical character of his fighting style: the music shows a touch of the Orient and a touch of mystery, a cross between Hitchcock and Zen; over the music we hear not the usual chaos of battle or the typical whitenoise of the jungle, but the enhanced sounds of Elias' passage through the brush; and the camera does not pan to catch his run, but follows him, the *mise en scene* of foliage between Elias and the lens blurred by the follow shot to enhance the sense of his speed. Elias comes by his warrior's mastery through his own semi-magical communion with Vietnam, his chthonic affiliation with the underground. He presides over the underground haven of the platoon's drug subculture, and when a Viet Cong tunnel complex is found it is Elias who descends into its depths. His skill as a warrior thus shares common roots with his role as protector and as guide to the hell of Vietnam.

As mentioned, *Platoon* sets up the opposition between Barnes and Elias early, in their responses to Taylor during the opening march. Both have their followings from the start, as the camera demonstrates by crosscutting from Elias' underground den of drugs and soul music to the barracks run by Barnes, where the music is country and bourbon the drug of choice. The confrontation is truly set in motion, however, when Elias intervenes to prevent the killing of the Vietnamese girl. The result of the wrestling match is ambiguous: by the time it is broken up Barnes seems to have the upper hand, but the killing of the girl is avoided. The direct result of the tussle, Taylor tells us, is "A civil war in the platoon: half the men with Elias, half with Barnes." That civil war in turn establishes for Taylor the moral of the story, delivered as he flies out: "We fought ourselves, and the enemy was in us."

Not content with the merely allegorical level, Stone weights his characters further by mythological reference, drawing from Scripture. Elias' name is a variant for Elijah, the prophet of God who battled Ahab, worshipper of Baal, for the hearts and minds of the Hebrew people. Like his namesake, Elias is a prophet; it is he who tells Taylor, "We're gonna lose this war." To cement the identification, as they enter the village where Barnes will kill the old woman and where Elias and Barnes enter into direct battle, Taylor's voice-over tells us: "Barnes was the eye of our rage...our Captain Ahab." That Barnes is Captain Ahab touches on another level of Stone's metaphorical borrowing: Barnes in fact closely resembles Melville's Ahab, the scars on his face like Ahab's wooden leg, both characters carrying the same allegorical baggage of pacts with death and unholy pursuits. At the outset of *Moby Dick*, Elijah appears to the narrator to warn him away from Ahab and the Pequod.

Elijah has traditionally been taken by allegorical interpretations of the Old Testament to be a symbolic foreshadowing of Christ. In *Platoon*, Elias' identification with Christ is both explicitly stated and symbolically reinforced. Early in the film, after an argument about who will serve on night patrol, a disgruntled fellow soldier complains of Elias: "He thinks he's Jesus fucking Christ"; later in the film Barnes contemptuously refers to Elias as a "water-walker." If Elias is Christ, then Barnes, ruler of the "hell" of Vietnam, must be taken to be Satan. Their final confrontation draws heavily on both film cliché and symbol. As the platoon prepares to retreat, the lieutenant worries about Elias still being out on his patrol of the periphery; Barnes ambiguously replies, "I'll get him." When he reaches Taylor's position and tells him to pull back, Taylor also worries about Elias, and again Barnes responds, "I'll go get him." Which of course he does, with a trinity of bullets across the chest. The murder is staged as classic heroic encounter: Elias appears silently, almost magically, in front of Barnes; seeing Barnes, he smiles; Barnes does not smile back; the camera closes in, so that the screen contains nothing but the two opponent's eyes; we can see from the fading of the smile lines (since the lips are out of the picture's frame) Elias' smile dissolve; then the three shots. As Barnes retreats he encounters Taylor again. "Where's Elias?" Taylor asks; "He's dead," Barnes replies.

In fact Elias is not dead yet; the film literally resurrects him. As the helicopter evacuates the platoon, they see Elias below them with an army of VC at his back—running, being hit in the back, running on, hit again. In his final moments he raises his arms, taking on a cruciform pose. The swirling dust raised by the helicopter as it swoops low over the scene blurs together the two prophetic deaths: Christ's crucifixion, and Elijah's ascension into heaven in a whirlwind. Back in the underground den, Elijah's disciples discuss his death. One of them speaks with assurance of his ascension: "If there's a heaven...I know he's sitting up there drunk as a monkey."

Film critics seem confused about where Taylor's true identity lies— whether in the fight for "possession of my soul" Elias or Barnes wins out. The confusion perhaps originates in part in the film itself, in Taylor's voice-over declaration after the scene in the village that "I don't know what's right and what's wrong anymore," or in his final confession that he is the "child born by those two fathers." In fact, Taylor's identification with Elias is quite obvious, the parallels as clear as the first six letters of Chris Taylor's name (I would like to thank Ellen Berkowitz for bringing this point to my attention). Both Elias and Taylor are labelled "crusaders," Elias by Barnes and Taylor by the soldier to whom he confessed that he volunteered. It is into Elias' underground, not Barnes' barracks, that Taylor is initiated, and when he is first brought to the lair he is introduced: "This is Chris. He been resurrected." It is with Elias that Taylor's overt sympathies throughout the film lie. Before Elias' death, Taylor is already imitating his actions. Immediately after Elias prevents the killing of the child, Taylor intervenes to avert the rape of a couple Vietnamese girls. "Welcome to Nam, man," one of the would-be rapists tells him (the same phrase that greeted the fresh troops frozen by the sight of the body bags), "This ain't your place at all." As Taylor responds—"You don't fuckin' get it, do you, man. You just don't fuckin' get it"—he glances up to see Elias looking on like a guardian angel, standing beside a grazing water buffalo with his gun resting on his hip.

With the death of Elias, the hero's mantle falls on Taylor's shoulders. The actual transference has as its emblem the confrontational gaze: just as Barnes met Elias' gaze before shooting him, so in the helicopter after witnessing Elias' final death Taylor raises his eyes to meet Barnes' stare, the camera closing in on both sets of eyes. When Taylor tries to convince his companions (against the more obvious evidence of the NVA fusillade to which they were all witness) that it was Barnes who killed Elias, his argument is that "Proof's in the eyes, man." When Barnes interrupts the conversation to declare that "I am reality," and to dare the disciples to act ("So kill me," he challenges them), it is only Taylor who in fact does act, wrestling with Barnes as Elias had before him (and, more clearly than in Elias' case, losing).

All this sets the stage for Taylor's final battle. In that battle, Taylor emerges at last as a true warrior hero: ruthless, reckless, fearless, and impossible to kill. His salvation comes through the *deus ex machina* of an air strike: just as Barnes (who obviously sees in Taylor an Elias reborn) is about to bayonet him, the napalm bombs burst behind him and everything goes black. When Taylor arises from this hightech version of purifying fire, day has supplanted night, and all that lives in the fire-blackened circle of Taylor's final rite is Barnes. He makes an easy target.

The battle between Barnes and Elias, and then between Barnes and Taylor, forms the central plot of *Platoon*. The clearly allegorical character of that plot Stone underlines with a multiple layering of mythic referencing, to Scripture and to heroic quest as well as to literary and film genre conventions. Stone further plays the more mythic heroic quest off the genre convention of the *Bildungsroman* to enhance the symbolic meaning of Taylor's battlefield "education." He overlays the whole bundle of fictions with generous borrowings from other war film genre conventions—from the use of familiar stock characters to the focus on the platoon as a unit to the elegaic strings of Barber's recurrent *Adagio* (Berg 195; Paris 24; Norman II:17; O'Brien, "Reel Politics" 18). Even in small details *Platoon* follows time-worn convention: the soldier who shows Taylor the snapshot of his overweight girlfriend back home dies in the ambush that night; when a running grunt catches his foot on the tripwire of a booby-trap, the breaking of the wire is shown in ground-level slow motion, and a suspenseful pause precedes the expected explosion. The overall result is a film as dependent upon myths and upon the fictions of genre convention as any of the earlier Vietnam movies with which it has been compared. The questions that remain are thus not about the *Platoon*s "realism," but rather about why it has been so important for both Stone and his audience to insist on the movie's "documentary" character.

The tension between surface realism and the more central fictionality of *Platoon* results in a series of contradictions within the film itself, embracing aspects of both the movie's form and its content. In formal terms, for instance, the "letters home" device employed to justify the narrative voice-overs proves simply implausible. The style of the voice-overs is blatantly oral, thick with contractions and sentence fragments, and the placement of the voice-overs negates their status as letters. Taylor is never narrating from a place where he could possibly be writing; he speaks his monologues while on the march, on watch at night, during lulls in combat action, and his narration is consistently interrupted by events. Similar contradictions figure into the technical level of the film, as between the documentary-style camerawork and the careful contrivance that allows first Elias and Barnes, then Taylor and Barnes, to discover the other in a gaze.

More important, however, are the contradictions implicit between the content level of the film and the conventions Stone employs. The *Bildungsroman* framework depends upon war being a field for education, yet the explicit content of Taylor's voice-overs denies there is anything to learn. In a realm defined as "the impossibility of reason," what can be learned is senselessness. "Just another day, stayin' alive," Taylor tells us well into the film, "we drop a lot of bombs and then walk through the jungle like ghosts in a landscape." In his opening narration Taylor tells us, "A gook could be standing three feet in front of me and I wouldn't even know it," but late in the film he can only see what's "six inches in front of my face, not much else." The framework also depends on the transferability of the knowledge acquired by the audience. If the education is to be meaningful, it must be something that can in turn be taught—and if it cannot be taught, there is no reason to make the film. Taylor directly says as much in his closing monologue—his aim is now "to teach others what we know"—and the whole function of the voice-over convention presumes that there is something that can be explained. But the Vietnam experience resists explanation, as Taylor's own words suggest: "Tell mom and dad I...well, just tell 'em." After telling two other soldiers that they "just don't fucking get it," he tells us, "I don't know what's right and what's wrong anymore." The envelope technique also works to negate the teaching function, by closing off the Vietnam experience from the film audience.

Equally problematic is Taylor's presumption that he can speak for the grunts, and the parallel presumption of Stone's that his film represents the experience of the ordinary soldier. The presumption is crippled at the outset by Taylor's special status—as a college boy and volunteer as well as a "crusader" in the more mythic sense. It is hampered by the technique of voice-over narration, which further privileges Taylor over the other soldiers. In addition, the allegorical plot removes the film not only from the reality of Vietnam, but from the reality of the ordinary soldier's experience. On the allegorical battlefield the struggle between good and evil is fought between only three characters, the rest of the cast serving merely as props for these central figures. Such a narrative strategy directly negates Stone's ostensible goal of creating a document to validate the war experience of the grunts elegized in Taylor's narration as "the best there is...heart and soul."

Most fundamentally, Stone contradicts the antiwar implications of *Platoon*'s realistic surface by rooting its plot action in the creation of a warrior hero. Such a result is not surprising given Stone's vision of Vietnam as the arena for a new *Iliad* (qtd. in McGilligan 21), but it contradicts much of the incidental event in the film and works against the presumably critical parts of Taylor's commentaries. The application of the *Bildungsroman* framework to the war experience bolsters this legitimation of war; the presumption that war (apparently even a senseless, lost war like Vietnam) can serve as a field for education and character building could come straight from a recruiting advertisement. The final stage of Stone's glamorization of the warrior is reached in the apocalyptic battle, where Taylor comes into his own as consummate killer and achieves his victory over Barnes by gunning him down. The combat sequence in which the final confrontation is embedded depends for its effect on precisely the thrill of battle that draws crowds to *Rambo*, and that the war film genre in general is designed to exploit. The effectiveness of the narrative strategy can be gauged by the audience cheers that greet the death of Barnes.

Critics have been enmeshed in a parallel set of contradictions. There are few reviewers who fully agree with William Shawcross that "there is nothing allegorical about *Platoon*." Most have simultaneously acclaimed the film's realism and noted the allegorical, even mythical elements in the plot. Vincent Canby, who dealt solely with the realism of the film in his first *New York Times* review of it, later concedes that *Platoon* is "still a work of fiction. It comes out of a long tradition of 'war' movies [and] uses a number of war-movie conventions." Canby also notes its mythic conventions—the "Christ-like image of a betrayed American soldier being crucified"—before going on to dismiss *Apocalypse Now* and *The Deer Hunter* because "both...saw the war in terms of mythology" (*"Platoon* Finds New Life" II:21, 31). Even more interestingly, David Halberstam directly confronts accusations that the two sergeants are unrealistic: "Some people have complained about his allegorical use of the two sergeants. I have no problem with them: both seem real enough to me." On the same page he goes on to describe them as the "sergeant of darkness" and the "sergeant of light" (II:38). Richard Allen recognizes in Elias "a martial saint: a St. George" (45), Stanley Kaufmann calls the voice-overs and soundtrack "the stuff of TV equivocation" (24), Richard Corliss notes plot echoes of war genre conventions (58), and Tom O'Brien sees in Taylor "a staple hero of combat literature since *The Red Badge of Courage*" ("Reel Politics" 17). All praise *Platoon*'s "realism."

The play of contradictions in their own view of the movie blinds reviewers to its more troubling subtexts. In particular, critics' claims for the film's realism lead them to ignore the elevation of the warrior hero and the glamorization of combat that are fundamental to its plot. It is precisely because of this blindness that critics find Taylor's murder of Barnes confusing or troubling. Richard Allen, for instance, after long consideration, concludes that *Platoon* is "morally ambiguous," much as the war that produced it was (45-46). There is in the film no ambiguity whatever: the culmination of Taylor's education is the creation of him as warrior hero, and warrior heroes kill their enemies, who are embodiments of evil whatever uniforms they wear.

Contradictions as plain as these could not be sustained unless they served a purpose. Cognitive dissonance generally marks points of tension within the ideologies of an individual or a group. The Vietnam War provides just such a point of tension, both for those who fought it and for those who participated in the public debate about it. Recent revisionary trends in interpretation have sought to paper over the ruptures the war introduced into central tenets of America's self-construction: beliefs about America's invincibility, moral high purposes, and world role. The response to *Platoon* must be understood within the framework of this revisionary climate, and within the context of the particular ideological needs of Stone as a Vietnam veteran and the moderate and liberal media as would-be shapers of political values.

For Stone, the most rudimentary level at which *Platoon* serves his personal needs is as explanation. The conflation of the allegorical plot and the realistic surface provides a basis for explaining the war in terms other than those of personal failure. If the loss of the war can be accounted for by Taylor's assertion that "we did not fight the enemy, we fought ourselves," then the loss ceases to be the defeat of American soldiers by the North Vietnamese enemy, and the training, will, and heroism of the individual American soldier need not be brought into question. This explanation can only work, however, if the allegorical battle within the American forces "really" took place, and so it must be validated by realistic detail in the film, and by emphasis on autobiography and the production of a "document" in the promotion of the film. The use of the realistic surface further serves the cause of explanation by allowing

Stone to subsume the major points (of surface detail, at least) of the antiwar position into his own view. Thus atrocities and cruelties by American troops are brought into the explanation itself and located in the "evil" side of the American forces. This maneuver both creates a justification for the presumed Manichean division on the American side, and redirects criticisms of the conduct of the war that could be taken as attacks on Stone as a Vietnam veteran.

In addition to explaining the war experience, however, *Platoon* also legitimizes it, creating in the war a source of meaning and value. This Stone accomplishes with the *Bildungsroman* framework, the overt message of which is that the war served as an education. Further, the war provided a sort of education not available to those who refused or avoided fighting in it; the point is specifically made by Taylor, when he explains that he dropped out of college because "I wasn't learning anything there." Stone asserts the special character of the battlefield education by the privileging of Taylor's narrative voice, in combination with the closure achieved by the narrative envelope. The special character of Taylor's knowledge can only be asserted, however, if the audience accepts the real status of this arena of education, which can only be accomplished with a convincing realism of surface. Once that realism is accepted by the film audience, the operation of closure removes the content of the film from criticism, and the allegorical plot is justified by the aura of authority given it by the narrative voice.

Perhaps most centrally, *Platoon* functions for Stone as a form of absolution. Both in purpose and in practice, the Vietnam War was morally ambiguous. Both the ostensible aims of the war and the methods by which the war was fought were widely questioned on fundamental moral grounds. The experience of the returned Vietnam veteran thus must include coming to terms with his own role in this moral ambiguity. The dichotomy of good and evil within the platoon allows Stone an easy avenue for evading his own moral responsibility; the prevalence of such dichotomies in other overtly autobiographical fictions of Vietnam suggests how much easier such an evasion is in comparison to a direct confrontation with one's own participation in an immoral conflict. Insofar as Barnes' allegorical identification with evil makes him the scapegoat for all immorality in the conduct of the war, it absolves all others of moral responsibility. But again, for the absolution to work, the posited dichotomy must be taken to be "real." The surface realism, and the incidental events introduced as partial confession (partial in that responsibility is evaded), provide a grounding for the allegorical in the "reality" of the war.

The critical reception of *Platoon* could, of course, reflect no more than the success with which Stone employs surface realism to legitimate or distract from the more fictional levels of his film. In this sense, the audience expectation for repetition in a Vietnam film of newsreel images and documentary patterns could be seen as ironically thwarted precisely by Stone's imitation of documentary and oral history styles in his fiction. Beyond such merely mechanical responses, however, the blindness to *Platoon*'s fictionality serves a number of clear purposes.

Two of those purposes correspond, though from a different point of view, with Stone's own: explanation and absolution. As an explanation of the war, it again partly justifies America's loss—much as it does for Stone, but without the overtone of answering a sense of personal failure. On another level, however, *Platoon* presumes to explain the veteran's experience to the non-veteran. For this to be successful at all requires the surface of realism to be convincing, but by layering that realism onto a framework of *Bildungsroman* and allegory Stone seeks to ensure that the evaluation of the veteran the film effects in its audience will be positive and meaningful. This corresponds to a real social need to reincorporate the veteran into society in such a way as to seal the rupture created by the drastic difference between the veteran's experience of the social world in Vietnam and the behaviors suited to the domestic social fabric.

The thematic of absolution answers to this need to resocialize the veteran. Insofar as the moral excesses of Vietnam were also antisocial excesses, which figured in the primarily negative representations of the veteran through most of the 1970s, absolution cleanses that image to promote social reincorporation. The Manichean dichotomy allows the excesses of the war to be relocated, shifted from all veterans to only some veterans (in *Platoon*, conveniently shifted to one left dead in the field), but again only if it is convincingly supported by realistic incident. Paradoxically, the incidental details in *Platoon* are there *not* to be examined, either in the interest of understanding or of revelation—they are, after all, exactly the events we expect, and function precisely to confirm those expectations. That the sources of the film's realism remain unexamined provides a basis for its wide appeal despite the unresolved debates about the nature and meaning of the war. Acceptance of the "realism" of the movie's incidental detail allows us to condemn the war without condemning the veteran (or alternatively to condemn neither the war nor the veteran), thus accomplishing the veteran's reincorporation without reopening political debates.

That the liberal press in particular has been integral in asserting *Platoon's* realism must be understood in the context of the prevalent mood of neoconservative revisionism. Liberal opinion has had to fight against what it must see as a double distortion, first against the obfuscation of successive presidents and then against the neoconservative rewriting of the past. Against the claims of Norman Podhoretz, for instance, that the Vietnam War was a just cause and could have been won, Stone's overt admission that atrocities took place (even when combined with the implicit suggestion that were it not for the "civil war" within U.S. ranks we might have won) must seem preferable. Put simply in cinematic terms, *Platoon* is more politically correct than *Rambo*.

Were it the case that *Platoon* merely served to solve the dilemmas of coming to terms with Vietnam faced by both veterans like Stone and domestic critics of the war—rebuilding ruptured ideologies, reintegrating society, and combatting neoconservative revisionism—the superficiality of the film's claims to be a realistic representation of the war would be no cause for concern. There are clear dangers, however, in the uncritical acceptance of such claims.

There is a danger first of all in the continued primacy of demands for "realism," based on documentary and newsreel versions of the real, as a criterion for Vietnam films. As Rick Berg has pointed out: "This continuing desire to see what we take for the real war, the real Vietnam, obscures any other understanding of Vietnam, as well as any other form of understanding.... We leave the films not only assured that we still know what Vietnam was and what it was all about, but also that our ways of knowing are still intact" (106). In *Platoon* this principle reveals itself in the paradox of the realistic detail mentioned above: that it exists not to be examined, but merely to fulfill our expectations. The consequence of the fulfillment of documentary-conditioned expectations in the surface play of realism is that the fictional elements of the film take on the legitimacy of the real. If *Platoon* asserts any mode of "understanding" Vietnam, it does so at the level of allegory; by underpinning that allegory with surface realism, it veils the grounds on which that understanding rests. By limiting our expectations of the Vietnam War film to documentary-style realism, we leave ourselves unprepared to deal with the proposed "understanding" on its actual ground. Thus reviewers hailed *Platoon*'s realism, and because they had done so had no framework appropriate to a discussion of conclusions drawn from allegory. The central question—Does this Manichean dichotomy in fact describe or explain the American experience in Vietnam?—remains largely unasked.

A related danger resides in the primacy of the personal as a mode of understanding. John Carlos Rowe, discussing the same centrality of personal experience in recent Vietnam documentaries and oral histories, concludes: "What has now assumed body and form in Sylvester Stallone's *Rambo: First Blood, Part II* is the distorted form of that radical individualism we so desperately want to salvage from the ashes of a lost war. The romance of *Rambo* has been made possible by our own romance of the real" (148). The re-glamorization of the warrior, common to both *Rambo* and *Platoon*, has its roots in precisely this emphasis on direct experience as the only route toward understanding. The connection is not just with romantic individualism, but with the limitations of direct experience accounts as well: they fail to deal with the causes and historical context of the war or with its consequences in the wider sphere of world politics. In *Platoon* there is no hint of why the war was being fought or what issues the fighting of it raised. The closest the film comes to such a statement is when Taylor tells us that, though the grunts at the front are "from the bottom of the barrel" of American society, "they're fighting for our society, and our freedom." At no point are those motives questioned—either as genuine motives for the soldier or as plausible justifications for the war. From the confines of its personal perspective, the only criticism *Platoon* can mount is of the conduct of the war.

By limiting its criticism to the realm of conduct, and by positing a "civil war" between good and evil elements of the American forces, *Platoon* makes common ground with those neoconservatives who would resurrect the myth that the war could have been won had we only fought it right. Taylor's voice-overs clearly suggest as much. "I can't believe we're fighting each other, when we should be fighting them," he laments after the confrontation in the village divides the platoon; he repeats the point in his final monologue. The suggestion that a united American force might have won the war is linked to the narrowing of perspective that follows from the primacy given to personal experience: nothing in *Platoon* suggests an awareness of the political struggle against the war in the United States, and nothing in it moves the film audience toward an understanding of what motivated the Viet Cong or the NVA in their struggles. By portraying the Vietnamese forces as shadowy, silent, and mysterious, Stone ensures that their cause cannot be addressed within the framework of the film. The danger of the resurrected myth is clear: it appears to address antiwar sentiment by criticizing the conduct of the war while preparing the ground for further conflict by claiming that American failure resulted only from internal division. In a war fought by a united American force, the allegorical internal battle would be dissolved; we could win the next one.

Finally, the prowar implications of the myth that we could have won in Vietnam must be seen as especially dangerous when featured in a movie where the warrior hero and the glamor of combat are so basic. Elias, the film's most idealized character, is not only the repository of *Platoon*'s moral values but its model of a guerrilla fighter as well. Taylor triumphs precisely when he masters the art of killing. Stone's dependence on genre conventions for his combat sequences ensures that none of the thrill will be lost however dubious the battle.

In its glorification of the warrior hero, *Platoon* differs little in effect from *Rambo*. What difference there is makes *Platoon* the more dangerous film: the adventures of *Rambo* are patently fantasy, but the realistic surface of *Platoon* makes the warrior hero seem a *real* possibility. That the mouthpieces of liberal opinion have largely remained blind to this level of meaning in *Platoon* exposes the dangers in their uncritical acceptance of the mythology of realism.

Works Cited

Allen, Richard. *"Platoon." Crisis*, April 1987: 43-45.

Ansen, David "A Ferocious Vietnam Elegy: Oliver Stone Brings It Brutally Back Home." *Newsweek*, 5 January 1987: 57.

Berg, Rick. "Losing Vietnam: Covering the War in an Age of Technology." *Cultural Critique* 3 (Spring 1986): 92-125.

Blake, Richard A. "Mind and Heart." *America*, 21 February 1987: 159.

Canby, Vincent. *"Platoon* Finds New Life in the Old War Movie." *New York Times*, 11 January 1987, III:21.

————— "The Vietnam War in Stone's Platoon." *New York Times*, 19 December 1986, III:12.

Corliss, Richard. *"Platoon:* Viet Nam As I Really Was, On Film." *Time*, 26 January 1987: 54-61.

Eco, Umberto. *The Role of the Reader*. Bloomington, IN: University of Indiana Press, 1979.

Halberstam, David. "Two Who Were There View *Platoon*: The Correspondent." *New York Times*, 8 March 1987, II:21.

Harmetz, Aljean. "Unwanted *Platoon* Finds Success as US Examines the Vietnam War." *New York Times*, 9 February 1987, III:13.

Hyam, Jay. *War Movies*. New York: W.H. Smith, 1984.

Kael, Pauline. "Little Shocks, Big Shocks." *New Yorker*, 12 January 1987: 94-96.

Kaufmann, Stanley. "An American Tragedy." *New Republic*, 19 January 1987: 24-25.

Maslin, Janet. "Movie Bloodlines Lead to Rambo." *New York Times*, 1 March 1987, II:21.

McGilligan, Pat. "Point Man." *Film Comment*, February 1987: 11-14.

Norman, Michael. *"Platoon* Grapples with Vietnam." *New York Times*, 21 December 1986, II:17.

O'Brien, Tim. "Oscars Step Out: Studios vs. the Judges." *Commonweal*, 13 March 1987: 147-149.

O'Brien, Tom. "Reel Politics." *Commonweal*, 16 January 1987: 17-18.

Paris, Michael. "The American Film Industry and Vietnam." *History Today* 37 (April 1987): 19-26.

"Platoon Meets Rambo." *New York Times*, 22 January 1987, I;26.

Rowe, John Carlos. "Eye Witness: Documentary Styles in the American Representations of Vietnam." *Cultural Critique* 3 (Spring 1986): 126-150.

Shawcross, William. "The Unseen Enemy." *Times Literary Supplement*, 24 April 1987: 438.

Simon, John. "Found in the Mud." *National Review*. 13 March 1987: 54-57.

Trainor, Richard. "Two Who Were There View *Platoon*: The Marine Officer." *New York Times*, 8 March 1987, II:21.

"TRB from Washington." *New Republic*, 9 March 1987: 4+.